THIRD EDITION

Exploring Social Life

READINGS TO ACCOMPANY

ESSENTIALS OF SOCIOLOGY

A Down-to-Earth Approach

SEVENTH EDITION

Edited by

James M. Henslin

Southern Illinois University, Edwardsville

PEARSON

Allyn and Bacon

Boston ■ New York ■ San Francisco
Mexico City ■ Montreal ■ Toronto ■ London ■ Madrid ■ Munich ■ Paris
Hong Kong ■ Singapore ■ Tokyo ■ Cape Town ■ Sydney

Senior Series Editor: Jeff Lasser
Series Editorial Assistant: Lauren Houlihan
Marketing Manager: Kelly May
Editorial Production Service: Omegatype Typography, Inc.
Composition Buyer: Linda Cox
Manufacturing Manager: Megan Cochran
Electronic Composition: Omegatype Typography, Inc.
Cover Administrator: Joel Gendron

For related titles and support materials, visit our online catalog at www.ablongman.com.

ISBN-13: 978-0-205-53053-3 ISBN-10: 0-205-53053-2

Printed in the United States of America

10 9 8 7 6 5 4 3 2 1 11 10 09 08 07

Exploring Social Life

Contents

Preface

It is gratifying to see that students and instructors alike have responded so favorably to *Essentials of Sociology: A Down-to-Earth Approach*. Because so many instructors want to give their students the opportunity to read original sociological research, I have designed this brief anthology as a companion for *Essentials of Sociology*. Because these readings follow the text's outline chapter for chapter, it is easy to incorporate them into the course. In keeping with the *Essentials* theme, there is a single reading for each chapter. The one exception is the addition of a reading on human sexuality for those who incorporate this topic into their course.

As always, a selection may have several subthemes. This allows a reading to be incorporated into a different chapter than the one I have assigned it, or to be included in the course even though a particular chapter is not assigned.

Also in keeping with the *Essentials* theme, I will keep this preface brief. If you have any suggestions for the next edition of this reader, please let me know. As always, I look forward to hearing from you.

Jim Henslin
Henslin@aol.com

Exploring Social Life

PART

I The Sociological Perspective

All of us, at least to some degree, want to understand social life. We may want to know why some people boast and tell lies, whereas others will undergo personal hardship to tell the truth. These are important questions, and they affect our everyday lives. So do issues on a much broader scale, such as why certain types of jobs are drying up around us, why we need more and more education to get a good job, why the divorce rate is so high, why people are prejudiced, why people are marrying later, or why cohabitation, which most people used to consider shameful behavior, is so common now. Then, too, there is the question of why nations go to war despite the common sentiment that war is evil and should be avoided.

The tool that sociology offers in our quest for understanding is called the *sociological perspective* (also known as the *sociological imagination*). Basically, the sociological perspective means that no behavior or event stands in isolation. Rather, it is connected to other events that surround it. To understand any particular behavior or event, we need to view it within the context in which it occurs. The sociological perspective sensitizes us to the need to uncover those connections.

C. Wright Mills, a sociologist who back in the 1950s and 1960s wrote on large-scale events such as war and politics, noted that world events were coming to play an increasingly significant role in our personal lives. More than ever, this is so today. What transpires in countries on the other side of the globe has profound effects on our own lives. An economic downturn in Europe, for example, can pinch our own economy—and may force us to put our lives on hold. When jobs are hard to get, we may decide that it is better to postpone getting married—no matter how much we are in love. Very reluctantly, we may even determine that it is prudent to move back in with our parents. If our country goes to war in some far-off region, it can have similar effects.

Economies surge, then tumble. Empires grow to a peak of power, then overreach and decline. Wars come and go, becoming a seemingly regular but strange part of our lives. New forms of communication change the way we do business, and even the way we write letters and do our homework. Morals change, and what was once considered wrong comes to be accepted as part of everyday life. What once were luxuries come to be considered as necessities.

Such far-reaching events affect both the ways we look at the world and how we see ourselves. Our aspirations—and our other innermost desires—do not originate within us. Instead, as we view them from the sociological perspective, we see that they are transplanted inside us. Most such influences on our personal desires, though, remain invisible to us. We tend to perceive only what we experience directly—our feelings, our interactions, our friendships, our problems—with causes and consequences beyond this intimate or personal level perceived only dimly.

In short, we cannot understand our lives by merely looking inside ourselves—at our own abilities, emotions, desires, or aspirations. Nor is it sufficient to look only at our own family, friends, and neighborhood, though they, too, are important. We have to also consider a world far beyond our immediate environment.

All these—our personal feelings, our everyday interactions, our associations, and events around the globe—come together in the *sociological perspective.* Learning to see ourselves and others from this perspective is a fascinating journey.

To begin this journey, we open the book with a selection that has become a classic in sociology. Peter Berger invites you to consider the excitement that comes with exploring social life. We follow this with a reading by Napoleon Chagnon, who recounts his fascinating adventure with a tribe in South America. In the third selection, Gwynne Dyer examines the techniques that the U.S. Marine Corps uses to turn boys into soldiers who will not hesitate to kill when the order is given. In the article that concludes this part, John Coleman shares his experiences as a homeless person, giving us a unique understanding of these people's lives.

READING 1

Invitation to Sociology

Peter L. Berger

introduction

To grasp the *sociological perspective* is to see the social world in a new light. As your angle of vision changes, no longer do things look the same. As you peer beneath the surface of human relationships, other realities begin to emerge. The taken-for-granted may take on an unfamiliar hue. For example, if you place the sociological lens on something as familiar as friendship, you will find that rather than being a simple matter, friendship is based on complex rights and obligations. As you analyze friendship, the implicit understandings on which it is based will begin to emerge. You will make visible its reciprocal obligations (how social debts accumulate when your friend does something for you that you are expected to repay). Although seldom stated, these implicit understandings provide the background that rules the relationship. Violate them and you risk severing the friendship.

Uncovering realities that lie beneath the surface and attaining a different understanding of social life are part of the fascination of sociology. Regardless of a sociologist's topic—whether as common and familiar as friendship or as uncommon and unfamiliar as how young women become prostitutes (Reading 6)—as Peter Berger points out in this selection, the sociologist's overriding motivation is curiosity, a desire to know and discover more about some aspect of social life.

Thinking Critically

As you read this selection, ask yourself:

1. What is the difference between a sociologist and a pollster?
2. What does Berger mean by saying "Statistical data by themselves do not make sociology"?
3. What does Berger mean when he says that "an invitation to sociology is an invitation to a special kind of passion"?

It is gratifying from certain value positions (including some of this writer's) that sociological insights have served in a number of instances to improve the lot of groups of human beings by uncovering morally shocking conditions or by clearing away collective illusions or by showing that socially desired results could be obtained in more humane fashion. One might point, for example, to some applications of sociological knowledge in the penological practice of Western countries. Or one might cite the use made of sociological studies in the Supreme Court decision of 1954 on racial segregation in the public schools. Or one could look at the applications of other sociological studies to the humane planning of urban redevelopment. Certainly the sociologist who is morally and politically sensitive will derive gratification from such instances. But, once more, it will be well to keep in mind that what is at issue here is not sociological understanding as such but certain applications of this understanding. It is not difficult to see how the same understanding could be applied with opposite intentions. Thus the sociological understanding of the dynamics of racial prejudice can be applied effectively by those promoting intragroup hatred as well as by those wanting to spread tolerance. And the sociological understanding of the nature of human solidarity can be employed in the service of both totalitarian and democratic regimes....

One image [of the sociologist is that of] a gatherer of statistics about human behavior.... He* goes out with a questionnaire, interviews people selected at random, then goes home [and] enters his tabulations [into computers].... In all of this, of course, he is supported by a large staff and a very large budget. Included in this image is the implication that the results of all this effort are picayune, a pedantic restatement of what everybody knows anyway. As one observer remarked pithily, a sociologist is a fellow who spends $100,000 to find his way to a house of ill repute.

This image of the sociologist has been strengthened in the public mind by the activities of many agencies that might well be called parasociological, mainly agencies concerned with public opinion and market trends. The pollster has become a well-known figure in American life, inopportuning people about their views from foreign policy to toilet paper. Since the methods used in the pollster business bear close resemblance to sociological research, the growth of this image of the sociologist is understandable.... The fundamental sociological question, whether concerned with premarital petting or with Republican votes or with the incidence of gang knifings, is always presumed to be "how often?" or "how many?"...

Now it must be admitted, albeit regretfully, that this image of the sociologist and his trade is not altogether a product of fantasy.... [A good] part of the sociological enterprise in this country continues to consist of little studies of obscure fragments of social life, irrelevant to any broader theoretical concern. One glance at the table of contents of the major sociological journals or at the list of papers read at sociological conventions will confirm this statement....

*Some classic articles in sociology that are reprinted in this anthology were written when "he" and "man" were generic, when they referred to both men and women. So it is with "his," "him," and so on. Although the writing style has changed, the sociological ideas have not.

Statistical data by themselves do not make sociology. They become sociology only when they are sociologically interpreted, put within a theoretical frame of reference that is sociological. Simple counting, or even correlating different items that one counts, is not sociology. There is almost no sociology in the Kinsey reports. This does not mean that the data in these studies are not true or that they cannot be relevant to sociological understanding. They are, taken by themselves, raw materials that can be used in sociological interpretation. The interpretation, however, must be broader than the data themselves. So the sociologist cannot arrest himself at the frequency tables of premarital petting or extramarital pederasty. These enumerations are meaningful to him only in terms of their much broader implications for an understanding of institutions and values in our society. To arrive at such understanding the sociologist will often have to apply statistical techniques, especially when he is dealing with the mass phenomena of modern social life. But sociology consists of statistics as little as philology consists of conjugating irregular verbs or chemistry of making nasty smells in test tubes.

Sociology has, from its beginnings, understood itself as a science.... [T]he allegiance of sociologists to the scientific ethos has meant everywhere a willingness to be bound by certain scientific canons of procedure. If the sociologist remains faithful to his calling, his statements must be arrived at through the observation of certain rules of evidence that allow others to check on or to repeat or to develop his findings further. It is this scientific discipline that often supplies the motive for reading a sociological work as against, say, a novel on the same topic that might describe matters in much more impressive and convincing language....

The charge that many sociologists write in a barbaric dialect must...be admitted.... Any scientific discipline must develop a terminology. This is self-evident for a discipline such as, say, nuclear physics that deals with matters unknown to most people and for which no words exist in common speech. However, terminology is possibly even more important for the social sciences, just because their subject matter *is* familiar and just because words *do* exist to denote it. Because we are well acquainted with the social institutions that surround us, our perception of them is imprecise and often erroneous. In very much the same way most of us will have considerable difficulty giving an accurate description of our parents, husbands or wives, children or close friends. Also, our language is often (and perhaps blessedly) vague and confusing in its references to social reality. Take for an example the concept of *class*, a very important one in sociology: There must be dozens of meanings that this term may have in common speech—income brackets, races, ethnic groups, power cliques, intelligence ratings, and many others. It is obvious that the sociologist must have a precise, unambiguous definition of the concept if his work is to proceed with any degree of scientific rigor. In view of these facts, one can understand that some sociologists have been tempted to invent altogether new words to avoid the semantic traps of the vernacular usage.

Finally, we would look at an image of the sociologist not so much in his professional role as in his being, supposedly, a certain kind of person. This is the image of the sociologist as a detached, sardonic observer, and a cold manipulator of men. Where this image prevails, it may represent an ironic triumph of the sociologist's own efforts to be accepted as a genuine scientist. The sociologist here becomes the self-appointed superior man, standing off from the warm vitality of common existence, finding his satisfactions not in living but in coolly appraising the lives of others, filing them away in little categories, and thus presumably missing the real significance of what he is observing. Further, there is the notion that, when he involves himself in social processes at all, the sociologist does so as an uncommitted technician, putting his manipulative skills at the disposal of the powers that be.

This last image is probably not very widely held.... The problem of the political role of the social scientist is, nevertheless, a very genuine one. For instance, the employment of sociologists by certain branches of industry and government raises moral questions that ought to be faced more widely than they have been so far. These are, however, moral questions that concern all men in positions of responsibility....

How then are we to conceive of the sociologist? In discussing the various images that abound in the popular mind we have already brought out certain elements that would have to go into our conception....

The sociologist, then, is someone concerned with understanding society in a disciplined way. The nature of this discipline is scientific. This means that what the sociologist finds and says about the social phenomena he studies occurs within a certain rather strictly defined frame of reference. One of the main characteristics of this scientific frame of reference is that operations are bound by certain rules of evidence. As a scientist, the sociologist tries to be objective, to control his personal preferences and prejudices, to perceive clearly rather than to judge normatively. This restraint, of course, does not embrace the totality of the sociologist's existence as a human being, but is limited to his operations *qua* sociologist. Nor does the sociologist claim that his frame of reference is the only one within which society can be looked at. For that matter, very few scientists in any field would claim today that one should look at the world only scientifically. The botanist looking at a daffodil has no reason to dispute the right of the poet to look at the same object in a very different manner. There are many ways of playing. The point is not that one denies other people's games but that one is clear about the rules of one's own. The game of the sociologist, then, uses scientific rules. As a result, the sociologist must be clear in his own mind as to the meaning of these rules. That is, he must concern himself with methodological questions. Methodology does not constitute his goal. The latter, let us recall once more, is the attempt to understand society. Methodology helps in reaching this goal. In order to understand society, or that segment of it that he is studying at the moment, the sociologist will use a variety of means. Among these are statistical techniques. Statistics can be very useful in answering certain sociological questions. But statistics does not constitute sociology. As a scientist, the sociologist will have to be concerned with the exact significance of the terms he is using. That is, he will have to be careful about terminology. This does not have to mean that he must invent a new language of his own, but it does mean that he cannot naively use the language of everyday discourse. Finally, the interest of the sociologist is primarily theoretical. That is, he is interested in understanding for its own sake. He may be aware of or even concerned with the practical applicability and consequences of his findings, but at that point he leaves the sociological frame of reference as such and moves into realms of values, beliefs and ideas that he shares with other men who are not sociologists....

[W]e would like to go a little bit further here and ask a somewhat more personal (and therefore, no doubt, more controversial) question. We would like to ask not only what it is that the sociologist is doing but also what it is that drives him to it. Or, to use the phrase Max Weber used in a similar connection, we want to inquire a little into the nature of the sociologist's demon. In doing so, we shall evoke an image that is not so much ideal-typical in the above sense but more confessional in the sense of personal commitment. Again, we are not interested in excommunicating anyone. The game of sociology goes on in a spacious playground. We are just describing a little more closely those we would like to tempt to join our game.

We would say then that the sociologist (that is, the one we would really like to invite to our game) is a person intensively, endlessly, shamelessly interested in the doings of men. His natural habitat is all the human gathering places of the world, wherever men come together. The sociologist may be interested in many other things. But his consuming interest remains in the world of men, their institutions, their history, their passions. And since he is interested in men, nothing that men do can be altogether tedious for him. He will naturally be interested in the events that engage men's ultimate beliefs, their moments of tragedy and grandeur and ecstasy. But he will also be fascinated by the common place, the everyday. He will know reverence, but this reverence will not prevent him from wanting to see and to understand. He may sometimes feel revulsion or contempt. But this also will not deter him from wanting to have his questions answered. The sociologist, in his quest for understanding, moves through the world of men without respect for the usual lines of demarcation. Nobility and degradation, power and obscurity, intelligence and folly—these are equally *interesting* to him, however unequal they may be in his personal values or tastes. Thus his questions may lead him to all possible levels of society, the best and the least known places, the most respected and the most despised. And, if he is a good sociologist, he will find himself in all these places because his own questions have so taken possession of him that he has little choice but to seek for answers.

It would be possible to say the same things in a lower key. We could say that the sociologist, but for the grace of his academic title, is the man who must listen to gossip despite himself, who is tempted to look through keyholes, to read other people's mail, to open closed cabinets. Before some otherwise unoccupied psychologist sets out now to construct an aptitude test for sociologists on the basis of sublimated voyeurism, let us quickly say that we are speaking merely by way of analogy. Perhaps some little boys consumed with curiosity to watch their maiden aunts in the bathroom later become inveterate sociologists. This is quite uninteresting. What interests us is the curiosity that grips any sociologist in front of a closed door behind which there are human voices. If he is a good sociologist, he will want to open that door, to understand these voices. Behind each closed door he will anticipate some new facet of human life not yet perceived and understood.

The sociologist will occupy himself with matters that others regard as too sacred or as too distasteful for dispassionate investigation. He will find rewarding the company of priests or of prostitutes, depending not on his personal preferences but on the questions he happens to be asking at the moment. He will also concern himself with matters that others may find much too boring. He will be interested in the human interaction that goes with warfare or with great intellectual discoveries, but also in the relations between people employed in a restaurant or between a group of little girls playing with their dolls. His main focus of attention is not the ultimate significance of what men do, but the action in itself, as another example of the infinite richness of human conduct. So much for the image of our playmate.

In these journeys through the world of men the sociologist will inevitably encounter other professional Peeping Toms. Sometimes these will resent his presence, feeling that he is poaching on their preserves. In some places the sociologist will meet up with the economist, in others with the political scientist, in yet others with the psychologist or the ethnologist. Yet chances are that the questions that have brought him to these same places are different from the ones that propelled his fellow-trespassers. The sociologist's questions always remain essentially the same: "What are people doing with each other here?" "What are their relationships to each other?" "How are these relationships organized in institutions?" "What are the collective ideas that move men and institutions?" In trying to answer these questions in specific instances, the sociologist will, of course, have to deal with economic or political matters, but he will do so in a way rather different from that of the economist or the political scientist. The scene that he contemplates is the same human scene that these other scientists concern themselves with. But the sociologist's angle of vision is different. When this is understood, it becomes clear that it makes little sense to try to stake out a special enclave within which the sociologist will carry on business in his own right. There is, however, one traveler whose path the sociologist will cross more often than anyone else's on his journeys. This is the historian. Indeed, as soon as the sociologist turns from the present to the past, his preoccupations are very hard indeed to distinguish from those of the historian. However, we shall leave this relationship to a later part of our considerations. Suffice it to say here that the sociological journey will be much impoverished unless it is punctuated frequently by conversation with that other particular traveler.

Any intellectual activity derives excitement from the moment it becomes a trail of discovery. In some fields of learning this is the discovery of worlds previously unthought and unthinkable. This is the excitement of the astronomer or of the nuclear physicist on the antipodal boundaries of the realities that man is capable of conceiving. But it can also be the excitement of bacteriology or geology. In a different way it can be the excitement of the linguist discovering new realms of human expression or of the anthropologist exploring human customs in faraway countries. In such discovery, when undertaken with passion, a widening of awareness, sometimes a veritable transformation of consciousness, occurs. The universe turns out to be much more wonder-full than one had ever dreamed. The excitement of sociology is usually of a different sort. Sometimes, it is true, the sociologist penetrates into worlds that had previously been quite unknown to him—for instance, the world of crime, or the world of some bizarre religious sect, or the world fashioned by the exclusive concerns of some group such as medical specialists or military leaders or advertising executives. However, much of the time the sociologist moves in sectors of experience that are familiar to him and to most people in his society. He investigates communities, institutions and activities that one can read about every day in the newspapers. Yet there is another excitement of discovery beckoning in his investigations. It is not the excitement of coming upon the totally unfamiliar, but rather the excitement of finding the familiar becoming transformed in its meaning. The fascination of sociology lies in the fact that its perspective makes us see in a new light the very world in which we have lived all our lives. This also constitutes a transformation of consciousness. Moreover, this transformation is more relevant existentially than that of many other intellectual disciplines, because it is more difficult to segregate in some special compartment of the mind. The astronomer does not live in the remote galaxies, and the nuclear physicist can, outside his laboratory, eat and laugh and marry and vote without thinking about the insides of the atom. The geologist looks at rocks only at appropriate times, and the linguist speaks English with his wife. The sociologist lives in society, on the job and off it. His own life, inevitably, is part of his subject matter. Men being what they are, sociologists too manage to segregate their professional insights from their everyday affairs. But it is a rather difficult feat to perform in good faith.

The sociologist moves in the common world of men, close to what most of them would call real. The categories he employs in his analyses are only refinements of the categories by which other men live—power, class, status, race, ethnicity. As a result, there is a deceptive simplicity and obviousness about some sociological investigations. One reads them, nods at the familiar scene, remarks that one has heard all this before and don't people have better things to do than to waste their time on truisms—until one is suddenly brought up against an insight that radically questions everything one had previously assumed about this familiar scene. This is the point at which one begins to sense the excitement of sociology.

Let us take a specific example. Imagine a sociology class in a Southern college where almost all the students are white Southerners. Imagine a lecture on the subject of the racial system of the South. The lecturer is talking here of matters that have been familiar to his students from the time of their infancy. Indeed, it may be that they are much more familiar with the minutiae of this system than he is. They are quite bored as a result. It seems to them that he is only using more pretentious words to describe what they already know. Thus he may use the term "caste," one commonly used now by American sociologists to describe the Southern racial system. But in explaining the term he shifts to traditional Hindu society, to make it clearer. He then goes on to analyze the magical beliefs inherent in caste tabus, the social dynamics of commensalism and connubium, the economic interests concealed within the system, the way in which religious beliefs relate to the tabus, the effects of the caste system upon the industrial development of the society and vice versa—all in India. But suddenly India is not very far away at all. The lecture then goes back to its Southern theme. The familiar now seems not quite so familiar any more. Questions are raised that are new, perhaps raised angrily, but raised all the same. And at least some of the students have begun to understand that there are functions involved in this business of race that they have not read about in the newspapers (at least not those in their hometowns) and that their parents have not told them—partly, at least, because neither the newspapers nor the parents knew about them.

It can be said that the first wisdom of sociology is this—things are not what they seem. This too is a deceptively simple statement. It ceases to be simple after a while. Social reality turns out to have many layers of meaning. The discovery of each new layer changes the perception of the whole.

Anthropologists use the term "culture shock" to describe the impact of a totally new culture upon a newcomer. In an extreme instance such shock will be experienced by the Western explorer who is told, halfway through dinner, that he is eating the nice old lady he had been chatting with the previous day—a shock with predictable physiological if not moral consequences. Most explorers no longer encounter cannibalism in their travels today. However, the first encounters with polygamy or with puberty rites or even with the way some nations drive their automobiles can be quite a shock to an American visitor. With the shock may go not only disapproval or disgust but a sense of excitement that things can *really* be that different from what they are at home. To some extent, at least, this is the excitement of any first travel abroad. The experience of sociological discovery could be described as "culture shock" minus geographical displacement. In other words, the sociologist travels at home—with shocking results. He is unlikely to find that he is eating a nice old lady for dinner. But the discovery, for instance, that his own church has considerable money invested in the missile industry or that a few blocks from his home there are people who engage in cultic orgies may not be drastically different in emotional impact. Yet we would not want to imply that sociological discoveries are always or even usually outrageous to moral sentiment. Not at all. What they have in common with exploration in distant lands, however, is the sudden illumination of new and unsuspected facets of human existence in society. This is the excitement and, as we shall try to show later, the humanistic justification of sociology.

People who like to avoid shocking discoveries, who prefer to believe that society is just what they were taught in Sunday School, who like the safety of the rules and the maxims of what Alfred Schuetz has called the "world-taken-for-granted," should stay away from sociology. People who feel no temptation before closed doors, who have no curiosity about human beings, who are content to admire scenery without wondering about the people who live in those houses on the other side of that river, should probably also stay away from sociology. They will find it unpleasant or, at any rate, unrewarding. People who are interested in human beings only if they can change, convert or reform them should also be warned, for they will find sociology much less useful than they hoped. And people whose interest is mainly in their own conceptual constructions will do just as well to turn to the study of little white mice. Sociology will be satisfying, in the long run, only to those who can think of nothing more entrancing than to watch men and to understand things human....

To be sure, sociology is an individual pastime in the sense that it interests some men and bores others. Some like to observe human beings, others to experiment with mice. The world is big enough to hold all kinds and there is no logical priority for one interest as against another. But the word "pastime" is weak in describing what we mean. Sociology is more like a passion. The sociological perspective is more like a demon that possesses one, that drives one compellingly, again and again, to the questions that are its own. An introduction to sociology is, therefore, an invitation to a very special kind of passion.

READING 2

The Fierce People

Napoleon Chagnon

introduction

The many cultures of humans are fascinating. Each human group has its own culture, whether the group be an urban gang in the United States or a tribe in the jungles of South America. Like an envelope, our culture encloses us into a particular area of life, directing our thoughts, behaviors, and perceptions. It sets boundaries and dictates what is significant and insignificant. It provides the rules for how we should interact with one another. Culture also provides the framework from which we view life. Understand a people's culture, and you come a long way to understanding why they think, feel, and act as they do.

Understanding and appreciation are two different things. To understand a group does not necessarily mean that you appreciate it. Understanding might help, but not necessarily. In this selection, Napoleon Chagnon recounts his harrowing stay with the Yąnomamö, a tribe in South America. As you read this selection, you will see how uncomfortable he was during his lengthy fieldwork.

Thinking Critically

As you read this selection, ask yourself:

1. Why didn't Chagnon develop an appreciation for the way of life of the Yąnomamö?
2. Why was Chagnon so stingy with his food—and so reluctant to accept food from others?
3. How does the culture of the Yąnomamö compare with your own culture? Be sure to compare gender relations (relationships among men and women).

The Yąnomamö Indians live in southern Venezuela and the adjacent portions of northern Brazil. Some 125 widely scattered villages have populations ranging from 40 to 250 inhabitants, with 75 to 80 people the most usual number. In total numbers their population probably approaches 10,000 people, but this is merely a guess. Many of the villages have not yet been contacted by outsiders, and nobody knows for sure exactly how many uncontacted villages there are, or how many people live in them. By comparison to African or Melanesian tribes, the Yąnomamö population is small. Still, they are one of the largest unacculturated tribes left in all of South America.

But they have a significance apart from tribal size and cultural purity: The Yąnomamö are still actively conducting warfare. It is in the nature of man to fight, according to one of their myths, because the blood of "Moon" spilled on this layer of the cosmos, causing men to become fierce. I describe the Yąnomamö as "the fierce people" because that is the most accurate single phrase that describes them. That is how they conceive themselves to be, and that is how they would like others to think of them.

I spent nineteen months with the Yąnomamö during which time I acquired some proficiency in their language and, up to a point, submerged myself in their culture and way of life. The thing that impressed me most was the importance of aggression in their culture. I had the opportunity to witness a good many incidents that expressed individual vindictiveness on the one hand and collective bellicosity on the other. These ranged in seriousness from the ordinary incidents of wife beating and chest pounding to dueling and organized raiding by parties that set out with the intention of ambushing and killing men from enemy villages. One of the villages was raided approximately twenty-five times while I conducted the fieldwork, six times by the group I lived among....

This is not to state that primitive man everywhere is unpleasant. By way of contrast, I have also done limited fieldwork among the Yąnomamö's northern neighbors, the Carib-speaking Makiritare Indians. This group was very pleasant and charming, all of them anxious to help me and honor bound to show any visitor the numerous courtesies of their system of etiquette. In short, they approached the image of primitive man that I had conjured up, and it was sheer pleasure to work with them....

My first day in the field illustrated to me what my teachers meant when they spoke of "culture shock." I had traveled in a small, aluminum rowboat propelled by a large outboard motor for two and a half days. This took me from the Territorial capital, a small town on the Orinoco River, deep into Yąnomamö country. On the morning of the third day we reached a small mission settlement, the field "headquarters" of a group of Americans who were working in two Yąnomamö villages. The missionaries had come out of these villages to hold their annual conference on the progress of their mission work, and were conducting their meetings when I arrived. We picked up a passenger at the mission station, James P. Barker, the first non-Yąnomamö to make a sustained, permanent contact with the tribe (in 1950). He had just returned from a year's furlough in the United States, where I had earlier visited him before leaving for Venezuela. He agreed to accompany me to the village I had selected for my base of operations to introduce me to the Indians. This village was also his own home base, but he had not been there for over a year and did not plan to join me for another three months. Mr. Barker had been living with this particular group about five years.

We arrived at the village, Bisaasi-teri, about 2:00 P.M. and docked the boat along the muddy bank at the terminus of the path used by the Indians to fetch their drinking water. It was hot and muggy, and my clothing was soaked with perspiration.

It clung uncomfortably to my body, as it did thereafter for the remainder of the work. The small, biting gnats were out in astronomical numbers, for it was the beginning of the dry season. My face and hands were swollen from the venom of their numerous stings. In just a few moments I was to meet my first Yą̧nomamö, my first primitive man. What would it be like? I had visions of entering the village and seeing 125 social facts running about calling each other kinship terms and sharing food, each waiting and anxious to have me collect his genealogy. I would wear them out in turn. Would they like me? This was important to me; I wanted them to be so fond of me that they would adopt me into their kinship system and way of life, because I had heard that successful anthropologists always get adopted by their people. I had learned during my seven years of anthropological training at the University of Michigan that kinship was equivalent to society in primitive tribes and that it was a moral way of life, "moral" being something "good" and "desirable." I was determined to work my way into their moral system of kinship and become a member of their society.

My heart began to pound as we approached the village and heard the buzz of activity within the circular compound. Mr. Barker commented that he was anxious to see if any changes had taken place while he was away and wondered how many of them had died during his absence. I felt into my back pocket to make sure that my notebook was there and felt personally more secure when I touched it. Otherwise, I would not have known what to do with my hands.

I looked up and gasped when I saw a dozen burly, naked, filthy, hideous men staring at us down the shafts of their drawn arrows! Immense wads of green tobacco were stuck between their lower teeth and lips making them look even more hideous, and strands of dark-green slime dripped or hung from their noses. We arrived at the village while the men were blowing a hallucinogenic drug up their noses. One of the side effects of the drug is a runny nose. The mucus is always saturated with the green powder and the Indians usually let it run freely from their nostrils. My next discovery was that there were a dozen or so vicious, underfed dogs snapping at my legs, circling me as if I were going to be their next meal. I just stood there holding my notebook, helpless and pathetic. Then the stench of the decaying vegetation and filth struck me and I almost got sick. I was horrified. What sort of a welcome was this for the person who came here to live with you and learn your way of life, to become friends with you? They put their weapons down when they recognized Barker and returned to their chanting, keeping a nervous eye on the village entrances.

We had arrived just after a serious fight. Seven women had been abducted the day before by a neighboring group, and the local men and their guests had just that morning recovered five of them in a brutal club fight that nearly ended in a shooting war. The abductors, angry because they lost five of the seven captives, vowed to raid the Bisaasi-teri. When we arrived and entered the village unexpectedly, the Indians feared that we were the raiders. On several occasions during the next two hours the men in the village jumped to their feet, armed themselves, and waited nervously for the noise outside the village to be identified. My enthusiasm for collecting ethnographic curiosities diminished in proportion to the number of times such an alarm was raised. In fact, I was relieved when Mr. Barker suggested that we sleep across the river for the evening. It would be safer over there.

As we walked down the path to the boat, I pondered the wisdom of having decided to spend a year and a half with this tribe before I had even seen what they were like. I am not ashamed to admit, either, that had there been a diplomatic way out, I would have ended my fieldwork then and there. I did not look forward to the next day when I would be left alone with the Indians; I did not speak a word of their language, and they were decidedly different from what I had imagined them to be. The whole situation was depressing, and I wondered why I ever decided to switch from civil engineering to anthropology in the first place. I had not eaten all day, I was soaking wet from perspiration, the gnats were biting me, and I was covered with red pigment, the result of a dozen or so complete examinations I had been given by as many burly Indians. These examinations capped an otherwise grim day. The Indians would blow their noses into their hands, flick as much of the mucus off that would separate in a snap of the wrist, wipe the residue into their hair, and then carefully examine my face, arms, legs, hair, and the contents of my pockets. I asked Mr. Barker how to say "Your hands are dirty"; my comments were met by the Indians in the following way: They would "clean" their hands by spitting a quantity of slimy tobacco juice into them, rub them together, and then proceed with the examination.

Mr. Barker and I crossed the river and slung our hammocks. When he pulled his hammock out of a rubber bag, a heavy, disagreeable odor of mildewed cotton came with it. "Even the missionaries are filthy," I thought to myself. Within two weeks everything I owned smelled the same way, and I lived with the odor for the remainder of the fieldwork. My own habits of personal cleanliness reached such levels that I didn't even mind being examined by the Indians, as I was not much cleaner than they were after I had adjusted to the circumstances.

So much for my discovery that primitive man is not the picture of nobility and sanitation I had conceived him to be. I soon discovered that it was an enormously time-consuming task to maintain my own body in the manner to which it had grown accustomed in the relatively antiseptic environment of the northern United States. Either I could be relatively well fed and relatively comfortable in a fresh change of clothes and do very little fieldwork, or, I could do considerably more fieldwork and be less well fed and less comfortable.

It is appalling how complicated it can be to make oatmeal in the jungle. First, I had to make two trips to the river to haul the water. Next, I had to prime my kerosene stove with alcohol and get it burning, a tricky procedure when you are trying to mix powdered milk and fill a coffee pot at the same time: the alcohol prime always burned out before I could turn the kerosene on, and I would have to start all over. Or, I would turn the kerosene on, hoping that the element was still hot enough to vaporize the fuel, and not start a small fire in my palm-thatched hut as the liquid kerosene squirted all over the table and walls and ignited. It was safer to start over with the alcohol. Then I had to boil the oatmeal and pick the bugs out of it. All my supplies, of course, were carefully stored in Indian-proof, ratproof, moisture-proof, and insect-proof containers, not one of which ever served its purpose adequately. Just taking things out of the multiplicity of containers and repacking them afterward was a minor project in itself. By the time I had hauled the water to cook with, unpacked my food, prepared the oatmeal, milk, and coffee, heated water for dishes, washed and dried the dishes, repacked the food in the containers, stored the containers in locked trunks and cleaned up my mess, the ceremony of preparing breakfast had brought me almost up to lunch time.

Eating three meals a day was out of the question. I solved the problem by eating a single meal that could be prepared in a single container, or, at most, in two containers, washed my dishes only when there were no clean ones left, using cold river water, and wore each change of clothing at least a week to cut down on my laundry problem, a courageous undertaking in the tropics. I was also less concerned about sharing my provisions with the rats, insects, Indians, and the elements, thereby eliminating the need for my complicated storage process. I was able to last most of the day on *café con leche,* heavily sugared espresso coffee diluted about five to one with hot milk. I would prepare this in the evening and store it in a thermos. Frequently, my single meal was no more complicated than a can of sardines and a package of crackers. But at least two or three times a week I would do something sophisticated, like make oatmeal or boil rice and add a can of tuna fish or tomato paste to it. I even saved time by devising a water system that obviated the trips to the river. I had a few sheets of zinc roofing brought in and made a rain-water trap. I caught the water on the zinc surface, funneled it into an empty gasoline drum, and then ran a plastic hose from the drum to my hut. When the drum was exhausted in the dry season, I hired the Indians to fill it with water from the river.

I ate much less when I traveled with the Indians to visit other villages. Most of the time my travel diet consisted of roasted or boiled green plantains that I obtained from the Indians, but I always carried a few cans of sardines with me in case I got lost or stayed away longer than I had planned. I found peanut butter and crackers a very nourishing food, and a simple one to prepare on trips. It was nutritious and portable, and only one tool was required to prepare the meal, a hunting knife that could be cleaned by wiping the blade on a leaf. More importantly, it was one of the few foods the Indians would let me eat in relative peace. It looked too much like animal feces to them to excite their appetites.

I once referred to the peanut butter as the dung of cattle. They found this quite repugnant. They did not know what "cattle" were, but were generally aware that I ate several canned products of such an animal. I perpetrated this myth, if for no other reason than to have some peace of mind while I ate. Fieldworkers develop strange defense mechanisms, and this was one of my own forms of adaptation. On another occasion I was eating a can of frankfurters and growing very weary of the demands of one of my guests for a share in my meal. When he asked me what I was eating, I replied: "Beef." He then asked, "What part of the animal are you eating?" to which I replied, "Guess!" He stopped asking for a share.

Meals were a problem in another way. Food sharing is important to the Yąnomamö in the context of displaying friendship. "I am hungry," is almost a form of greeting with them. I could not possibly have brought enough food with me to feed the entire village, yet they seemed not to understand this. All they could see was that I did not share my food with them at each and every meal. Nor could I enter into their system of reciprocities with respect to food; every time one of them gave me something "freely," he would dog me for months to pay him back, not with food, but with steel tools. Thus, if I accepted a plantain from someone in a different village while I was on a visit, he would most likely visit me in the future and demand a machete as payment for the time that he "fed" me. I usually reacted to these kinds of demands by giving a banana, the customary reciprocity in their culture—food for food—but this would be a disappointment for the individual who had visions of that single plantain growing into a machete over time.

Despite the fact that most of them knew I would not share my food with them at their request, some of them always showed up at my hut during mealtime. I gradually became accustomed to this and learned to ignore their persistent demands while I ate. Some of them would get angry because I failed to give in, but most of them accepted it as just a peculiarity of the subhuman foreigner. When I did give in, my hut quickly filled with Indians, each demanding a sample of the food that I had given one of them. If I did not give all a share, I was that much more despicable in their eyes.

A few of them went out of their way to make my meals unpleasant, to spite me for not sharing; for example, one man arrived and watched me eat a cracker with honey on it. He immediately recognized the honey, a particularly esteemed Yąnomamö food. He knew that I would not share my tiny bottle and that it would be futile to ask. Instead, he glared at me and queried icily, "Shaki![1] What kind of animal semen are you eating on that cracker?" His question had the desired effect, and my meal ended.

Finally, there was the problem of being lonely and separated from your own kind, especially your family. I tried to overcome this by seeking personal friendships among the Indians. This only complicated the matter because all my friends simply used my confidence to gain privileged access to my cache of steel tools and trade goods, and looted me. I would be bitterly disappointed that my "friend" thought no more of me than to finesse our relationship exclusively with the intention of getting at any locked up possessions, and my depression would hit new lows every time I discovered this. The loss of the possession bothered me much less than the shock that I was, as far as most of them were concerned, nothing more than a source of desirable items; no holds were barred in relieving me of these, since I was considered something sub-human, a non-Yąnomamö.

The thing that bothered me most was the incessant, passioned, and aggressive demands the Indians made. It would become so unbearable that I would have to lock myself in my mud hut every once in a while just to escape from it: Privacy is one of Western culture's greatest achievements. But I did not want privacy for its own sake; rather, I simply had to get away from the begging. Day and night for the entire time I lived with the Yąnomamö I was plagued by such demands as: "Give me a knife, I am poor!"; "If you don't take me with you on your next trip to Widokaiyateri, I'll chop a hole in your canoe!"; "Don't point your camera at me or I'll hit you!"; "Share your food with me!"; "Take me across the river in your canoe and be quick about it!"; "Give me a cooking pot!"; "Loan me your flashlight so I can go hunting tonight!"; "Give me medicine…I itch all over!"; "Take us on a week-long hunting trip with your shotgun!"; and "Give me an axe, or I'll break into your hut when you are away visiting and steal one!" And so I was bombarded by such demands day after day, months on end, until I could not bear to see an Indian.

It was not as difficult to become calloused to the incessant begging as it was to ignore the sense of urgency, the impassioned tone of voice, or the intimidation and aggression with which the demands were made. It was likewise difficult to adjust to the fact that the Yąnomamö refused to accept "no" for an answer until or unless it seethed with passion and intimidation—which it did after six months. Giving in to a demand always established a new threshold; the next demand would be for a bigger item or favor, and the anger of the Indians even greater if the demand was not met. I soon learned that I had to become very much like the Yąnomamö to be able to get along with them on their terms: sly, aggressive, and intimidating.

Had I failed to adjust in this fashion I would have lost six months of supplies to them in a single day or would have spent most of my time ferrying them around in my canoe or hunting for them. As it was, I did spend a considerable amount of time doing these things and did succumb to their outrageous demands for axes and machetes, at least at first. More importantly, had I failed to demonstrate that I could not be pushed around beyond a certain point, I would have been the subject of far more ridicule, theft, and practical jokes than was the actual case. In short, I had to acquire a certain proficiency in their kind of interpersonal politics and to learn how to imply subtly that certain potentially undesirable consequences might follow if they did such and such to me. They do this to each other in order to establish precisely the point at which they cannot goad an individual any further without precipitating retaliation. As soon as I caught on to this and realized that much of their aggression was stimulated by their desire to discover my flash point, I got along much better with them and regained some lost ground. It was sort of like a political game that everyone played, but one in which each individual sooner or later had to display some sign that his bluffs and implied threats could be backed up. I suspect that the frequency of wife beating is a component of this syndrome, since men can display their ferocity and show others that they are capable of violence. Beating a wife with a club is considered to be an acceptable way of displaying ferocity and one that does not expose the male to much danger. The important thing is that the man has displayed his potential for violence and the implication is that other men better treat him with respect and caution.

After six months, the level of demand was tolerable in the village I used for my headquarters. The Indians and I adjusted to each other and knew what to expect with regard to demands on their part for goods, favors, and services. Had I confined my fieldwork to just that village alone, the field experience would have been far more enjoyable. But, as I was interested in the demographic pattern and social organization of a much larger area, I made regular trips to some dozen different villages in order to collect genealogies or to recheck those I already had. Hence, the intensity of begging and intimidation was fairly constant for the duration of the fieldwork. I had to establish my position in some sort of pecking order of ferocity at each and every village.

For the most part, my own "fierceness" took the form of shouting back at the Yąnomamö as loudly and as passionately as they shouted at me, especially at first, when I did not know much of their language. As I became more proficient in their language and learned more about their political tactics, I became more sophisticated in the art of bluffing. For example, I paid one young man a machete to cut palm trees and make boards from the wood. I used these to fashion a platform in the bottom of my dugout canoe to keep my possessions dry when I traveled by river. That afternoon I was doing informant work in the village; the long-awaited mission supply boat arrived, and most of the Indians ran out of the village to beg goods from the crew. I continued to work in the village for another hour or so and went down to the river to say "hello" to the men on the supply boat. I was angry when I discovered that the Indians had chopped up all my palm boards and used them to paddle their own canoes across the river. I knew that if I overlooked this incident I would have invited them to take even greater liberties with my goods in the future. I crossed the river, docked amidst their dugouts, and shouted for the Indians to come out and see me. A few of the culprits appeared, mischievous grins on their faces. I gave a spirited lecture about how hard I had worked to put those boards in my canoe, how I had paid a machete for the wood, and how angry I was that they destroyed my work in their haste to cross the river. I then pulled out my hunting knife and, while their grins disappeared, cut each of their canoes loose, set them into the current, and let them float away. I left without further ado and without looking back.

They managed to borrow another canoe and, after some effort, recovered their dugouts. The headman of the village later told me with an approving chuckle that I had done the correct thing. Everyone in the village, except, of course, the culprits, supported and defended my action. This raised my status.

Whenever I took such action and defended my rights, I got along much better with the Yąnomamö. A good deal of their behavior toward me was directed with the forethought of establishing the point at which I would react defensively. Many of them later reminisced about the early days of my work when I was "timid" and a little afraid of them, and they could bully me into giving goods away.

Theft was the most persistent situation that required me to take some sort of defensive action. I simply could not keep everything I owned locked in trunks, and the Indians came into my hut and left at will. I developed a very effective means for recovering almost all the stolen items. I would simply ask a child who took the item and then take that person's hammock when he was not around, giving a spirited lecture to the others as I marched away in a faked rage with the thief's hammock. Nobody ever attempted to stop me from doing this, and almost all of them told me that my technique for recovering my possessions was admirable. By nightfall the thief would either appear with the stolen object or send it along with someone else to make an exchange. The others would heckle him for getting caught and being forced to return the item.

With respect to collecting the data I sought, there was a very frustrating problem. Primitive social organization is kinship organization, and to understand the Yąnomamö way of life I had to collect extensive genealogies. I could not have deliberately picked a more difficult group to work with in this regard: They have very stringent name taboos. They attempt to name people in such a way that when the person dies and they can no longer use his name, the loss of the word in the language is not inconvenient. Hence, they name people for specific and minute parts of things, such as "toenail of some rodent," thereby being able to retain the words "toenail" and "(specific) rodent," but not being able to refer directly to the toenail of that rodent. The taboo is maintained even for the living: One mark of prestige is the courtesy others show you by not using your name. The sanctions behind the taboo seem to be an unusual combination of fear and respect.

I tried to use kinship terms to collect genealogies at first, but the kinship terms were so ambiguous that I ultimately had to resort to names. They were quick to grasp that I was bound to learn everybody's name and reacted, without my knowing it, by inventing false names for everybody in the village. After having spent several months collecting names and learning them, this came as a disappointment to me: I could not cross-check the genealogies with other informants from distant villages.

They enjoyed watching me learn these names. I assumed, wrongly, that I would get the truth to each question and that I would get the best information by working in public. This set the stage for converting a serious project into a farce. Each informant tried to outdo his peers by inventing a name even more ridiculous than what I had been given earlier, or by asserting that the individual about whom I inquired was married to his mother or daughter, and the like. I would have the informant whisper the name of the individual in my ear, noting that he was the father of such and such a child. Everybody would then insist that I repeat the name aloud, roaring in hysterics as I clumsily pronounced the name. I assumed that the laughter was in response to the violation of the name taboo or to my pronunciation. This was a reasonable interpretation, since the individual whose name I said aloud invariably became angry. After I learned what some of the names meant, I began to understand what the laughter was all about. A few of the more colorful examples are: "hairy vagina," "long penis," "feces of the harpy eagle," and "dirty rectum." No wonder the victims were angry.

I was forced to do my genealogy work in private because of the horseplay and nonsense. Once I did so, my informants began to agree with each other and I managed to learn a few new names, real names. I could then test any new informant by collecting a genealogy from him that I knew to be accurate. I was able to weed out the more mischievous informants this way. Little by little I extended the genealogies and learned the real names. Still, I was unable to get the names of the dead and extend the genealogies back in time, and even my best informants continued to deceive me about their own close relatives. Most of them gave me the name of a living man as the father of some individual in order to avoid mentioning that the actual father was dead.

The quality of a genealogy depends in part on the number of generations it embraces, and the name taboo prevented me from getting any substantial information about deceased ancestors. Without this information, I could not detect marriage patterns through time. I had to rely on older informants for this information, but these were the most reluctant of all. As I became more proficient in the language and more skilled at detecting lies, my informants became better at lying. One of them in particular was so cunning and persuasive that I was shocked to discover that he had been inventing his information. He specialized in making a ceremony out of telling me false names. He would look around to make sure nobody was listening outside my hut, enjoin me to never mention the name again, act very nervous and spooky, and then grab me by the head to whisper the name very softly into my ear. I was always elated after an informant session with him, because I had several generations of dead ancestors for the living people. The others refused to give me this information. To show my gratitude, I paid him quadruple the rate I had given the others. When word got around that I had increased the pay, volunteers began pouring in to give me genealogies.

I discovered that the old man was lying quite by accident. A club fight broke out in the village one day, the result of a dispute over the possession of a woman. She had been promised to Rerebawa, a particularly aggressive young man who had married into the village. Rerebawa had already been given her older sister and was enraged when the younger girl began having an affair with another man in the village, making no attempt to conceal it from him. He challenged the young man to a club fight, but was so abusive in his challenge that the opponent's father took offense and entered the village circle with his son, wielding a long club. Rerebawa swaggered out to the duel and hurled insults at both of them, trying to goad them into striking him on the head with their clubs. This would have given him the opportunity to strike them on the head. His opponents refused to hit him, and the fight ended. Rerebawa had won a moral victory because his opponents were afraid to hit him. Thereafter, he swaggered around and insulted the two men behind their backs. He was genuinely angry with them, to the point of calling the older man by the name of his dead father. I quickly seized on this as an opportunity to collect an accurate genealogy and pumped him about his adversary's ancestors. Rerebawa had been particularly nasty to me up to this point, but we became staunch allies: We were both outsiders in the local village. I then asked about other dead ancestors and got immediate replies. He was angry with the whole group and not afraid to tell me the names of the dead. When I compared his version of the genealogies to that of the old man, it was obvious that one of them was lying. I challenged his information, and he explained that everybody knew that the old man was deceiving me and bragging about it in the village. The names the old man had given me were the dead ancestors of the members of a village so far away that he thought I would never have occasion to inquire about them. As it turned out, Rerebawa knew most of the people in that village and recognized the names.

I then went over the complete genealogical records with Rerebawa, genealogies I had presumed to be in final form. I had to revise them all because of the numerous lies and falsifications they contained. Thus, after five months of almost constant work on the genealogies of just one group, I had to begin almost from scratch!

Discouraging as it was to start over, it was still the first real turning point in my fieldwork. Thereafter, I began taking advantage of local arguments and animosities in selecting my informants, and used more extensively individuals who had married into the group. I began traveling to other villages to check the genealogies, picking villages that were on strained terms with the people about whom I wanted information. I would then return to my base camp and check with local informants the accuracy of the new information. If the informants became angry when I mentioned the new names I acquired from the unfriendly group, I was almost certain that the information was accurate. For this kind of checking I had to use informants whose genealogies I knew rather well: They had to be distantly enough related to the dead person that they would not go into a rage when I mentioned the name, but not so remotely related that they would be uncertain of the accuracy of the information. Thus, I had to make a list of names that I dared not use in the presence of each and every informant. Despite the precautions, I occasionally hit a name that put the informant into a rage, such as that of a dead brother or sister that other informants had not reported. This always terminated the day's work with that informant, for he would be too touchy to continue any further, and I would be reluctant to take a chance on accidentally discovering another dead kinsman so soon after the first.

These were always unpleasant experiences, and occasionally dangerous ones, depending on the temperament of the informant. On one occasion I was planning to visit a village that had been raided about a week earlier. A woman whose name I had on my list had been killed by the raiders. I planned to check each individual on the list one by one to estimate ages, and I wanted to remove her name so that I would not say it aloud in the village. I knew that I would be in considerable difficulty if I said this name aloud so soon after her death. I called on my original informant and asked him to tell me the name of the woman who had been killed. He refused, explaining that she was a close relative of his. I then asked him if he would become angry if I read off all the names on the list. This way he did not have to say her name and could merely nod when I mentioned the right one. He was a fairly good friend of mine, and I thought I could predict his reaction. He assured me that this would be a good way of doing it. We were alone in my hut so that nobody could overhear us. I read the names softly, continuing to the next when he gave a negative reply. When I finally spoke the name of the dead woman he flew out of his chair, raised his arm to strike me, and shouted: "You son-of-a-bitch![2] If you ever say that name again, I'll kill you!" He was shaking with rage, but left my hut quietly. I shudder to think what might have happened if I had said the name unknowingly in the woman's village. I had other, similar experiences in different villages, but luckily the dead person had been dead for some time and was not closely related to the individual into whose ear I whispered the name. I was merely cautioned to desist from saying any more names, lest I get people angry with me.

I had been working on the genealogies for nearly a year when another individual came to my aid. It was Kaobawa, the headman of Upper Bisaasi-teri, the group in which I spent most of my time. He visited me one day after the others had left the hut and volunteered to help me on the genealogies. He was poor, he explained, and needed a machete. He would work only on the condition that I did not ask him about his own parents and other very close kinsmen who were dead. He also added that he would not lie to me as the others had done in the past. This was perhaps the most important single event in my fieldwork, for out of this meeting evolved a very warm friendship and a very profitable informant-fieldworker relationship.

Kaobawa's familiarity with his group's history and his candidness were remarkable. His knowledge of details was almost encyclopedic. More than that, he was enthusiastic and encouraged me to learn details that I might otherwise have ignored. If there were things he did not know intimately, he would advise me to wait until he could check things out with someone in the village. This he would do clandestinely, giving me a report the next day. As I was constrained by my part of the bargain to avoid discussing his close dead kinsmen, I had to rely on Rerebawa for this information. I got Rerebawa's genealogy from Kaobawa.

Once again I went over the genealogies with Kaobawa to recheck them, a considerable task by this time: they included about two thousand names, representing several generations of individuals from four different villages. Rerebawa's information was very accurate, and Kaobawa's contribution enabled me to trace the genealogies further back in time. Thus, after nearly a year of constant work on genealogies, Yąnomamö demography and social organization began to fall into a pattern. Only then could I see how kin groups formed and exchanged women with each other over time, and only then did the fissioning of larger villages into smaller ones show a distinct pattern. At this point I was able to begin formulating more intelligent questions because there was now some sort of pattern to work with. Without the help of Rerebawa and Kaobawa, I could not have made very much sense of the plethora of details I had collected from dozens of other informants.

Kaobawa is about 40 years old. I say "about" because the Yąnomamö numeration system has only three numbers: one, two, and more-than-two. He is the headman of Upper Bisaasi-teri. He has had five or six wives so far and temporary affairs with as many more women, one of which resulted in a child. At the present time he has just two wives, Bahimi and Koamashima. He has had a daughter and a son by Bahimi, his eldest and favorite wife. Koamashima, about 20 years old, recently had her first child, a boy. Kaobawa may give Koamashima to his youngest brother. Even now the brother shares in her sexual services. Kaobawa recently gave his third wife to another of his brothers because she was beshi: "horny." In fact, this girl had been married to two other men, both of whom discarded her because of her infidelity. Kaobawa had one daughter by her; she is being raised by his brother.

Kaobawa's eldest wife, Bahimi, is about thirty-five years old. She is his first cross-cousin. Bahimi was pregnant when I began my fieldwork, but she killed the new baby, a boy, at birth, explaining tearfully that it would have competed with Ariwari, her nursing son, for milk. Rather than expose Ariwari to the dangers and uncertainty of an early weaning, she killed the new child instead. By Yąnomamö standards, she and Kaobawa have a very tranquil household. He only beats her once in a while, and never very hard. She never has affairs with other men.

Kaobawa is quiet, intense, wise, and unobtrusive. He leads more by example than by threats and coercion. He can afford to be this way as he established his reputation for being fierce long ago, and other men respect him. He also has five mature brothers who support him, and he has given a number of his sisters to other men in the village, thereby putting them under some obligation to him. In short, his "natural" following (kinsmen) is large, and he does not have to constantly display his ferocity. People already respect him and take his suggestions seriously.

Rerebawa is much younger, only about twenty-two years old. He has just one wife by whom he has had three children. He is from Karohi-teri, one of the villages to which Kaobawa is allied. Rerebawa left his village to seek a wife in Kaobawa's group because there were no eligible women there for him to marry.

Rerebawa is perhaps more typical than Kaobawa in the sense that he is concerned about his reputation for ferocity and goes out of his way to act tough. He is, however, much braver than the other men his age and backs up his threats with action. Moreover, he is concerned about politics and knows the details of intervillage relationships over a large area. In this respect he shows all the attributes of a headman, although he is still too young and has too many competent older brothers in his own village to expect to move easily into the position of leadership there.

He does not intend to stay in Kaobawa's group and has not made a garden. He feels that he has adequately discharged his obligations to his wife's parents by providing them with fresh game for three years. They should let him take the wife and return to his own village with her, but they refuse and try to entice him to remain permanently in Bisaasi-teri to provide them with game when they are old. They have even promised to give him their second daughter if he will stay permanently.

Although he has displayed his ferocity in many ways, one incident in particular shows what his character is like. Before he left his own village to seek a wife, he had an affair with the wife of an older brother. When he was discovered, his brother attacked him with a club. Rerebawa was infuriated so he grabbed an axe and drove his brother out of the village after soundly beating him with the flat of the blade. The brother was so afraid that he did not return to the village for several days. I recently visited his village with him. He made a point to introduce me to this brother. Rerebawa dragged him out of his hammock by the arm and told me, "This is the brother whose wife I had an affair with," a deadly insult. His brother did nothing and slunk back into his hammock, shamed, but relieved to have Rerebawa release the vise-grip on his arm.

Despite the fact that he admires Kaobawa, he has a low opinion of the others in Bisaasi-teri. He admitted confidentially that he thought Bisaasi-teri was an abominable group: "This is a terrible neighborhood! All the young men are lazy and cowards and everybody is committing incest! I'll be glad to get back home." He also admired Kaobawa's brother, the headman of Monou-teri. This man was killed by raiders while I was doing my fieldwork. Rerebawa was disgusted that the others did not chase the raiders when they discovered the shooting: "He was the only fierce one in the whole group; he was my close friend. The cowardly Monou-teri hid like women in the jungle and didn't even chase the raiders!"

Even though Rerebawa is fierce and capable of being quite nasty, he has a good side as well. He has a very biting sense of humor and can entertain the group for hours on end with jokes and witty comments. And, he is one of few Yąnomamö that I feel I can trust. When I returned to Bisaasi-teri after having been away for a year, Rerebawa was in his own village visiting his kinsmen. Word reached him that I had returned, and he immediately came to see me. He greeted me with an immense bear hug and exclaimed, "Shaki! Why did you stay away so long? Did you know that my will was so cold while you were gone that at times I could not eat for want of seeing you?" I had to admit that I missed him, too.

Of all the Yąnomamö I know, he is the most genuine and the most devoted to his culture's ways and values. I admire him for that, although I can't say that I subscribe to or endorse these same values. By contrast, Kaobawa is older and wiser. He sees his own culture in a different light and criticizes aspects of it he does not like. While many of his peers accept some of the superstitions and explanatory myths as truth and as the way things ought to be, Kaobawa questions them and privately pokes fun at some of them. Probably, more of the Yąnomamö are like Rerebawa, or at least try to be.

NOTES

1. "Shaki," or, rather, "Shakiwa," is the name they gave me because they could not pronounce "Chagnon." They like to name people for some distinctive feature when possible. *Shaki* is the name of a species of noisome bees; they accumulate in large numbers around ripening bananas and make pests of themselves by eating into the fruit, showering the people below with the debris. They probably adopted this name for me because I was also a nuisance, continuously prying into their business, taking pictures of them, and, in general, being where they did not want me.

2. This is the closest English translation of his actual statement, the literal translation of which would be nonsensical in our language.

READING 3

Anybody's Son Will Do

Gwynne Dyer

introduction

To understand the term *socialization,* just substitute the word *learning.* Socialization does not refer only to children. All of us are being socialized all the time. Each time we are exposed to something new, we are being socialized. If we learn how to operate a new computer, play a new (or old) video game, watch a movie, read a book, or listen to a college lecture, we are being socialized. Even when we talk to a friend, socialization occurs. And socialization doesn't stop at a certain age. When we are old, we will still have experiences (even watching televised news) that influence the ways we look at ourselves and the world. Socialization, then, is a lifelong process. You could say that in this process we are becoming more and more a part of our culture (or of our subculture).

From the examples just given, you can see that socialization is usually gentle and gradual. But there are remarkable exceptions, and in this reading we look at one of them. Gwynne Dyer analyzes the process by which the U.S. Marine Corps turns young men into killers—and how this organization accomplishes such a drastic change in just a few weeks. As you will see, the Marines' techniques are brutal, swift, and effective.

Thinking Critically

As you read this selection, ask yourself:

1. How do the U.S. Marines socialize their recruits?
2. How do the socialization techniques of the Marines compare with the socialization techniques that have been used to bring you to your current place in life?
3. Why are the socialization techniques of the Marines so effective?

You think about it and you know you're going to have to kill but you don't understand the implications of that, because in the society in which you've lived murder is the most heinous of crimes...and you are in a situation in which it's turned the other way round....When you do actually kill someone the experience, my experience, was one of revulsion and disgust....

> *I was utterly terrified—petrified—but I knew there had to be a Japanese sniper in a small fishing shack near the shore. He was firing in the other direction at Marines in another battalion, but I knew as soon as he picked off the people there—there was a window on our side—that he would start picking us off. And there was nobody else to go…and so I ran towards the shack and broke in and found myself in an empty room.…*
>
> *There was a door which meant there was another room and the sniper was in that—and I just broke that down. I was just absolutely gripped by the fear that this man would expect me and would shoot me. But as it turned out he was in a sniper harness and he couldn't turn around fast enough. He was entangled in the harness so I shot him with a .45, and I felt remorse and shame. I can remember whispering foolishly, "I'm sorry" and then just throwing up.… I threw up all over myself. It was a betrayal of what I'd been taught since a child.*
>
> —William Manchester

Yet he did kill the Japanese soldier, just as he had been trained to—the revulsion only came afterward. And even after Manchester knew what it was like to kill another human being, a young man like himself, he went on trying to kill his "enemies" until the war was over. Like all the other tens of millions of soldiers who had been taught from infancy that killing was wrong, and had then been sent off to kill for their countries, he was almost helpless to disobey, for he had fallen into the hands of an institution so powerful and so subtle that it could quickly reverse the moral training of a lifetime.

The whole vast edifice of the military institution rests on its ability to obtain obedience from its members even unto death—and the killing of others. It has enormous powers of compulsion at its command, of course, but all authority must be based ultimately on consent. The task of extracting that consent from its members has probably grown harder in recent times, for the gulf between the military and the civilian worlds has undoubtedly widened: Civilians no longer perceive the threat of violent death as an everyday hazard of existence, and the categories of people whom it is not morally permissible to kill have broadened to include (in peacetime) the entire human race. Yet the armed forces of every country can still take almost any young male civilian and turn him into a soldier with all the right reflexes and attitudes in only a few weeks. Their recruits usually have no more than twenty years' experience of the world, most of it as children, while the armies have had all of history to practice and perfect their techniques.

> *Just think of how the soldier is treated. While still a child he is shut up in the barracks. During his training he is always being knocked about. If he makes the least mistake he is beaten, a burning blow on his body, another on his eye, perhaps his head is laid open with a wound. He is battered and bruised with flogging. On the march…they hang heavy loads round his neck like that of an ass.*
>
> —Egyptian, ca. 1500 B.C.

> *The moment I talk to the new conscripts about the homeland I strike a land mine. So I kept quiet. Instead, I try to make soldiers of them. I give them hell from morning to sunset. They begin to curse me, curse the army, curse the state.*

Then they begin to curse together, and become a truly cohesive group, a unit, a fighting unit.

—Israeli, ca. A.D. 1970

All soldiers belong to the same profession, no matter what country they serve, and it makes them different from everybody else. They have to be different, for their job is ultimately about killing and dying, and those things are not a natural vocation for any human being. Yet all soldiers are born civilians. The method for turning young men into soldiers—people who kill other people and expose themselves to death—is basic training. It's essentially the same all over the world, and it always has been, because young men everywhere are pretty much alike.

Human beings are fairly malleable, especially when they are young, and in every young man there are attitudes for any army to work with: the inherited values and postures, more or less dimly recalled, of the tribal warriors who were once the model for every young boy to emulate. Civilization did not involve a sudden clean break in the way people behave, but merely the progressive distortion and redirection of all the ways in which people in the old tribal societies used to behave, and modern definitions of maleness still contain a great deal of the old warrior ethic. The anarchic machismo of the primitive warrior is not what modern armies really need in their soldiers, but it does provide them with promising raw material for the transformation they must work in their recruits.

Just how this transformation is wrought varies from time to time and from country to country. In totally militarized societies—ancient Sparta, the samurai class of medieval Japan, the areas controlled by organizations like the Eritrean People's Liberation Front today—it begins at puberty or before, when the young boy is immersed in a disciplined society in which only the military values are allowed to penetrate. In more sophisticated modern societies, the process is briefer and more concentrated, and the way it works is much more visible. It is, essentially, a conversion process in an almost religious sense—and as in all conversion phenomena, the emotions are far more important than the specific ideas....

Armies know this. It is their business to get men to fight, and they have had a long time to work out the best way of doing it. All of them pay lip service to the symbols and slogans of their political masters, though the amount of time they must devote to this activity varies from country to country.... Nor should it be thought that the armies are hypocritical—most of their members really do believe in their particular national symbols and slogans. But their secret is that they know these are not the things that sustain men in combat.

What really enables men to fight is their own self-respect, and a special kind of love that has nothing to do with sex or idealism. Very few men have died in battle, when the moment actually arrived, for the United States of America or for the sacred cause of Communism, or even for their homes and families; if they had any choice in the matter at all, they chose to die for each other and for their own vision of themselves....

The way armies produce this sense of brotherhood in a peacetime environment is basic training: a feat of psychological manipulation on the grand scale which has been so consistently successful and so universal that we fail to notice it as remarkable. In countries where the army must extract its recruits in their late teens, whether voluntarily or by conscription, from a civilian environment that does not share the military values, basic training involves a brief but intense period of indoctrination whose purpose is not really to teach the recruits basic military skills, but rather to change their values and their loyalties. "I guess you could say we brainwash them a little bit," admitted a U.S. Marine drill instructor, "but you know they're good people."

The duration and intensity of basic training, and even its major emphases, depend on what kind of society the recruits are coming from, and on what sort of military organization they are going to. It is obviously quicker to train men from a martial culture than from one in which the dominant values are civilian and commercial, and easier to deal with volunteers than with reluctant conscripts. Conscripts are not always unwilling, however; there are many instances in which the army is popular for economic reasons....

It's easier if you catch them young. You can train older men to be soldiers; it's done in every major war. But you can never get them to believe that they like it, which is the major reason armies try to get their recruits before they are 20. There are other reasons too, of course, like the physical fitness, lack of dependents, and economic dispensability of teenagers, that make armies prefer them, but the most important qualities teenagers bring to basic training are enthusiasm and naiveté. Many of them actively want the discipline and the closely structured environment that the armed forces will provide, so there is no need for the recruiters to deceive the kids about what will happen to them after they join.

> *There is discipline. There is drill.... When you are relying on your mates and they are relying on you, there's no room for slackness or sloppiness. If you're not prepared to accept the rules, you're better off where you are.*
>
> —British army recruiting advertisement, 1976

> *People are not born soldiers, they become soldiers.... And it should not begin at the moment when a new recruit is enlisted into the ranks, but rather much earlier, at the time of the first signs of maturity, during the time of adolescent dreams.*
>
> —*Red Star* (Soviet army newspaper), 1973

Young civilians who have volunteered and have been accepted by the Marine Corps arrive at Parris Island, the Corps's East Coast facility for basic training, in a state of considerable excitement and apprehension: Most are aware that they are about to undergo an extraordinary and very difficult experience. But they do not make their own way to the base; rather, they trickle in to Charleston airport on various flights throughout the day on which their training platoon is due to form, and are held there, in a state of suppressed but mounting nervous tension, until late in the evening. When the buses finally come to carry them the seventy-six miles to Parris Island, it is often after midnight—and this is not an administrative oversight. The shock treatment they are about to receive will work most efficiently if they are worn out and somewhat disoriented when they arrive.

The basic training organization is a machine, processing several thousand young men every month, and every facet and gear of it has been designed with the sole purpose of turning civilians into Marines as efficiently as possible. Provided it can have total control over their bodies and their environment for approximately three months, it can practically guarantee converts. Parris Island provides that controlled environment, and the recruits do not set foot outside it again until they graduate as Marine privates eleven weeks later.

> *They're allowed to call home, so long as it doesn't get out of hand—every three weeks or so they can call home and make sure everything's all right, if they haven't gotten a letter or there's a particular set of circumstances. If it's a case of an emergency call coming in, then they're allowed to accept that call; if not, one of my staff will take the message....*
>
> *In some cases I'll get calls from parents who haven't quite gotten adjusted to the idea that their son had cut the strings—and in a lot of cases that's what they're doing. The military provides them with an opportunity to leave home but they're still in a rather secure environment.*
>
> —Captain Brassington, USMC

For the young recruits, basic training is the closest thing their society can offer to a formal rite of passage, and the institution probably stands in an unbroken line of descent from the lengthy ordeals by which young males in precivilized groups were initiated into the adult community of warriors. But in civilized societies it is a highly functional institution whose product is not anarchic warriors, but trained soldiers.

Basic training is not really about teaching people skills; it's about changing them, so that they can do things they wouldn't have dreamt of otherwise. It works by applying enormous physical and mental pressure to men who have been isolated from their normal civilian environment and placed in one where the only right way to think and behave is the way the Marine Corps wants them to. The key word the men who run the machine use to describe this process is *motivation.*

> *I can motivate a recruit and in third phase, if I tell him to jump off the third deck, he'll jump off the third deck. Like I said before, it's a captive audience and I can train that guy; I can get him to do anything I want him to do.... They're good kids and they're out to do the right thing. We get some bad kids, but you know, we weed those out. But as far as motivation—here, we can motivate them to do anything you want, in recruit training.*
>
> —USMC drill instructor, Parris Island

The first three days the raw recruits spend at Parris Island are actually relatively easy, though they are hustled and shouted at continuously. It is during this time that they are documented and inoculated, receive uniforms, and learn the basic orders of drill that will enable young Americans (who are not very accustomed to this aspect of life) to do everything simultaneously in large groups. But the most important thing that happens in "forming" is the surrender of the recruits' own clothes, their hair—all the physical evidence of their individual civilian identities.

During a period of only 72 hours, in which they are allowed little sleep, the recruits lay aside their former lives in a series of hasty rituals (like being shaven to the scalp) whose symbolic significance is quite clear to them even though they are quite deliberately given absolutely no time for reflection, or any hint that they might have the option of turning back from their commitment. The men in charge of them know how delicate a tightrope they are walking, though, because at this stage the recruits are still newly caught civilians who have not yet made their ultimate inward submission to the discipline of the Corps.

> *Forming Day One makes me nervous. You've got a whole new mob of recruits, you know, 60 or 70 depending, and they don't know anything. You don't know what kind of a reaction you're going to get from the stress you're going to lay on them, and it just worries me the first day....*
>
> *Things could happen, I'm not going to lie to you. Something might happen. A recruit might decide he doesn't want any part of this stuff and maybe take a poke at you or something like that. In a situation like that it's going to be a spur-of-the-moment thing and that worries me.*
>
> —USMC drill instructor

But it rarely happens. The frantic bustle of forming is designed to give the recruit no time to think about resisting what is happening to him. And so the recruits emerge from their initiation into the system, stripped of their civilian clothes, shorn of their hair, and deprived of whatever confidence in their own identity they may previously have had as 18-year-olds, like so many blanks ready to have the Marine identity impressed upon them.

The first stage in any conversion process is the destruction of an individual's former beliefs and confidence, and his reduction to a position of helplessness and need. It isn't really as drastic as all that, of course, for three days cannot cancel out 18 years; the inner thoughts and the basic character are not erased. But the recruits have already learned that the only acceptable behavior is to repress any unorthodox thoughts and to mimic the character the Marine Corps wants. Nor are they, on the whole, reluctant to do so, for they *want* to be Marines. From the moment they arrive at Parris Island, the vague notion that has been passed down for a thousand generations that masculinity means being a warrior becomes an explicit article of faith, relentlessly preached: To be a man means to be a Marine.

There are very few 18-year-old boys who do not have highly romanticized ideas of what it means to be a man, so the Marine Corps has plenty of buttons to push. And it starts pushing them on the first day of real training: The officer in charge of the formation appears before them for the first time, in full dress uniform with medals, and tells them how to become men.

> *The United States Marine Corps has 205 years of illustrious history to speak for itself. You have made the most important decision in your life...by signing your name, your life, pledge to the Government of the United States, and even more importantly, to the United States Marine Corps—a brotherhood, an elite unit. In 10.3 weeks you are going to become a member of that history, those traditions, this organization—if you have what it takes....*

> *All of you want to do that by virtue of your signing your name as a man. The Marine Corps says that we build men. Well, I'll go a little bit further. We develop the tools that you have—and everybody has those tools to a certain extent right now. We're going to give you the blueprints, and we are going to show you how to build a Marine.* You've *got to build a Marine—you understand?*
>
> —Captain Pingree, USMC

The recruits, gazing at him with awe and adoration, shout in unison, "Yes, sir!" just as they have been taught. They do it willingly, because they are volunteers—but even conscripts tend to have the romantic fervor of volunteers if they are only 18 years old. Basic training, whatever its hardships, is a quick way to become a man among men, with an undeniable status, and beyond the initial consent to undergo it, it doesn't even require any decisions.

> *I had just dropped out of high school and I wasn't doing much on the street except hanging out, as most teenagers would be doing. So they gave me an opportunity—a recruiter picked me up, gave me a good line, and said that I could make it in the Marines, that I have a future ahead of me. And since I was living with my parents, I figured that I could start my own life here and grow up a little.*
>
> —USMC recruit

> *I like the hand-to-hand combat and...things like that. It's a little rough going on me, and since I have a small frame I would like to become deadly, as I would put it. I like to have them words, especially the way they've been teaching me here.*
>
> —USMC recruit (from Brooklyn), Parris Island

The training, when it starts, seems impossibly demanding physically for most of the recruits—and then it gets harder week by week. There is a constant barrage of abuse and insults aimed at the recruits, with the deliberate purpose of breaking down their pride and so destroying their ability to resist the transformation of values and attitudes that the Corps intends them to undergo. At the same time the demands for constant alertness and for instant obedience are continuously stepped up, and the standards by which the dress and behavior of the recruits are judged become steadily more unforgiving. But it is all carefully calculated by the men who run the machine, who think and talk in terms of the stress they are placing on the recruits: "We take so many c.c.'s of stress and we administer it to each man—they should be a little bit scared and they should be unsure, but they're adjusting." The aim is to keep the training arduous but just within most of the recruits' capability to withstand. One of the most striking achievements of the drill instructors is to create and maintain the illusion that basic training is an extraordinary challenge, one that will set those who graduate apart from others, when in fact almost everyone can succeed.

There has been some preliminary weeding out of potential recruits even before they begin training, to eliminate the obviously unsuitable minority, and some people do "fail" basic training and get sent home, at least in peacetime. The standards of acceptable performance in the U.S. armed forces, for example, tend to rise and fall in inverse proportion to the number and quality of recruits available to fill the forces to the authorized manpower levels. But there are very few young men who cannot be turned into passable soldiers if the forces are willing to invest enough effort in it.

Not even physical violence is necessary to effect the transformation, though it has been used by most armies at most times.

> *It's not what it was 15 years ago down here. The Marine Corps still occupies the position of a tool which the society uses when it feels like that is a resort that they have to fall to. Our society changes as all societies do, and our society felt that through enlightened training methods we could still produce the same product—and when you examine it, they're right.... Our 100 c.c.'s of stress is really all we need, not two gallons of it, which is what used to be.... In some cases with some of the younger drill instructors it was more an initiation than it was an acute test, and so we introduced extra officers and we select our drill instructors to "fine-tune" it.*
>
> —Captain Brassington, USMC

There is, indeed, a good deal of fine-tuning in the roles that the men in charge of training any specific group of recruits assume. At the simplest level, there is a sort of "good cop–bad cop" manipulation of the recruits' attitudes toward those applying the stress. The three younger drill instructors with a particular serial are quite close to them in age and unremittingly harsh in their demands for ever higher performance, but the senior drill instructor, a man almost old enough to be their father, plays a more benevolent and understanding part and is available for individual counseling. And generally offstage, but always looming in the background, is the company commander, an impossibly austere and almost godlike personage.

At least these are the images conveyed to the recruits, although of course all these men cooperate closely with an identical goal in view. It works: In the end they become not just role models and authority figures, but the focus of the recruits' developing loyalty to the organization.

> *I imagine there's some fear, especially in the beginning, because they don't know what to expect.... I think they hate you at first, at least for a week or two, but it turns to respect.... They're seeking discipline, they're seeking someone to take charge, 'cause at home they never got it.... They're looking to be told what to do and then someone is standing there enforcing what they tell them to do, and it's kind of like the father-and-son game, all the way through. They form a fatherly image of the DI whether they want to or not.*
>
> —Sergeant Carrington, USMC

Just the sheer physical exercise, administered in massive doses, soon has the recruits feeling stronger and more competent than ever before. Inspections, often several times daily, quickly build up their ability to wear the uniform and carry themselves like real Marines, which is a considerable source of pride. The inspections also help to set up the pattern in the recruits of unquestioning submission to military authority: Standing stock-still, staring straight ahead, while somebody else examines you closely for faults is about as extreme a ritual act of submission as you can make with your clothes on.

But they are not submitting themselves merely to the abusive sergeant making unpleasant remarks about the hair in their nostrils. All around them are deliberate reminders—the flags and insignia displayed on parade, the military music, the marching formations and drill instructors' cadenced calls—of the idealized organization, the "brotherhood" to which they will be admitted as full members if they submit and conform. Nowhere in the armed forces are the military courtesies so elaborately observed, the staffs' uniforms so immaculate (some DIs change several times a day), and the ritual aspects of military life so highly visible as on a basic training establishment.

Even the seeming inanity of close-order drill has a practical role in the conversion process. It has been over a century since mass formations of men were of any use on the battlefield, but every army in the world still drills its troops, especially during basic training, because marching in formation, with every man moving his body in the same way at the same moment, is a direct physical way of learning two things a soldier must believe: that orders have to be obeyed automatically and instantly, and that you are no longer an individual, but part of a group.

The recruits' total identification with the other members of their unit is the most important lesson of all, and everything possible is done to foster it. They spend almost every waking moment together—a recruit alone is an anomaly to be looked into at once—and during most of that time they are enduring shared hardships. They also undergo collective punishments, often for the misdeed or omission of a single individual (talking in the ranks, a bed not swept under during barracks inspection), which is a highly effective way of suppressing any tendencies toward individualism. And, of course, the DIs place relentless emphasis on competition with other "serials" in training: there may be something infinitely pathetic to outsiders about a marching group of anonymous recruits chanting, "Lift your heads and hold them high, 3313 is a-passin' by," but it doesn't seem like that to the men in the ranks.

Nothing is quite so effective in building up a group's morale and solidarity, though, as a steady diet of small triumphs. Quite early in basic training, the recruits begin to do things that seem, at first sight, quite dangerous: descend by ropes from fifty-foot towers, cross yawning gaps hand-over-hand on high wires (known as the Slide for Life, of course), and the like. The common denominator is that these activities are daunting but not really dangerous: the ropes will prevent anyone from falling to his death off the rappelling tower, and there is a pond of just the right depth—deep enough to cushion a falling man, but not deep enough that he is likely to drown—under the Slide for Life. The goal is not to kill recruits, but to build up their confidence as individuals and as a group by allowing them to overcome apparently frightening obstacles.

> *You have an enemy here at Parris Island. The enemy that you're going to have at Parris Island is in every one of us. It's in the form of cowardice. The most rewarding experience you're going to have in recruit training is standing on line every evening, and you'll be able to look into each other's eyes, and you'll be able to say to each other with your eyes: "By God, we've made it one more day! We've defeated the coward."*
>
> —Captain Pingree

> *Number on deck, sir, 45... highly motivated, truly dedicated, rompin', stompin', bloodthirsty, kill-crazy United States Marine Corps recruits, SIR!*
>
> —Marine chant, Parris Island

If somebody does fail a particular test, he tends to be alone, for the hurdles are deliberately set low enough that most recruits can clear them if they try. In any large group of people there is usually a goat: someone whose intelligence or manner or lack of physical stamina marks him for failure and contempt. The competent drill instructor, without deliberately setting up this unfortunate individual for disgrace, will use his failure to strengthen the solidarity and confidence of the rest. When one hapless young man fell off the Slide for Life into the pond, for example, his drill instructor shouted the usual invective—"Well, get out of the water. Don't contaminate it all day"—and then delivered the payoff line: "Go back and change your clothes. You're useless to your unit now."

"Useless to your unit" is the key phrase, and all the recruits know that what it means is "useless in *battle.*" The Marine drill instructors at Parris Island know exactly what they are doing to the recruits, and why. They are not rear-echelon people filling comfortable jobs, but the most dedicated and intelligent NCOs the Marine Corps can find; even now, many of them have combat experience. The Corps has a clear-eyed understanding of precisely what it is training its recruits for—combat—and it ensures that those who do the training keep that objective constantly in sight.

The DIs "stress" the recruits, feed them their daily ration of synthetic triumphs over apparent obstacles, and bear in mind all the time that the goal is to instill the foundations for the instinctive, selfless reactions and the fierce group loyalty that is what the recruits will need if they ever see combat. They are arch-manipulators, fully conscious of it, and utterly unashamed. These kids have signed up as Marines, and they could well see combat; this is the way they have to think if they want to live.

> *I've seen guys come to Vietnam from all over. They were all sorts of people that had been scared—some of them had been scared all their life and still scared. Some of them had been a country boy, city boys—you know, all different kinds of people—but when they got in combat they all reacted the same—99 percent of them reacted the same.... A lot of it is training here at Parris Island, but the other part of it is survival. They know if they don't conform—conform I call it, but if they don't react in the same way other people are reacting, they won't survive. That's just it. You know, if you don't react together, then nobody survives.*
>
> —USMC drill instructor, Parris Island

> *When I went to boot camp and did individual combat training they said if you walk into an ambush what you want to do is just do a right face—you just turn right or left, whichever way the fire is coming from, and assault. I said, "Man, that's crazy. I'd never do anything like that. It's stupid."...*
>
> *The first time we came under fire, on Hill 1044 in Operation Beauty Canyon in Laos, we did it automatically. Just like you look at your watch to see what time it is. We done a right face, assaulted the hill—a fortified position with concrete bunkers emplaced, machine guns, automatic weapons—and we took it. And we killed—I'd estimate probably 35 North Vietnamese soldiers in the assault, and we only lost three killed. I think it was about two or three, and about eight or ten wounded....*
>
> *But you know, what they teach you, it doesn't faze you until it comes down to the time to use it, but it's in the back of your head, like, What do you do when you come to a stop sign? It's in the back of your head, and you react automatically.*
>
> —USMC sergeant

Combat is the ultimate reality that Marines—or any other soldiers, under any flag—have to deal with. Physical fitness, weapons training, battle drills, are all indispensable elements of basic training, and it is absolutely essential that the recruits learn the attitudes of group loyalty and interdependency which will be their sole hope of survival and success in combat. The training inculcates or fosters all of those things, and even by the halfway point in the 11-week course, the recruits are generally responding with enthusiasm to their tasks....

In basic training establishments,...the malleability is all one way: in the direction of submission to military authority and the internalization of military values. What a place like Parris Island produces when it is successful, as it usually is, is a soldier who will kill because that is his job.

READING 4

Diary of a Homeless Man

John R. Coleman

introduction

When I was doing research on the homeless, I slept in homeless shelters across the nation–in about a dozen U.S. cities and one in Canada. The research was emotionally draining. I was challenged continuously to be alert to conduct the seemingly endless interviews and to watch out for danger that appeared to lurk around every comer. (I dictated one of my recordings squatted next to a building, describing the arrival of the police and medics to take a homeless man to the hospital. He had been attacked by another homeless man.)

I had built in a break with my brother and his family in California. When he and his wife went to work the day after I arrived, I was left alone in the house. It was at this point that I realized what a marvelous luxury a living room is. I could lie on the couch and flip TV channels to my heart's content. I had always taken the living room for granted, and only by being with the homeless who had no living rooms did the significance of "living room" hit me. The room actually took on a different meaning.

For thousands of people, the city street is their living room. These discards of the advanced technological society have been left behind in our culturally mandated frenetic pursuit for material wealth. Like others, John Coleman, the president of a small, private college, had seen these strange people on the streets of the city. Like others, he wondered what their life was like. And like a few of us–very few–he decided to find out first hand, by experiencing their world. He, too, left his comfortable, upper-middle-class home and joined the street people. This is his engrossing account of that experience.

Thinking Critically

As you read this selection, ask yourself:

1. How do you think that the problem of homelessness can be solved? You must be practical; that is, you should try to come up with workable solutions.
2. Why do you think that the homeless are treated with such disdain (lack of respect)?
3. Assume that we will continue to have homeless people. How can we improve the way they are treated? Cite specific instances from the reading that you would try to solve.

WEDNESDAY, 1/19

Somehow, 12 degrees at 6 A.M. was colder than I had counted on. I think of myself as relatively immune to cold, but standing on a deserted sidewalk outside Penn Station with the thought of ten days ahead of me as a homeless man, the immunity vanished. When I pulled my collar closer and my watch cap lower, it wasn't to look the part of a street person; it was to keep the wind out.

My wardrobe wasn't much help. I had bought my "new" clothes—flannel shirt, baggy sweater, torn trousers, the cap and the coat—the day before on Houston Street for $19. "You don't need to buy shoes," the shop-keeper had said. "The ones you have on will pass for a bum's." I was hurt; they were shoes I often wore to the office.

Having changed out of my normal clothes in the Penn Station men's room and stowed them in a locker, I was ready for the street. Or thought so.

Was I imagining it, or were people looking at me in a completely different way? I felt that men, especially the successful-looking ones in their forties and over, saw me and wondered. For the rest, I wasn't there.

At Seventh Avenue and 35th Street, I went into a coffee shop. The counterman looked me over carefully. When I ordered the breakfast special—99 cents plus tax—he told me I'd have to pay in advance. I did (I'd brought $40 to see me through the ten days), but I noticed that the other customers were given checks, and paid only when they left.

By 9:30, I had read a copy of the *Times* retrieved from a trash basket; I had walked most of the streets around the station; I had watched the construction at the new convention center. There was little else to do.

Later, I sat and watched the drug sales going on in Union Square. Then I went into the Income Maintenance Center on 14th Street and watched the people moving through the welfare lines. I counted the trucks on Houston Street.

I vaguely remembered a quote to the effect that "idleness is only enjoyable when you have a lot to do." It would help to be warm, too.

There was ample time and incentive to stare at the other homeless folk on the street. For the most part, they weren't more interesting than the typical faces on Wall Street or upper Madison Avenue. But the extreme cases caught and held the eye. On Ninth Avenue, there was a man on the sidewalk directing an imaginary (to me) flow of traffic. And another, two blocks away, tracing the flight of planes or birds—or spirits—in the winter sky. And there was a woman with gloves tied to her otherwise bare feet.

Standing outside the Port Authority Bus Terminal was a man named Howard. He was perhaps my age, but the seasons had left deeper marks on his face. "Come summertime, it's all going to be different," he told me. "I'm going to have a car to go to the beach. And I'm going to get six lemons and make me a jug of ice-cold lemonade to go with the car.

"This whole country's gone too far with the idea of one person being at the top. It starts with birthday parties. Who gets to blow out the candle? One person. And it takes off from there. If we're ever going to make things better, we gotta start with those candles."

From *New York* Magazine, February 21, 1982. Reprinted by permission of the author.

Was there any chance of people like us finding work?

"Jobs are still out there for the young guys who want them," Howard said. "But there's nothing for us. Never again. No, I stopped dreaming about jobs a long time ago. Now I dream about cars. And lemonade."

Drugs and alcohol are common among the homeless. The damage done by them was evident in almost every street person I saw. But which was cause, and which was effect? Does it matter, once this much harm has been done?

My wanderings were all aimless. There was no plan, no goal, no reason to be anywhere at any time. Only hours into this role, I felt a useless part of the city streets. I wasn't even sure why I was doing this....

A weathered drifter told me about a hideaway down in the bowels of the station, where it was warm and quiet. I found my way there and lay down on some old newspapers to sleep.

How long did I sleep? It didn't seem long at all. I was awakened by a flashlight shining in my eyes, and a voice, not an unkind one, saying, "You can't sleep here. Sorry, but you have to go outside."

I hadn't expected to hear that word "sorry." It was touching.

I left and walked up to 47th Street, between Fifth and Madison Avenues, where I knew there was a warm grate in the sidewalk. (I've been passing it every morning for over five years on my way to work.) One man was asleep there already. But there was room for two, and he moved over.

THURSDAY, 1/20

When you're spending the night on the street, you learn to know morning is coming by the kinds of trucks that roll by. As soon as there are other than garbage trucks—say, milk or bread trucks—you know the night will soon be over.

I went back to Penn Station to clean up in the washroom. The care with which some of the other men with me bathed themselves at the basins would have impressed any public-health officer. And I couldn't guess from the appearance of their clothes who would be the most fastidious.

I bought coffee and settled back to enjoy it out of the main traffic paths in the station. No luck. A cop found me and told me to take it to the street.

After breakfast ($1.31 at Blimpie), I walked around to keep warm until the public library opened. I saw in a salvaged copy of the *Times* that we had just had our coldest night of the year, well below zero with the windchill factor, and that a record 4,635 people had sought shelter in the city's hostels.

The library was a joy. The people there treated me the same as they might have had I been wearing my business suit. To pass the time, I got out the city's welfare reports for 50 years ago. In the winter of 1933, the city had 4,524 beds available for the homeless, and all were said to be filled every night. The parallel to 1983 was uncanny. But, according to the reports, the man in charge of the homeless program in 1933, one Joseph A. Manning, wasn't worried about the future. True, the country was in the midst of a depression. But there had been a slight downturn in the numbers served in the shelters in the two months immediately preceding his report. This meant, wrote Manning, that "the depression, in the parlance of the ring, is K.O.'d."

Already, I notice changes in me. I walk much more slowly. I no longer see a need to beat a traffic light or to be the first through a revolving door. Force of habit still makes me look at my wrist every once in a while. But there's no watch there, and it wouldn't make any difference if there were. The thermometer has become much more important to me now than any timepiece could be....

The temperature rose during the day. Just as the newspaper headlines seem to change more slowly when you're on the streets all day long, so the temperature seems to change more rapidly and tellingly.

At about 9 P.M., I went back to the heated grate on 47th Street. The man who had been there last night was already in place. He made it clear that there was again room for me:

I asked him how long he had been on the streets.

"Eleven years, going on twelve," he said.

"This is only my second night."

"You may not stick it out. This isn't for every man."

"Do you ever go into the shelters?"

"I couldn't take that. I prefer this anytime."

FRIDAY, 1/21

When I left my grate mate—long before dawn—he wished me a good day. I returned the gesture: He meant his, and I meant mine.

In Manhattan's earliest hours, you get the feeling that the manufacture and removal of garbage is the city's main industry. So far, I haven't been lucky or observant enough to rescue much of use from the mounds of trash waiting for the trucks and crews. The best find was a canvas bag that will fit nicely over my feet at night.

I'm slipping into a routine: Washing up at the station. Coffee on the street. Breakfast at Blimpie. A search for the *Times* in the trash baskets. And then a leisurely stretch of reading in the park.

Some days bring more luck than others. Today I found 20 cents in a pay-phone slot and heard a young flutist playing the music of C.P.E. Bach on Sixth Avenue between 9th and 10th streets. A lot of people ignored her, even stepped over her flute case as if it were litter on the sidewalk. More often than not, those who put money in the case looked embarrassed. They seemed to be saying, "Don't let anyone see me being appreciative."

By nightfall, the streets were cruelly cold once again....

I headed for the 47th Street grate again but found my mate gone. There was no heat coming up through it. Do they turn it off on Friday nights? Don't we homeless have any rights?

On the northwest corner of Eighth Avenue and 33rd Street, there was a blocked-off subway entrance undergoing repair. I curled up against the wall there under some cardboard sheets. Rain began to fall, but I stayed reasonably dry and was able to get to sleep.

At some point, I was awakened by a man who had pulled back the upper piece of cardboard.

"You see my partner here. You need to give us some money."

I was still half-asleep. "I don't have any."

"You must have something, man."

"Would I be sleeping here in the rain if I did?"

His partner intervened. "C'mon. Leave the old bastard alone. He's not worth it."

"He's got something. Get up and give it to us."

I climbed to my feet and began fumbling in my pocket. Both men were on my left side. That was my chance. Suddenly I took off and ran along 33rd Street toward Ninth Avenue. They gave no chase. And a good thing, too, because I was too stiff with cold to run a good race.

SATURDAY, 1/22

A man I squatted next to in a doorway on 29th Street said it all: "The onliest thing is to have a warm place to sleep. That and having somebody care about you. That'd be even onlier."

He had what appeared to be rolls of paper toweling wrapped around one leg and tied with red ribbon. But the paper, wet with rain by now, didn't seem to serve any purpose.

I slept little. The forecast was for more rain tomorrow, so why wish the night away?

The morning paper carried news of Mayor Koch's increased concern about the homeless.

But what can he do? He must worry that the more New York does to help, the greater the numbers will grow. At the moment he's berating the synagogues for not doing anything to take street people in.

Watching people come and go at the Volvo tennis tournament at Madison Square Garden, I sensed how uncomfortable they were at the presence of the homeless. Easy to love in the abstract, not so easy face to face.

It's no wonder that the railway police are under orders to chase us out of sight.

Perhaps a saving factor is that we're not individuals. We're not people anybody knows. So far I've had eye contact with only three people who know me in my other life. None showed a hint of recognition. One was the senior auditor at Arthur Andersen & Company, the accounting firm that handles the Clark Foundation, my employer. One was a fellow lieutenant in the Auxiliary Police Force, a man with whom I had trained for many weeks. And one was an owner in the cooperative apartment where I live....

Early in the evening I fell asleep on the Seventh Avenue steps outside the Garden. Three Amtrak cops shook me awake to ask if two rather good-looking suitcases on the steps were mine. I said that I had never seen them.

One cop insisted that I was lying, but then a black man appeared and said they belonged to a friend of his. The rapid-fire questioning from two of the cops soon made that alibi rather unlikely. The third cop was going through the cases and spreading a few of the joints he found inside on the ground.

As suddenly as it had begun, the incident was over. The cops walked away, and the man retrieved the bags. I fell back to sleep. Some hours later when I woke up again, the black man was still there, selling.

SUNDAY, 1/23

A new discovery of a warm and dry, even scenic, place to sit on a rainy day: the Staten Island Ferry.

For one 25-cent fare, I had four crossings of the harbor, read all I wanted of the copy of the Sunday *Times* I'd found, and finished the crossword puzzle.

When I got back to the Garden, where the tennis tournament was in its last hours, I found the police were being extra diligent in clearing us away from the departing crowds. One older woman was particularly incensed at being moved. "You're ruining my sex life," she shouted. "That's what you're doing. My sex life. Do you hear?"

A younger woman approached me to ask if I was looking for love. "No, ma'am. I'm just trying to stay out of the rain."...

So, back to the unused subway entrance, because there was still no heat across town on the 47th Street grate.

The night was very cold. Parts of me ached as I tried to sleep. Turning over was a chore, not only because the partially wet cardboard had to be re-arranged with such care, but also because the stiffer parts of my body seemed to belong to someone else. Whatever magic there was in those lights cutting down through the fog was gone by now. All I wanted was to be warm and dry once more. Magic could wait.

MONDAY, 1/24

Early this morning I went to the warren of employment agencies on 14th Street to see if I could get a day's work. There was very little action at most of these last-ditch offices, where minimum wages and sub-minimum conditions are the rule.

But I did get one interview and thought I had a dishwashing job lined up. I'd forgotten one thing. I had no identification with me. No identification, no job.

There was an ageless, shaggy woman in Bryant Park this morning who delivered one of the more interesting monologues I've heard. For a full ten minutes, with no interruption from me beyond an occasional "Uh huh," she analyzed society's ills without missing a beat.

Beginning with a complaint about the women's and men's toilets in the park being locked ("What's a poor body to do?"), she launched into the strengths of the Irish, who, though strong, still need toilets more than others, and the weaknesses of the English and the Jews, the advantages of raising turkeys over other fowl, and the wickedness of Eleanor Roosevelt in letting the now Queen Mother and that stuttering king of hers rave so much about the hot dogs served at Hyde Park that we had no alternative but to enter World War II on their side. The faulty Russian satellite that fell into the Indian Ocean this morning was another example of shenanigans, she said. It turns out the Russians and Lady Diana, "that so-called Princess of Wales," are in cahoots to keep us so alarmed about such things far away from home that we don't get anything done about prayer in schools or the rest of it. But after all, what would those poor Protestant ministers do for a living if the children got some real religion in school, like the kind we got from the nuns, God bless them?

That at least was the gist of what she said. I know I've missed some of the finer points.

At 3:30 P.M., with more cold ahead, I sought out the Men's Shelter at 8 East 3rd Street. This is the principal entry point for men seeking the city's help. It provides meals for 1,300 or so people every day and beds for some few of those. I had been told that while there was no likelihood of getting a bed in this building I'd be given a meal here and a bed in some other shelter.

I've seen plenty of drawings of London's workhouses and asylums in the times of Charles Dickens. Now I've seen the real thing, in the last years of the twentieth century in the world's greatest city.

The lobby, and the adjacent "sitting room" were jammed with men standing, sitting, or stretched out in various positions on the floor. It was as lost a collection of souls as I could have imagined. Old and young, scarred and smooth, stinking and clean, crippled and hale, drunk and sober, ranting and still, parts of another world and parts of this one. The city promises to take in anyone who asks. Those rejected everywhere else find their way to East 3rd Street.

The air was heavy with the odors of Thunderbird wine, urine, sweat, and, above all, nicotine and marijuana. Three or four Human Resources Administration police officers seemed to be keeping the violence down to tolerable levels, but barely so.

After a long delay, I got a meal ticket for dinner and was told to come back later for a lodging ticket.

It was time to get in line to eat. This meant crowding into what I can only compare to a cattle chute in a stockyard. It ran along two walls of the sitting room and was already jammed. A man with a bullhorn kept yelling at us to stand up and stay in line. One very old and decrepit (or drunk?) man couldn't stay on his feet. He was helped to a chair, from which he promptly fell onto the floor. The bullhorn man had some choice obscenities for him, but they didn't seem to have any effect. The old man just lay there; and we turned our thoughts back to the evening meal.

I made a quick, and probably grossly unfair, assessment of the hundreds of men I could see in the room. Judging them solely by appearance, alertness, and body movements, I decided that one-quarter of them were perfectly able to work; they, more likely than not, were among the warriors who helped us win the battle against inflation by the selfless act of joining the jobless ranks. Another quarter might be brought back in time into job-readiness by some counseling and some caring for them as individuals. But the other half seemed so ravaged by illness, addiction, and sheer neglect that I couldn't imagine them being anything but society's wards from here on out to—one hopes—a peaceful end.

At the appointed hour, we were released in groups of twenty or thirty to descend the dark, filthy steps to the basement eating area. The man with the bullhorn was there again, clearly in charge and clearly relishing the extra power given to his voice by electric amplification. He insulted us collectively and separately without pause, but because his vocabulary was limited it tended to be the same four-letter words over and over.

His loudest attack on me came when I didn't move fast enough to pick up my meal from the counter. His analysis of certain flaws in my white ancestry wasn't hard to follow, even for a man in as much of a daze as I was.

The shouting and the obscenities didn't stop once we had our food. Again and again we were told to finish and get out. Eating took perhaps six minutes, but those minutes removed any shred of dignity a man might have brought in with him from the street.

Back upstairs, the people in charge were organizing the people who were to go to a shelter in Brooklyn. Few had volunteered, so there was more haranguing.

In the line next to the one where I was waiting for my lodging ticket a fight suddenly broke out. One man pulled a long knife from his overcoat pocket. The other man ran for cover, and a police officer soon appeared to remove the man with the knife from the scene. The issue, it seems, was one of proper places in the line.

There still weren't enough Brooklyn volunteers to suit the management, so they brought in their big gun: Mr. Bullhorn. "Now, listen up," he barked. "There aren't any buses going to Ft. Washington [another shelter] until 11:30, so if you want to get some sleep, go to Brooklyn. Don't ask me any questions. Just shut up and listen. It's because you don't listen up that you end up in a place like this."

I decided to ask a question anyway, about whether there would still be a chance for me to go Brooklyn once I got my lodging ticket. He turned on me and let me have the full force of the horn: "Don't ask questions, I said. You're not nobody."

The delays at the ticket-issuing window went on and on. Three staff members there seemed reasonably polite and even efficient. The fourth and heaviest one—I have no idea whether it was a man or woman—could not have moved more slowly without coming to a dead halt. The voice of someone who was apparently a supervisor came over the public-address system from time to time to apologize for the delay in going to the Ft. Washington shelter, which was in an armory, but any good he did from behind the scenes was undone by the staff out front and a "see-no-work, hear-no-work, do-no-work" attendant in the office.

As 11:30 approached, we crowded back into the sitting room to get ready to board the buses. A new martinet had appeared on the scene. He got as much attention through his voice, cane, and heavy body as Mr. Bullhorn had with his amplifying equipment. But this new man was more openly vile and excitable; he loved the power that went with bunching us all up close together and then ordering us to stretch out again in a thinner line. We practiced that routine several times....

Long after the scheduled departure, the lines moved. We sped by school buses to the armory at Ft. Washington Avenue and 168th Street. There we were met, just before 2:30 A.M., by military police, social workers, and private guards. They marched us into showers (very welcome), gave us clean underwear, and sent us upstairs to comfortable cots arranged in long rows in a room as big as a football field.

There were 530 of us there for the night, and we were soon quiet.

TUESDAY, 1/25

We were awakened at 6 A.M. by whistles and shouting, and ordered to get back onto the buses for the return trip to lower Manhattan as soon as possible.

Back at 8 East 3rd Street, the worst of the martinets were off duty. So I thought breakfast might be a bit quieter than dinner had been. Still, by eight, I had seen three incidents a bit out of the ordinary for me.

A man waiting for breakfast immediately ahead of me in the cattle chute suddenly grabbed a chair from the adjoining area and prepared to break it over his neighbor's head. In my haste to get out of the way, I fell over an older man sleeping against the wall. After some shouts about turf, things cooled off between the fighters, and the old man forgave me.

In the stairwell leading down to the eating area, a young man made a sexual advance to me. When I withdrew from him and stupidly reached for my coat pocket, he thought I was going for a weapon. He at once pinned me against the wall and searched my pockets; there was nothing there.

As I came out of the building onto East 3rd Street, two black Human Resources Administration policemen were bringing two young blacks into the building. One officer had his man by the neck. The other officer had his man's hands cuffed behind his back and repeatedly kicked him hard in the buttocks.

My wanderings were still more aimless today. I couldn't get East 3rd Street out of my mind. What could possibly justify some of that conduct? If I were a staff member there, would I become part of the worst in that pattern? Or would I simply do as little, and think as little, as possible?

At day's end I can't recall much of where I went or why I went there.

Only isolated moments remain with me. Like...staring at the elegant crystal and silver in the shops just north of Madison Square Park and wondering what these windows say to the people I'd spent the night with.

Much too soon it was time to go back to the shelter for dinner and another night. At first I thought I didn't have the guts to do it again. Does one have to do *this* to learn who the needy are? I wanted to say, "Enough! There's only so much I need to see."

But I went back to the shelter anyway, probably because it took more guts to quit than it did to go ahead.

A man beside me in the tense dinner line drove one truth of this place home to me. "I never knew hell came in this color," he said.

I was luckier in my assignment for the night. I drew the Keener Building, on Wards Island, a facility with a capacity of 416 men. The building was old and neglected, and the atmosphere of a mental hospital, which it once was, still hung over it. But the staff was polite, the rooms weren't too crowded (there were only twelve beds in Room 326), the single sheet on each bed was clean, and there was toilet paper in the bathroom.

There were limits and guards and deprivations, but there was also an orderliness about the place. Here, at least, I didn't feel I had surrendered all of my dignity at the door.

WEDNESDAY, 1/26

...Back to the shelter on East 3rd Street for dinner.

There is simply no other situation I've seen that is so devoid of any graces at all, so tense at every moment, or so empty of hope. The food isn't bad, and the building is heated; that's all it has going for it.

The only cutlery provided is a frail plastic spoon. With practice you can spread hard oleo onto your bread with the back of one. If there's liver or ham, you don't have to cut it; just put it between the two pieces of bread that go with each meal. Everything else—peas, collard greens, apple pudding, plums—can be managed with the spoon. And talk over dinner or sipping, rather than gulping, coffee isn't all that important.

What is hardest to accept is the inevitable jungle scene during the hour you stand in line waiting to eat. Every minute seems to be one that invites an explosion. You know instinctively that men can't come this often to the brink without someone going over. One person too many is going to try to jump ahead in line. One particular set of toes is going to be stepped on by mistake. And the lid is going to blow.

The most frightening people here are the many young, intensely angry blacks. Hatred pours out in all of their speech and some of their actions. I could spend a lot of time imagining how and why they became so completely angry—but if I were the major, the counselor, or the man with the bullhorn, I wouldn't know how to divert them from that anger any more. Hundreds and hundreds of men here have been destroyed by alcohol or drugs. A smaller, but for me more poignant, number are being destroyed by hate.

Their loudest message—and because their voices are so strong it is very loud indeed—is "Respect me, man." The constant theme is that someone or some group is putting them down, stepping on them, asking them to conform to a code they don't accept, getting in their way, writing them off.

So most of the fights begin over turf. A place in line. A corner to control. The have-nots scrapping with the have-nots....

Tonight, I chose the Brooklyn shelter because I thought the buses going there would leave soonest. The shelter, a converted school, is on Williams Avenue and has about 400 beds.

We left in fairly good time but learned when we got to the shelter that no new beds would be assigned until after 11 P.M. We were to sit in the auditorium until then.

At about ten, a man herded as many of us newcomers as would listen to him into a corner of the auditorium. There he delivered an abusive diatribe outlining the horror that lay ahead for our possessions and our bodies during the night to come. It made the ranting at East 3rd Street seem tame.

It's illustrative of what the experience of homelessness and helplessness does to people that all of us—regardless of age, race, background, or health—listened so passively.

Only at midnight, when some other officials arrived, did we learn that this man had no standing whatsoever. He was just an underling who strutted for his time on the stage before any audience cowed enough to take what he dished out....

THURSDAY, 1/27

Back on the street this morning, I became conscious of how little time I had left to live this way. There seemed so much still to do, and so little time in which to do it.

One part of me tells me I have been fully a part of this. I know I walk with slower steps and bent shoulders.... I know I worry a lot more about keeping clean.

But then I recall how foolish that is, I'm acting. This will end tomorrow night. I can quit any time I want to. And unlike my mate from 47th Street, I haven't the slightest idea of what eleven years of sleeping on a grate amount to.

Early this afternoon, I went again to the Pavilion restaurant, where I had eaten five times before. I didn't recognize the man at the cash register.

"Get out," he said.

"But I have money."

"You heard me. Get out." His voice was stronger.

"That man knows me," I said, looking toward the owner in the back of the restaurant.

The owner nodded, and the man at the register said, "Okay, but sit in the back."

If this life in the streets had been real, I'd have gone out the door at the first "Get out." And the assessment of me as not worthy would have been self-fulfilling; I'd have lost so much respect for myself that I wouldn't have been worthy of being served the next time. The downward spiral would have begun.

Until now I haven't understood the extent of nicotine addiction. Dependencies on drugs and alcohol have been around me for a long time, but I thought before that smoking was a bad habit rather easy to overcome.

How many times have I, a nonsmoker, been begged for a cigarette in these days? Surely hundreds. Cigarettes are central. A few folks give them away, a small number sell them for up to 8 cents apiece, and almost all give that last pathetic end of a butt to the first man who asks for what little bit is left. I know addiction now as I didn't before.

Tonight, after a repeat of the totally degrading dinner-line scene at East 3rd Street, I signed up for Keener once again. No more Brooklyn for me.

Sitting upstairs with the other Keener-bound men, I carelessly put my left foot on the rung of the chair in front of me, occupied by a young black.

"Get your foot off, yo."

("Yo" means "Hey, there," "Watch yourself," "Move along," and much more.)

I took it off. "Sorry," I said.

But it was too late. I had broken a cardinal rule. I had violated the man's turf. As we stood in the stairwell waiting for the buses, he told a much bigger, much louder, much angrier friend what I had done.

That man turned on me.

"Wait till we get you tonight, whitey. You stink. Bad. The worst I've ever smelled. And when you put your foot on that chair, you spread your stink around. You better get yourself a shower as soon as we get there, but it won't save you later on.... And don't sit near me or him on the bus. You hear, whitey?"

I didn't reply.

The bombardment went on as we mounted the bus. No one spoke up in my defense. Three people waved me away when I tried to sit next to them. The next person, black and close to my age, made no objection when I sat beside him.

The big man continued to tirade for a while, but he soon got interested in finding out from the driver how to go about getting a bus-driver's license. Perhaps he had come down from a high.

I admit I was scared. I wrote my name, address, and office telephone number on a piece of paper and slipped it into my pocket. At least someone would know where to call if the threats were real. I knew I couldn't and wouldn't defend myself in this setting.

While we stood in line on Wards Island waiting for our bed assignments, there were plenty of gripes about the man who was after me. But no one said anything directly to him. Somehow it didn't seem that this was the night when the meek would inherit the earth.

I slept fitfully. I don't like lying with the sheet hiding my face.

FRIDAY, 1/28

I was up and out of Keener as early as possible. That meant using some of my little remaining money for a city-bus ride back to Manhattan, but it was worth it to get out of there.

After breakfast on East 3rd Street, I was finished with the public shelters. That was an easy break for me to make, because I had choices and could run.

The day was cold and, for the early hours, clear. I washed the memory of the big man at 3rd Street out of my mind by wandering through the Fulton Fish Market. I walked across the Brooklyn Bridge and even sang as I realized how free I was to relax and enjoy its beauty.

With a cup of coffee and the *Times*, I sat on a cinder block by the river and read. In time, I wandered through the Wall Street district and almost learned the lay of some of the streets.

I walked up to the Quaker Meeting House at Rutherford Place and 15th Street. Standing on the porch outside, I tried hard to think how the doctrine that "there is that of God in every person" applied to that man last night and to some of the others I had encountered in these ten days. I still think it applies, but it isn't always easy to see how....

Darkness came. I got kicked out of both the bus terminal and Grand Central. I got my normal clothes out of the locker at Penn Station, changed in the men's room, and rode the AA train home.

My apartment was warm, and the bed was clean.

That's the onliest thing.

PART

II Social Groups and Social Control

It is easy to lose sight of the sociological significance of where we are born, that our birth ushers us into a world that already exists. For the most part, we yawn at such a statement. It seems to be an "of-course-we-all-know-that" type of thing, and ordinarily we fail to grasp its profound implications. That the world we enter is already constructed means that we join a human group with established ways of "doing social life." That is, we enter a group that has constructed an arbitrary system of norms and ideas that we are expected to follow. From birth, we are immersed in this sea of expectations. They may pinch, but we are only individuals. The group has already made the rules within which we are to live our lives. The game is in progress, and we have little choice but to play it.

Like a game, for social life to exist, rules are absolutely necessary. If you can't depend on people to do things, everything falls apart. For social groups to function, then—to do whatever they have set out to do—they must be able to depend on their members. This applies to all social groups, whether they be as small as our family or as large as a multinational corporation.

Deviance, however, is as inevitable as rules are necessary. Where there are rules, there will be rule breakers. *All* of us violate some of our group's many rules; that is, we all fail to meet some of the expectations that others have of us. When we do this, we become deviants. In sociology, *deviant* simply means someone who has deviated from the rules, someone who has wandered from the path that he or she was expected to follow. Deviant does *not* mean a horrible person—although horrible people are included in the term.

It has been said that the first rule of sociology is that nothing is as it appears, that behind the scenes lies a different reality. If so, then it is a goal of sociology to expose this hidden reality, the one that groups so carefully put forward for public consumption. We only have to peer deeply enough.

Sociologists have found that participant observation (reviewed in Chapter 1 of *Essentials*) is a good way of peering behind the scenes. It helps us explore this parallel reality that usually opens only to insiders. Just as the preceding article gave us a behind-the-scenes glimpse of the life of homeless people, so in the opening article of this part, Daniel Chambliss takes us behind the scenes of the hospital to reveal what really goes on there. This enables us to grasp a perspective that contrasts sharpley with the one that is usually presented to us. To probe behind the scenes, sociologists also use in-depth interviews. In the second and concluding selection of this part, Nanette Davis turns the sociological lens on how young women become prostitutes. From her interviews, she found that theirs is not a conscious decision. Instead, they drift from promiscuity to prostitution. As you read this article, note how the self-identity of these women changes as they move from one status to another.

READING 5

Just Another Routine Emergency

Daniel F. Chambliss

introduction

Just as buildings have façades—attractive, carefully manicured front exteriors that are designed to give a good impression of what might be inside—so social groups and organizations have façades. Some organizations hire public relations firms to put out favorable messages. Others contribute to charitable causes to cultivate images of caring. Even oil companies that exploit the environment publish expensive, full-page glossy ads in national magazines to convince the public that they care more about the environment than does *Greenpeace* or *The Sea Shepards.*

Behind the social façade put out for public consumption lies a different reality. As in the case of some oil companies, the reality may conflict greatly with the cultivated public image. But in the typical case, the hidden reality has more to do with dissension among the group's members, or with less dedication to the group's goals, than the organization wants to reveal. At times, the façade may have more to do with maintaining an appearance of competence and order, whereas the reality is a looming incompetence and disorder. This selection by Daniel Chambliss takes a look behind the social façade of the hospital, revealing a reality that few of us are familiar with.

Thinking Critically

As you read this selection, ask yourself:

1. How do the personnel of hospitals keep outsiders from seeing past their social façade?
2. What did this participant observation study reveal about hospitals that we otherwise would not have known?
3. Use this reading to prove or disprove this statement: From their callous and inappropriate humor, we can see that doctors and nurses don't really care about their patients.

Every unit in the hospital...has its own normality, its own typical patients, number of deaths, and crises to be faced. But just as predictably, every unit has its emergencies that threaten the routine and challenge the staff's ability to maintain workaday attitudes and practices. Emergencies threaten the staff's ability to carry on as usual, to maintain their own distance from the patient's suffering, and to hold at bay their awe at the enormity of events. Occasionally breakdowns occur in unit discipline or the ability to do the required work.

Staff follow several strategies when trying to manage the threat of breakdowns: they will keep outsiders outside, follow routinization rituals, or use humor to distance themselves. Finally, even when all efforts fail, they will keep going, no matter what. Consider in turn each of these implicit maxims:

1. KEEP OUTSIDERS OUTSIDE

Every hospital has policies about visiting hours, designed not only to "let patients rest" but also to protect staff from outsiders' interference in their work. Visitors are limited to certain hours, perhaps two to a patient room for fifteen-minute visits; they may have to be announced before entering the unit or may be kept waiting in a room down the hall. No doubt many such policies are good for the patient. No doubt, too, they keep visitors out of the nurse's way, prevent too many obtrusive questions or requests for small services, and prevent curious laypersons from seeing the messier, less presentable sides of nursing care.

When visitors cannot be physically excluded, they can still be cognitively controlled, that is, prevented from knowing that something untoward is happening. Typically, the staff behave in such episodes as if everything were OK, even when it is not. This is similar to what Erving Goffman observed in conversations: when the shared flow of interaction is threatened by an accidental insult or a body failure such as a sneeze or flatulence, people simply try to ignore the break in reality and carry on as if nothing has happened. Such "reality maintenance" is often well-orchestrated, requiring cooperation on the part of several parties. For Goffman, normal people in normal interactions accept at face value each other's presentation of who they are:

> A state where everyone temporarily accepts everyone else's line is established. This kind of mutual acceptance seems to be a basic structural feature of interaction, especially the interaction of face-to-face talk. It is typically a "working" acceptance, not a "real" one.[1]

And when this routine breaks down, the immediate strategy is simple denial:

> When a person fails to prevent an incident, he can still attempt to maintain the fiction that no threat to face has occurred. The most blatant example of this is found where the person acts as if an event that contains a threatening expression has not occurred at all.[2]

In the hospital, the unexpected entrance of outsiders into a delicate situation can disrupt the staff's routine activities and create unmanageable chaos. To avoid this, the staff may pretend to outsiders that nothing special is happening; this pretense itself can be part of the routine. During a code (resuscitation) effort I witnessed, there were three such potential disruptions by outsiders: another patient calling for help, a new incoming patient being wheeled in, and the new patient's family members entering the unit. All three challenges were handled by the staff diverting the outsiders from the code with a show, as if nothing were happening:

> Code in CCU [Cardiac Care Unit]...woman patient, asystole [abnormal ventricle contractions]. Doc (res[ident]) pumping chest—*deep* pumps, I'm struck by how far down they push. Serious stuff. Matter of factness of process is striking. This was a surprise code, not expected. Patient was in Vtak [ventricular fibrillation], pulse started slowing, then asystole. N[urse]s pumping for a while, RT [Respiratory Therapist] ambu-bagging [pumping air into lungs]. Maybe 7–8 people in patient's room working. Calm, but busy. Occasionally a laugh.
>
> Pt in next room (no more than 10 feet away) called for nurse—a doc went in, real loose and casual, strolled in, pt said something; doc said, "There's something going on next door that's taking people's time; we'll get to you"—real easy, like nothing at all happening. Then strolls back to code room. Very calm...
>
> Two N[urse]s came into unit wheeling a new patient. One said, "Uh, oh, bad time," very quietly as she realized, going in the door, that a code was on. Somebody said, "Close the door"—the outside door to the unit, which the Ns with the new pt were holding open...
>
> When the new pt was brought in and rolled into his room, the family with him was stopped at unit door, told to stay in waiting room and "we'll call you" with a casual wave of hand, as if this is routine. [No one said a code was on. Patient lying on gurney was wheeled in, went right by the code room and never knew a thing.] [Field Notes]

This is a simple example of protecting the routine from the chaos of a panicking patient or a horrified family; the outsiders never knew that a resuscitation was occurring fifteen feet away. The staff's work was, in their own eyes, routine; their challenge was protecting that routine from outside disruption.

2. FOLLOW ROUTINIZATION RITUALS

The staff's sense of routine is maintained by the protective rituals of hospital life. Under stress, one may use them more and more compulsively, falling back on the old forms to reconvince oneself that order is still present. Frantic prayers in the foxhole are the prototype cases.

Most prominent of such rituals in hospitals are "rounds," the standard ritual for the routine handling of patient disasters in the hospital. "Rounds" is the generic term for almost any organized staff group discussion of patients' conditions. "Walking rounds" refers to a physician walking through the hospital, usually trailed by various residents and interns, going from patient to patient and reviewing their condition. "Grand rounds" are large meetings of the medical staff featuring the presentation of an interesting case, with elaborate discussion and questions, for the purpose of education and review of standard practices. Nursing rounds usually consist of a meeting between the staff for one (outgoing) shift reporting to the staff of the next (incoming) shift on the condition of all patients on the floor. Here the staff collectively explains what has happened and why, bringing every case into the staff's framework of thinking, and systematically enforcing the system's capability for handling medical problems without falling to pieces. In rounds, the staff confirm to each other that things are under control. Once a week, for instance, the Burn Unit at one hospital holds rounds in their conference room with a group of residents, one or two attending, several nurses, the social workers, dieticians, and physical therapists. The patients here are in terrible shape; one can sometimes hear moans in the hallway outside as patients are taken for walks by the nurses. But rounds continue:

> Macho style of the docs very evident.... Resident will present a case, then the attendings take rapid-fire shots at what he [the resident] had done: wrong dressing, wrong feeding schedule, failure to note some abnormality in the lab results. Much of the talk was a flurry of physiological jargon, many numbers and abbreviations. The intensity of the presentation, the mercilessness of the grilling, is surprising.... Focus is on no errors made in situation of extreme pressure—i.e., both in patient treatment and then here in rounds presenting the case. Goal here is to be predictable, *controlled,* nothing left out. [Field Notes]

3. USE HUMOR TO DISTANCE YOURSELF

Keeping outsiders away and following the standard rituals for maintaining normality can help, but sometimes the pathos of hospital life becomes psychologically threatening to staff members. One response is to break down, cry, and run out, but this is what they are trying to avoid; the more common reaction is the sort of black humor that notoriously characterizes hospitals and armies everywhere. Humor provides an outlet; when physical space is not available, humor is a way to separate oneself psychologically from what is happening. It says both that I am not involved and that this really isn't so important. (In brain surgery, when parts of that organ are, essentially, vacuumed away, one may hear comments like "There goes 2d grade, there go the piano lessons," etc.) With laughter, things seem less consequential, less of a burden. What has been ghastly can perhaps be made funny:

> Today they got a 600-gram baby in the Newborn Unit. When Ns heard [the baby] was in Delivery, they were praying, "Please God let it be under 500 grams"—because that's the definite cutoff under which they won't try to save it—but the doc said admit it anyway. Ns unhappy.
>
> I came in the unit tonight; N came up to me and said brightly, with a big smile, "Have you seen our fetus?" Ns on the Newborn Unit have nicknames for some. There's "Fetus," the 600-gram one; "Munchkin"; and "Thrasher," in the corner, the one with constant seizures. Grim humor, but common. ["Fetus" was born at 24 weeks, "Munchkin" at 28.] [Field Notes]

The functions of such humor for medical workers have been described in a number of classic works of medical sociology. Renée Fox, writing in her book *Experiment Perilous* about physicians on a metabolic research unit, says, "The members of the group were especially inclined to make jokes about events that disturbed them a good deal," and she summarizes that

> by freeing them from some of the tension to which they were subject, enabling them to achieve greater detachment and equipoise, and strengthening their resolve to do something about the problems with which they were faced, the grim medical humor of the Metabolic Group helped them to come to terms with their situation in a useful and professionally acceptable way.[3]

Fox and other students of hospital culture (notably Rose Coser)[4] have emphasized that humor fills a functional purpose of "tension release," allowing medical workers to get on with the job in the face of trauma; their analyses usually focus on jokes explicitly told in medical settings. This analysis is correct as far as it goes, but in a sense I think it almost "explains away" hospital humor—as if to say that "these people are under a lot of strain, so it's understandable that they tell these gruesome jokes." It suggests, in a functionalist fallacy, that jokes are made because of the strain and that things somehow aren't "really" funny.

But they are. An appreciation of hospital life must recognize that funny things—genuinely funny, even if sometimes simultaneously horrible—do happen. Hospitals are scenes of irony, where good and bad are inseparably blended, where funny things happen, where to analytically excuse laughter as a defense mechanism is simultaneously to deny the human reality, the experience, that even to a non-stressed outsider *this is funny.*[5] The humor isn't found only in contrived jokes but in the scenes one witnesses; laughter can be spontaneous, and it's not always nervous. True, one must usually have a fairly normalized sense of the hospital to laugh here, but laugh one does.

Certainly, the staff make jokes:

> In the OR [operating room]:
>
> "This is his [pt's] 6th time [for a hernia repair]."
> "After two, I hear you're officially disabled."
> "Oh good, does that mean he gets a special parking place?"
> [Field Notes]
> In the ICU [Intensive Care Unit], two Ns—one male, one female—working on pt.
> Nurse 1 (male): "This guy has bowel sounds in his scrotum."
> Nurse 2 (female): "In his scrotum?"
> Nurse 1: "Yeah, didn't you pick that up?"
> Nurse 2: "I didn't put my stethoscope there!" (Big laughs.) [Field Notes]

Sometimes jokes are more elaborate and are obviously derived from the tragedy of the situation:

> In another ICU, staff member taped a stick to the door of the unit, symbolizing (for them) "The Stake," a sign of some form of euthanasia [perhaps the expression sometimes used, "to stake" a patient, derives from the myth that vampires can only be killed by driving a stake through the heart]. Periodically word went around that a resident had just won the "Green Stake Award," meaning that he or she had, for the first time, allowed or helped a patient to die. [Field Notes]
>
> Some colorful balloons with "Get Well Soon" were delivered to a patient's room. The patient died the following night. Someone on the staff moved the balloons to the

> door of another patient's room; that patient died! Now the staff has put the balloons at the door of the patient they believe is "most likely to die next." [Field Notes]

But jokes have to be contrived; they are deliberate efforts at humor and so make a good example of efforts to distance oneself, or to make the tragic funny. But the inherent irony of the hospital is better seen in situations that spontaneously provoke laughter. These things are funny in themselves; even an outsider can laugh at them:

> Nurse preparing to wheel a patient into the OR tells him, "Take out your false teeth, take off your glasses...," and continuing, trying to make a joke, "Take off your leg, take out your eyes." The patient said, "Oh, I almost forgot—" and pulled out his [false] eye! [Interview]

Or:

> Lady patient [Geriatric floor] is upset because she called home, there's no answer; she's afraid her husband has died. Sylvia [a nurse] told her he probably just went somewhere for lunch, but patient said he would have called. She's afraid.
>
> [Later] Sylvia went back in lady's room—she's crying. Husband called! Sylvia happy, smiling, "You should be happy!" "But," says the old lady, "he called to say he was out burying the dog!"
>
> Sylvia had to leave the room because she was starting to laugh; she and Janie laughing at this at the N's station, saying it's really sad but funny at the same time. [Field Notes]

Or:

> In looking at X-rays of a patient's colon, the resident explains to the team a shadow on the film: "Radiology says it could be a tumor, or it might just be stool." Jokes all around about how "helpful" Rays [Radiology] is. [Field Notes]

One needn't be under pressure to find such things funny. People do laugh to ease pressure or to distance oneself. But sometimes the distance comes first: laughter is made possible by the routinization that has gone before.

4. WHEN THINGS FALL APART, KEEP GOING

Sometimes routinization fails: outsiders come into the room and, seeing their dead mother, break down, screaming and wailing; or a longtime, cared-for patient begins irretrievably to "decompensate" and lose blood pressure, sliding quickly to death; or emergency surgery goes bad, the trauma shakes the staff, and there are other patients coming in from the ambulances. Any of these can destroy the staff's sense of "work as usual." In such cases, the typical practice seems to be, remarkably: just keep going. Trauma teams specialize in the psychological strength (or cold-bloodedness, perhaps) to continue working when the world seems to be falling apart. Finally, nurses and physicians are notable for continuing to work even, in the final case, after the patient is for almost all purposes dead, or will be soon.

> A resident said to the attending [physician] on one floor, discussing a terminal patient: "If we transfuse him, he might get hepatitis."
> Another resident: "By the time he gets hepatitis he'll be dead."
> Attending: "OK, so let's transfuse." [Field Notes]

Perseverance is a habit; it's also a moral imperative, a way of managing disaster as if it were routine.

In every unit there are nurses known for being good under pressure. These are people who, whatever their other skills (and, typically, their other skills are quite good), are able to maintain their presence of mind in any crisis. Whereas "being organized" is a key quality for nurses in routine situations, staying calm is crucial in emergency situations. Compare two nurses known for remaining calm (Mavis and Anna) to two others who are prone to alarm (Linda and Julie):

> Mavis [in Neonatal ICU] is cited as a good nurse (great starting IVs, e.g.) who doesn't get shook, even in a code, even if her pt is dying, she still keeps doing what you're supposed to do. Linda, by contrast, is real smart, very good technically, but can freak out, start yelling, etc., if things are going badly. [Field Notes]
>
> Julie [in Medical ICU], hurrying around, looks just one step ahead of disaster, can't keep up, etc. Doc says something about the patient in room 1. Julie says, walking past, "He's not mine," keeps going. But Anna, calm, walks in pt's room—pt with oxygen mask, wants something. Anna goes out, calmly, comes back in a minute w/cup of crushed ice, gives pt a spoonful to ease thirst. She *always* seems to be doing that little thing that others "don't have time for"—never flustered and yet seems to get more done than anyone else. [Field Notes, Interview]

But to "keep going" depends not so much on the individual fortitude of nurses such [as] Mavis and Anna, but on the professional and institutional habits of the nursing staff and the hospital. The continuance of care even in the face of obvious failure of efforts is itself a norm. Whatever one's personal disposition, one keeps working; the staff keep working, often when the patient is all but dead, or "dead" but not officially recognized as such:

> Dr. K., walking rounds with four residents, discussing a 30-year-old male patient, HIV-positive, gone totally septic [has bloodstream infection, a deadly problem], no hope at all of recovery—Dr. K. says this is a "100 percent mortality" case; so they decide how to proceed with minimal treatment, at the end of which Dr. K. says brightly, "And if he codes—code him!" [Field Notes]

Coding such a patient is an exercise in technique; there is no hope entailed, no optimism, no idea that he might be saved. There is only the institutional habit which substitutes for hope, which in many cases obviates the staff's pessimism or lack of interest. When standard procedure is followed, courage is unnecessary. It is one thing to be routinely busy, caring for vegetative patients; it happens every day. It is quite another to handle emergency surgery with no time and a life at stake. Sometimes such a case will challenge all the staff's resources—their personal fortitude, their habitualization of procedures, the self-protection offered by an indefatigable sense of humor. To maintain one's composure while under tremendous pressures of time and fatefulness requires all the courage a staff can muster.

One such case was that of emergency surgery on a thirty-five-year-old woman who came to Southwestern Regional hospital in severe abdominal pain; she was diagnosed with a ruptured ectopic [tubal] pregnancy estimated at sixteen weeks. The case provides us with a dramatic example of the pressure placed on the staff to retain their composure in the face of disaster.

The long description which follows is graphic. The scene was more than bloody; it was grotesque. More than one staff member—including one member of the surgical team itself—left the room during the operation, sickened. Other nurses, even very experienced ones, told me they have never witnessed such a scene and hope never to witness one. I include it here, in some detail, to exemplify both what health professionals face in their work and how, incredibly, some of them can carry on. The description is reconstructed from Field Notes (some written at the time on the inside of a surgical mask, some on sheets of paper carried in a pocket), and from interviews afterward with participants:

> Saturday night OR suite; hasn't been busy. Only one case so far, a guy who got beat up with a tire iron (drug deal), finished about 8:30 P.M. It's about 10:00. 2 Ns—the Saturday night staff—sitting around in the conference room, just chatting and waiting for anything that happens.
>
> Call comes over intercom: ruptured tubal (pregnancy) just came in OR, bringing to the crash room. 35-year-old black woman, very heavy—250 pounds maybe—apparently pregnant for 16 weeks, which means she's been in pain for 10 weeks or more without coming in. Friends brought her to ER screaming in pain. Blood pressure is at "60 over palpable," i.e., the diastolic doesn't even register on the manometer. She's obviously bleeding bad internally, will die fast if not opened up. Ns run to OR and set up fast. I've never seen people work so quickly here, no wasted motion at all. This is full speed *emergency.*
>
> When patient is rolled in, fully conscious, there are more than a dozen staff people in the room, including three gynecological surgery residents, who will operate; all three are women. The surgeons are scrubbed and gowned and stand in a line, back from the table, watching without moving, the one in charge periodically giving orders to the nurses who are setting up. At one point there are twelve separate people working on the patient—IVs going into both arms, anesthesiologist putting mask on pt to gas, nurse inserting a Foley [bladder] catheter, others tying pt's arms to the straightout arms of the table, others scrubbing the huge belly, an incredible scene. The patient is shaking terribly, in pain and fear. Her eyes are bugging out, looking around terribly fast. She's whimpering, groaning as needles go in, crying out softly. No one has time even to speak to her; one nurse briefly leans over and speaks into her ear something like "try not to worry, we're going to take care of you," but there is no time for this. I've never seen anyone so afraid, sweating and crying and the violent shaking.
>
> As soon as they have prepped her—the belly cleansed and covered with Opsite, in a matter of minutes, very, very fast, the anesthesiologist says, "All set?" And someone says "yes," and they gas her. I'm standing right by her head, looking to the head side of the drape which separates her head from her body; the instant that her eyes close, I look to the other side—and the surgeon has already slit her belly open. No hesitation at all, maybe before the patient was out.

What happened next, more extraordinary than the very fast prep, was the opening. Usually in surgery the scalpel makes the skin cut, then slowly scissors are used, snipping piece by piece at muscle, the Bovie cauterizing each blood vessel on the way, very methodical and painstaking. This was nothing like that. It was an entirely different style. They cut fast and deep, sliced her open deep, just chopped through everything, in a—not a panic, but something like a "blitzkrieg," maybe—to get down into the Fallopian tube that had burst and was shooting blood into the abdomen.

When they first got into the abdominal cavity, usually there would be some oozing blood; here as they opened blood splattered out all over the draping on the belly. It was a godawful mess, blood everywhere. They had one surgeon mopping up with gauze sponges, another using a suction pump, a little plastic hose, trying to clean the way. Unbelievable. They got down to the tubes, reaching down and digging around with their hands. And then they found it—suddenly out of this bloody mess down in the abdomen, with the surgeons groping around trying to feel where things were, out of this popped up, right out of the patient and, literally, onto the sheet covering her, the 16-week fetus itself. Immediately one surgeon said mock-cheerfully, "It's a boy!" "God, don't do that," said the scrub tech, turning her head away.

The scrub tech then began to lose it, tears running down her cheeks. Two other people on the team—there were maybe six around the table—said about the same time, nearly together, "Damien!" and "Alien!" recalling recent horror movies, "children of the devil" themes. The fetus lay on the sheet just below the open abdomen for a few moments. The head surgery resident, working, just kept working. The scrub tech should have put the fetus into a specimen tray, but she was falling to pieces fast, crying, and starting to have trouble handing the proper tools to the surgeon, who said something like, "What are you doing?" At this point the circulating nurse, a man, said, "If nobody else will do it," picked up the fetus and put it in a specimen tray, which he then covered with a towel and put aside. He then told another nurse to help him into a gown—he wasn't scrubbed. This violates sterile technique badly, for him to start handling tools, but the scrub tech was becoming a problem. The circulating nurse then quickly gowned and gloved, gently pulled the scrub tech aside and said, "I'll do it." The scrub tech ran out of the room in tears. And the circulating nurse began passing tools to the surgeons himself. It is the circulating nurse's responsibility to handle problems this way, and he did. Another nurse had gone out to scrub properly, and when she came back, maybe ten minutes later, she gowned and gloved and relieved him; so he (the circulating nurse) went back to his regular job of charting the procedure, answering the phone, etc.

By this time, things were under control; the bleeding was stopped, the tube tied off. The other tube was OK and left alone so the pt can get pregnant again. The blood in the abdomen was cleaned up—over 1500 cc's were lost, that's just under a half-gallon of blood. The pt would have died fast if they hadn't gotten in there.

Within two hours after the patient had first rolled in, the room was quiet, only three staff members left, two surgeons and the scrub nurse closing up and talking quietly. Most of the mess—the bloody sponges, the used tools, and all—was gone, cleared away, and all the other staff people, including the chief surgeon, had left. Very calm. The patient, who two hours ago was on the end of a fast terrible death, will be out of the hospital in two days with no permanent damage beyond the loss of one Fallopian tube. [Field Notes, Interviews]

In this situation, we can see two somewhat distinct problems in maintaining the routine order of things: first, the challenge simply in getting the work done; and second, the challenge of upholding the moral order of the hospital.[6] The first issue was resolved by replacing the scrub tech so the operation could continue. The second issue is trickier. The scrub tech's response appeared to be set off not by the horror of what she saw—the bloody fetus—but by the reaction of the assisting surgeon—"It's a boy!" I can only guess that the joke was too much for her. In continuing to work without her, and continuing without noticeable change of demeanor, the surgical team was asserting not only the imperative to protect the operational routine but also, I think, to protect the moral order of emergency surgery as well. That order includes:

1. The job comes first, before personal reactions of fear or disgust.
2. Cynicism is an acceptable form of expression if it helps to maintain composure and distance.
3. The medical team is rightfully in charge and above what may be happening in the OR [operating room].
4. Preserving life is the central value; others (such as niceties of language or etiquette) fall far behind.

There is clearly a morality here. Just as clearly, it is not the morality of everyday life.

NOTES

1. Erving Goffman, "On Face-Work," in *Interaction Ritual: Essays on Face-to-Face Behavior* (New York: Pantheon Books, 1967), p. 11.
2. Ibid., pp. 17–18.
3. Renée C. Fox, *Experiment Perilous* (New York: Free Press, 1959; reprint ed., Philadelphia: University of Pennsylvania Press, 1974), pp. 80–82.
4. Rose Laub Coser, "Some Social Functions of Laughter," in Lewis Coser, *The Pleasures of Sociology,* edited and with an introduction and notes by Lewis Coser (New York: New American Library, 1980), pp. 81–97.
5. The genius of Shem's *House of God* is that it accepts this fact and presents it honestly.
6. I am indebted to Robert Zussman, who suggested these in his review of the manuscript.

READING 6

Becoming a Prostitute

Nanette J. Davis

introduction

Society is set up to produce conforming individuals. As we learn the ways of our culture, we learn how we *ought* to act, think, and evaluate people, events, and ourselves. We learn what is expected of us if we are to be considered members of society in good standing. We learn this lesson as we are socialized within our family and later within other social institutions. The overall message we receive is to conform–in behavior and thought. And conformity is necessary, because if society is to survive, there must be rules, or norms, that allow its members to interact cooperatively with one another. This requires that people know what to expect of one another.

Most of us do conform most of the time, but not always. All of us break at least some of the rules, and some of us seem to break most of the rules. Most of us manage to skirt the rules when we want to, yet conform sufficiently to remain members of society in good standing. Some, however, flout the norms to such a degree that they are labeled outsiders. They know the label they receive, and this, in turn, affects how they think of themselves. Note how the women that Davis analyzes gradually move from one set of norms into another.

Thinking Critically

As you read this selection, ask yourself:

1. Why did these young women become prostitutes?
2. How does identifying with hustler norms facilitate entry into prostitution?
3. If you were appointed by the mayor of Minneapolis to develop a program to decrease the prostitution of young women, based on this article what program would you propose?

The source of data for this study is provided by a jail sample of thirty prostitutes from three correctional institutions (reformatory, workhouse, and training school) in Minnesota. Included are seventeen white women, twelve black women, and one Indian woman. The age range was fifteen to thirty-four, with an average age of twenty-one.

From "Becoming a Prostitute," by Nanette J. Davis. In James M. Henslin (Ed.), *Studies in the Sociology of Sex*.

All of the thirty women were legally classified as "common prostitute," although only twenty-four of the thirty informants reported that they were professional prostitutes. The women operated at the "street-walker" level of prostitution, that is, lounging in bars or on streetcorners and openly soliciting clients. Data were elicited through structured interviews, with emphasis, however, on the informants' verbalized statements. The interviews averaged one and one-half to two hours in length. Official records also were used. Further, informal data were gained through participant observation....

THE PROCESS OF DRIFT FROM PROMISCUITY TO THE FIRST ACT OF PROSTITUTION

Age at First Sexual Experience

The women in this sample were initiated into sexual experiences at an early age. The mean age at which they first had sexual intercourse was 13.6, with a range of seven to eighteen. Rape experiences, reported by two women, account for the lower age level (seven and nine years, respectively). Three other informants noted traumatic sexual experiences with brothers, step-father, or father, at age twelve or under. Nineteen of the thirty women report they had sexual intercourse by age thirteen, although almost one-half of the white girls had experienced intercourse by age twelve. The most characteristic pattern was coitus with a boyfriend, who was typically five or six years older than the girl was. Four informants were sexually initiated by another girl with heterosexual relations occurring within a year after such lesbian contacts.... First sexual contacts typically involved sexual intercourse, with only one girl reporting an initial petting experience.

Preconditions for those characterized by "early sexuality" are: (1) high levels of familial permissiveness led to association with older males at parties, neighboring houses, or street pickups, (2) familial social control was often lacking or inconsistent, (3) peer group norms encouraged early sexuality, and (4) sexuality was associated with freedom (a movement away from a disliked family) or, conversely, security (the certainty of male companionship). Three girls, on the other hand, did not experience their first sexual intercourse until age seventeen or eighteen. Those having this "late sexuality" experienced these typical conditions: (1) sexual matters were taboo areas in the family, (2) the mother was highly protective, exerting strong religious and familial controls with consequent little freedom of opportunity in early adolescence, and (3) a rebellion pattern eventually developed in opposition to the rigidity of the controls.

Almost all of the women (twenty-eight of thirty) report that their first sex experience was either meaningless or distasteful; for example, "It was nothing," "I did it just to please him," "I really didn't like it," "I disliked it," "It was awful," "I was scared," "It made me sick." A need for conformity seems to be the most salient motive for this first sexuality, as:

> I did it just to belong. Everybody was doing it.
>
> I was the only virgin in the crowd (age fifteen). Five of my girlfriends had kids at sixteen....

The promiscuous pattern which developed for most girls (three women had early pregnancies which were followed by marriage, with promiscuity and prostitution occurring *after* these events) seems to reflect associates' expectations, the desire to attract males ("The boys were always hot after me"), and an opportunity structure which facilitated the behavior.

Perception of Childhood and Adolescent Years

The promiscuous pattern may provide one condition which can lead to informal labeling ("bad" girl, "easy mark") and subsequent stigmatization by parents, teachers, and conventional associates. But other circumstances may arise, prior to or following this sexual behavior.... These women perceived their childhood and adolescent years as marked by negative or degrading interactions with society, as the following data indicate:

1. Familial instability was typical for almost all of the white girls (sixteen of seventeen) and two-thirds of the blacks (eight of twelve). Such instability included a drunken, violent or absentee parent (usually the father), extreme poverty, or families larger than the parents could cope with. Conditions within the family were eventually brought to the attention of neighbors, welfare board, or court. Such attention was defined as humiliating or demoralizing.

2. More than half of the informants (eighteen of thirty) have spent one year or more of their childhood (under twelve) in foster homes, living with relatives, or in other separations from the nuclear family.

3. Almost all of the informants (twenty-eight) report that parents, neighbors, and/or teachers considered them "trouble-makers," "slow learners," or generally inadequate in relation to expectations.

4. The black women (nine of twelve), especially, reported "unfair" treatment by white teachers or students, inability to gain and/or hold a job, and frustration in cases where self-improvement was attempted.

5. Twenty-three of the thirty informants reported that they had been sentenced to a juvenile home or training school as adolescents for truancy, incorrigibility, or sex delinquency....

In the interactional processes with significant others (parents, teachers, neighbors, and friends), the girl [is seen as] "different." She is a person who is expected to behave in unconventional ways. Absenteeism from school, chronic disobedience at home, and later, promiscuity, categorize the girl as difficult, if not impossible to control. Low family cohesion with consequent weak affectional ties between parents and daughter leads the girl to seek street associates....

[T]he rationale for promiscuity, and initially for prostitution, is a hedonistic concern for fun, new experiences, excitement, and a response to peer group expectations. Sex as a status tool is exploited to gain male attention. The adolescent urge for liberation from the confines of the family and controls of school and job leads to involvement in drinking parties or hustler groups, where differential identification with sophisticated delinquents occurs.

The Drift from Promiscuity to First Act of Prostitution

Regardless of the age at which the girl first experienced intercourse, there then followed a *"drift" or "slide" process from promiscuity to prostitution,* with the girl first prostituting herself in late adolescence (mean = 17.3 years). There was a range, however, of fourteen to twenty-five years. The early age of prostitution was facilitated by a definition of the deviant situation as similar to sexual promiscuity—excitement and desire for male attention:...

> It was either jump in bed, and go with every Tom, Dick, and Harry, and just give it away, so I decided to turn tricks instead.... The money was so easy to get....

My data strongly suggest that the movement from casual delinquency to the first phase of [prostitution] is facilitated by the policy of confining deviants to correctional institutions. The adolescent girl who is labeled a sex offender for promiscuity or "mixing" (white girls associating with black males) may initially experience a conflict about her identity. Intimate association with sophisticated deviants, however, may provide an incentive to learn the hustler role ("The girls told me about it—I was such an avid listener."), and thus resolve the status anxiety by gaining prestige through association with deviants, and later, experimentation in the deviant role. Frequent and predictable escapes from the open institution are common. Lines of communication between urban vice neighborhoods and training school inmates assures the escapee of finding accommodations during a "run."

As an outlaw, the girl cannot seek the security of parents or the home neighborhood. Thus, isolated from conventional associates or activities, and dependent on deviant contacts for financial and social support, the girl may come to define the situation as one that inevitably leads her into enacting the deviant role, as:

> I ran away from the institution. I went and visited my girlfriends. I was out of the institution about a month, just loafing around. I talked to some friends of mine who were hustlers. Someone suggested I try it. I had been sponging off everybody. I got sick of sponging. I'd sleep here one night, and there another....
>
> I had run away (from the training school). I had no money or anything. I went walking the street. The older girls (institutionalized associates) told me about it.

Roads to Recruitment

Adolescent institutionalization, then, often prior to the actual commitment of a deviant act, may act as a structural condition which facilitates the learning of a deviant role. Induction into the career, on the other hand, proceeds through alternative routes, chief of which are: (1) response to peer group expectations, (2) involvement in a pimp-manager relationship, and (3) adolescent rebellion.

Response to *peer group expectations* undoubtedly provides the major avenue to recruitment ("It's the environment. Everyone is doing it.") Associating with hustlers, "party girls," or pimps, while viewed as prestigious, can only be maintained by "trying out" the behavior. Clearly, for twenty-eight of the thirty informants, differential identification with deviant associates accounts, in part, for the movement into prostitution.

> I was on run...I didn't get up until 3 P.M. I was staying with my boyfriend. He was unemployed. He was planning to set me up [for prostitution]. We had been talking about it. I took long precautions.... A friend helped me out. Everything happened so fast. It was kind of like prearranged for me. Crazy! We were staying in a hotel with lots of pimps and prostitutes living there. The first time was at the World's Series. I was dressed like a normal teenager....

Involvement in a *pimp-manager relationship* provides a typical method of entrance for some under-age girls (eight informants.) In other instances, the pimp may not have initially arranged the first contact, but he typically appears relatively early on the scene to direct the girl's activities. The uninitiated girl views the pimp relationship as a means of security in an otherwise rejecting world.

> I always had a need to belong.... A pimp moves in, and he sees you're attractive, and he sees you want to belong. Pimps are the most understanding. They're the least educated persons, though. I thought my pimp was my knight in shining armor....

The pimp's ability to "set the girl up" by arranging clients is a measure of the girl's arrival on the deviant scene. One informant, whose first experience was such an arrangement, recalled how the system operated.

> I was living with a girlfriend.... She wasn't a hustler—and started going with this one boy. He introduced me to this pimp. He asked me if I would [hustle]. I was against it, but they all said how easy it was. I went to this pimp's house. I was a call girl. There were three of us [hustlers]. The pimps would come in. They got all the contacts, and they'd say to the tricks, "Lookee here, I got these girls, see," and he'd line up the tricks. Then he'd say to the girls that there was a trick in this hotel, and you'd go to a room number.

Another girl commented that the pimp used alternate techniques of violence ("He hit me on the head when I said no") and persuasion: "He told me, 'I can put you in big business. You won't have to hustle hard.' I saw the girls and how they did it. It was like a dream."

Adolescent rebellion operates for girls who have experienced oppressive familial controls (six women), forming another typical pattern.

> Well, I started hustling, I suppose, because the party group I ran around with were always talking about it. My mother had always picked my friends. She wouldn't allow any bad influences—the square friends only, the goody-goody club activities at church. My parents were very old-fashioned. They didn't drink or smoke, and were very church-going. But when I got in with this group, it was really different, man!...

Dominant Motives During the First Stage

Underlying these main roads to recruitment into prostitution are curiosity and a desire for new experience, defined idleness, identification with hustler norms, and a strong present-time orientation.

Curiosity and access to new experiences (or "kicks") act as a dominant motive to the naive girl who seeks esteem from the hustler group. "I was unemployed at the time, just hanging around with a group. I wanted some excitement—kicks, you know."

Remarks such as, "It was the glamor and game of it," "I did it just for the fun of it," "There's a lot of excitement to that—the cops on you and everything," indicate a perception of deviance as part of the excitement and risk of street life....

Idleness is typical for most of the women (twenty-three of thirty). Separations from family, school, job, or other conventional activities characterize this first deviant phase. For the runaway training school girl, prostitution may relieve the dullness of an otherwise undirected existence.

> I was sixteen and on the run, just loafing around my girlfriend's house. One of my girlfriends gave me the pointers, so I decided to try it.
>
> I had run away—like I was lost or something. I had been walking the streets all day, and at 6 P.M. I met this guy. I was really looking for love and attention, but not necessarily the men.

Identification with hustler norms undoubtedly accounts for the frequently expressed (twenty-seven of thirty) money rationale. However, economic deprivation is not the dominant element for most girls. Only two women, for instance, expressed intense financial need because of child support. Independence, isolation from conventional supports, and the lure of "easy" money, were major considerations.

> I was on run—no job or anything. I was by myself. It was about 8. I went out, went downtown. My boyfriend worked in the ________ Hotel. He called me up to say that he had a man who had fifty dollars to get a girl, and so there it was. I got forty-five dollars the first night—for four men. Everyone was doing it, anyway. Then I walked back downtown, and had three more, and then went back to my apartment.

A strong present-time orientation characterizes the younger girl particularly, who conceives of the act as satisfying immediate needs only, without considering long-range implications.

> The first time I did it was to buy a present for my boyfriend. The next time just to have some spending money. I've been asked to hustle lots of times. I know all the gimmicks, and how to do it...all that stuff.
>
> I was going to school and I wanted to go to this dance the night after. I needed new clothes. I went out at ten o'clock and home at twelve. I had three tricks the first time, and fifteen dollars for every trick.

Whatever the mode of recruitment, or the dominant motives involved, this study shows certain common elements present at this state of deviant involvement.

These generally include: informal labeling which early categorizes the girl as unconventional or "troublemaker"; isolation from conventional family, friends, or associates; response to deviant associates' expectations; and expressed need for economic self-sufficiency while "on run" or probation. Such motives indicate that: (1) episodic involvement, or *a drift into deviance,* is characteristic of prostitutes and is related to hedonistic and short-term concerns; and (2) stigmatized persons may respond to a morally degraded status by seeking associates who may reward the deviant behavior.

Transitional Deviance and Professionalization

Twenty-one of the thirty women interviewed experienced an "occasional" or "transitional" stage of deviance. Of the nine other labeled prostitutes, four repudiated the role after three or more deviant episodes, while five women moved directly into full-time deviance. The transitional stage lasted an average of six months (with a range from two weeks to four years). It could be viewed as an on-the-job learning period....

Motivational ambivalence during the transitional phase creates a zig-zag pattern of deviance for most prostitutes. They vacillate between conventionality and deviance. The conventional life, for instance, is not yet denied. Some girls make verbal commitments to stop, or even attempt to return to home, school, job or to set themselves up in an apartment with conventional associates. Conventional motives involve expressed reluctance to move into the act because of fear of discovery, interracial contacts, or belief that such conduct is immoral. ("It's not the right thing to do. I would get a bad reputation.")...

During this phase, they indicate indecision and confusion regarding their role. By hustling only occasionally, not more than two or three times a week, or engaging in prostitution "only when I wanted to," or "sometimes when I'm lonesome," or for "just something to do," the individual perceives that she is in control of the situation....

[T]he drift into deviance...occurs through *normalization of the act*.... [This] may occur through rationalizations appropriate for promiscuity—the desire for male attention....

> I'm a person who likes to walk. There's nothing wrong with picking somebody up while you're walking. I always like walking around at night, and girls will be tempted. Girls like the offer. They like to see what the guy is going to say.

The "gaming" element, which revolves around the excitement of the "pickup" and independence on the street, is also linked to a promiscuous, rather than deviant, orientation. The promiscuous girl with conventional in-group supports may not define herself as a prostitute at this point.

In certain cases, role ambivalence may even lead to repudiation of the "trial" role after a few experiences (four informants). Negative experiences with a client, pimp, or policeman, for instance, may lead her to reject the role. Inadequate motivation is a typical condition leading to role failure in many areas of life. It was expressed by one seventeen-year old informant who had hustled on-and-off for about a month before her career had been interrupted by jail:

> Hustling—I don't get no kicks from it. I wouldn't go out and do it for a living. There are better ways to make money. I couldn't go through everything a prostitute goes through. I really don't have the guts for it. A prostitute picks up anyone off the street, and gets money for it. The tricks I had it with I did it just for sex, but not for me—not the whole self. I knew I couldn't make a career out of it. When you don't care about the guy, sex isn't for that.

Sex with affection, uncontaminated by money, still operates as a norm for the deviant dropout.

Their continuation in this sexually deviant behavior, on the other hand, is contingent on strong economic motivation (twenty-one women), loneliness (three), and/or expressed entrapment because of pimp control (six). For two girls, drug addiction acted as an inducement for continuation of the deviant role. Continuation in the deviant role is further contingent on an adequate learning period uninterrupted by police harassment or jail sentencing....

Delayed definitions of the act as immoral, degrading or repulsive (fifteen women report intense dissatisfaction or disgust with the situation) can no longer be postponed if situations occur that force unequivocal perception of a deviant self. Self-discovery, for instance, may be inevitable for some prostitutes when the pimp's behavior shifts from lover to exploiter, and, for example, nightly money quotas become the primary condition for the relationship ("I was just another one of his hustlers").... Another typical experience is contact with the police, court, or jail, where the label "common prostitute" is assigned. After the legal confrontation, public exposure proceeds in rapid order. Listing the girl's name in the paper, or passing the information to parents from "inside" sources, implies that, as a consequence, the girl soon renounces the pretense of conventional commitments. At this point, she may cut herself off from family and conventional others' support. Informants report such responses to the labeling procedure:

> They sent me up for something I didn't do, so I might as well do it. I wasn't afraid of anything.
>
> Society is really uninformed. They don't put themselves to the trouble to understand. There are lots worse things besides prostitution that happen. Society isn't helping at all. There's not a chance to be decent. Society has put the brand on us.

Personal integrity at earlier phases of the career had been maintained by secrecy regarding the deviant behavior. Role segmentation breaks down, however, if the woman has internalized the streetwalker's myth—"once a girl is on the streets, everyone knows what she is." For example,

> At first I was scared. The news gets out so fast. Everyone knows when a girl's on the streets a couple of nights. I thought about stopping, you know, but I just went on....

In-service training for this streetwalker group during the transitional period includes: (1) willingness to satisfy a broad range of client requests, requiring certain social and sexual skills; (2) elimination of fears regarding clients who are defined as "odd" (sadomasochists); (3) adaptation to police surveillance and entrapment procedures; (4) avoidance of drunken clients, or those unable or unwilling to pay; and (5) substitution of a "business" ethic for the earlier one of "gaming" or excitement....

[After a woman has gone through this process of learning and of making the required adjustment in her identity, she has *become* a prostitute. Sex has become her vocation.]

NOTE

This study is based on an unpublished Master's thesis, "Prostitution and Social Control: An Empirical Inquiry into the Socialization Process of Deviant Behavior" (1967) University of Minnesota, under the direction of Professor David A. Ward.

The writer wishes to express appreciation to James M. Henslin, Peter K. Manning, Bernard N. Meltzer, John Petras, and Ira Reiss for their helpful comments.

The selection is a condensed version of the author's more detailed analysis appearing in *Studies in the Sociology of Sex,* James M. Henslin, ed. New York: Appleton-Century-Crofts, 1971: 297–322, and the revised edition, *The Sociology of Sex: An Introductory Reader,* James M. Henslin and Edward Sagarin, eds. New York: Schocken Books, 1978: 195–222.

PART III Social Inequality

It is socially impossible to have a society of equals. Despite the laudable desires of some to build an egalitarian society, every society will have inequality. Always there will be what sociologists call *social stratification.*

Each social group has a value system. That is, it values certain things above others. In a tribal group, this could be running, shooting arrows, throwing spears, or showing bravery. Some members of the tribe will have greater abilities to do the particular things that their group values—no matter what those things may be. Their skills and accomplishments will mark them as different. These people will be looked up to, and they will likely be treated differently.

By considering skills and accomplishments, as in a tribal group, we can see why social distinctions are inevitable. Social stratification, however, is based on much more than ability and accomplishment. In fact, ability and achievement are seldom the bases of social stratification. Much more common are inherited factors.

Every society stratifies its members according to whatever particular values and characteristics it cherishes. That is, every human group divides its people into layers, and treats each layer differently. Once a society is stratified, birth ushers children into different positions. By virtue of where their parents are located, children inherit some of the social distinctions of their parents. These can be their religion (Christian, Jew, Muslim), social class (upper, middle, lower), caste (Brahmin, Shudra, Dalit), or any other distinction that their group makes.

Because their group has already set up the rules, children also inherit *statuses* (positions) based on their sex. With these come wide-ranging expectations of behaviors and attitudes, which sociologists call *gender.* So it may be with their race–ethnicity. In addition, with today's geopolitical arrangements, their birth also ushers them onto a world stage, where they inherit their country's position in what is known as *global stratification.* Their nation may be rich and powerful or poor and weak. Wherever a nation is located on the world scene, this, too, has fundamental consequences for their lives.

In this third part of the book, we look at some of the major aspects of social inequality. We begin with a view of global stratification. Mary Beth Mills' opening article makes it evident that where your nation is located in the global scheme of things makes a fundamental difference for what happens to you in life. Herbert Gans follows with a provocative analysis of poverty. Using a functionalist perspective, he suggests that poverty is inevitable because poor people perform valuable services for society. In his report on the social inequality of race, Clarence Page, a journalist, recounts his experiences with race, with an emphasis on how he learned to take his place in a race-conscious and -driven society. With Robert Edgerton's controversial suggestion that some societies may be "sick," we close this part with a focus on the social inequality of gender.

READING 7

From the Village to the Factory

Mary Beth Mills

introduction

One of the world's most significant changes is the globalization of capitalism. Capitalism won the Cold War, and except for a few holdouts (Cuba, North Korea, and China), socialism has been vanquished. Victorious with its heady success, capitalism is expanding rapidly into every nook and cranny of the planet. Part of this process is the so-called undeveloped nations (undeveloped only in a chauvinistic, ethnocentric sense of Western imperialistic cultural and economic dominance, for they all have fully developed, intricate cultures). Eyeing the material wealth of the industrialized West and Japan, and mindful of the West's economic, political, and military power, like a separated lover, these nations long to embrace capitalism. For their part, the Most Industrialized Nations view the Least Industrialized Nations as vast sources of cheap labor and natural resources.

Downsizing, a fancy way of saying that a company is firing workers, is part of the globalization of capitalism. In their pursuit of the bottom line, U.S. firms, followed more reluctantly by the Europeans and the Japanese, have laid off millions of workers. From the point of view of profit, which is capitalism's bottom line, this makes sense: In the Least Industrialized Nations, millions of workers eagerly await the crumbs of the industrialized world. This is a capitalist's dream: workers willing to accept peanuts for wages and glad to get them. What motivates these workers? What are their lives like? Mills answers such questions as she gives us an inside view of women workers in Thailand.

Thinking Critically

As you read this selection, ask yourself:

1. What are the dominant perspectives of young village women who move to Bangkok? If you were to move to Bangkok and worked alongside these women, how do you think your views of working in a Bangkok factory would differ from theirs? Why?
2. Why do these women workers feel such ambivalence?
3. How are the Bangkok factories part of the globalization of capitalism? How do you benefit from them? For young village women, are the factories exploitation or opportunities?

> *A friend who had been working in Bangkok came back to visit [our village]. She wore beautiful clothes. When she saw me, her greeting was, "Oh ho! How did you get so run-down looking? Want to come work with me?" . . . [That night] I lay thinking, "I ought to go give it a try." I dreamed that I would go [to the city], work really hard and save money to help my family. I lay unable to stop thinking about this until I slept. I got up early in the morning and at once rushed to find my friend. I was so happy that I could go with her. I got my clothes ready and said good-bye to my brothers, sisters, father and mother.*
>
> Khem, Bangkok textile worker, age 21

In this brief passage, a young Thai labor migrant gives an account of how she left home to begin urban employment at the age of sixteen. Central to this narrative is the moral obligation of a dutiful daughter—"I would work really hard and save money to help my family"—anchoring Khem's story in the intimate world of village kinship and rural poverty. But this projection of virtue and self-sacrifice stands alongside a portrait of the confident returning migrant with her "beautiful clothes" and teasing disdain for the sorry existence of her friend. It is this image of urban sophistication and accumulation, as much as her concern for household needs, that occupies Khem's waking thoughts before sleep and propels her rapid departure the next morning.

Khem's narrative, placing kinship-based morality alongside desires for autonomy and commodified display, highlights widespread themes within rural-urban migration in contemporary Thailand. In these few sentences Khem constructs two potential selves: the "good daughter" motivated by emotional ties and a deep sense of responsibility to rural family, and the "modern woman" whose independence and mobility are tied to her experience with urban society. For Khem and thousands of other young women working in the capital city of Bangkok, both these self-images are desirable, both play a key role in their decisions to leave home; however, both are also potentially at odds. Each rests on a different set of priorities: saving money to assist family or spending it to acquire the commodities and experiences associated with urban status and modern style. Consequently, rural-urban migration involves much more than a shift in physical location. As young Thai women move into Bangkok employment they also engage in a process of self-construction, laying claim to, negotiating and at times contesting these different aspects of gender identity.

Khem is but one among the hundreds of thousands of rural women whose labor in Bangkok manufacturing and service jobs has sustained Thailand's successful drive to attract global capital investment and compete with other industrializing nations around the world. Indeed, women like Khem—unmarried, in their late teens and early twenties—now constitute the preferred work force of many Bangkok employers. Few if any communities in rural Thailand remain untouched by this youthful outflow. In many rural areas it is a virtual cliché to observe that "there is no one left in the villages but the old people and little children." While it is by no means

"Contesting the Margins of Modernity: Women, Migration, and Consumption in Thailand," by Mary Beth Mills from *American Ethnologist*, 24(1), pp. 37–61. Used by permission of The University of California Press.

true that all young people leave the countryside for urban employment, still the high rates at which they are leaving often makes it more meaningful to ask not whether adolescent children will go to Bangkok but when.

Young women without the responsibilities of a family are expected to have a limited commitment to wage employment, working for a few months or years before marriage, and consequently can be expected to put up with low pay, limited benefits, and job insecurity.

However, if young women in Thailand and elsewhere appeal to employers as a presumably quiescent and inexpensive labor force, this tells us little about why women themselves take up wage work nor how they understand their experiences of it. To try and answer these questions I conducted anthropological fieldwork with rural-urban migrants both in Bangkok's industrial zones and in rural sending communities in Thailand's northeastern region during the late 1980s and early 1990s. When I began this research I expected to find that young women moving into Bangkok were the unwitting victims of their country's headlong pursuit of national development: their entry into urban labor markets a sacrifice demanded by rural families desperate to make ends meet.

Although they were well aware of the hardships they encountered as low wage laborers, the women I met certainly did not see themselves as victims. Rather, young women like Khem almost always took credit for the decision to leave the village and find urban work, sometimes with the active support of their parents, sometimes quite the opposite. Nor were the economic returns to rural households from daughters' employment always clear; parents with whom I spoke often complained about infrequent or inadequate wage remittances. Furthermore, women's out-migration was not limited to the more impoverished segments of a community but involved families across social strata: poor, middle, and even quite well-off peasant households. I quickly realized that the entry of young rural women into urban labor was a product of complex motivations.

As Khem's words themselves reveal, labor mobility reflects social and cultural tensions within households and within the individual herself. Women's migration is not just a response to dominant ideals of filial obligation (to "save money to help my family") but to equally powerful perceptions of status lost to already mobile peers and desires for "beautiful clothes" and other commodified signifiers of urban glamour and sophistication. In other words, the movement of young women into Bangkok has as much to do with aspirations for particular kinds of personhood as with specific material goals. In particular, the idea of working in Bangkok offers young rural women an experience of personal independence that is largely unavailable to them within the village setting as unmarried daughters subordinate to parents and other elders. For the adolescent whose peers are all working in Bangkok, the tales told by friends on visits home invoke images of glamour and style she might otherwise only see on television broadcasts.

MIGRATION AND DISCOURSES OF MODERNITY

When young migrants speak of their decision to go to Bangkok, as in Khem's account, their stories almost always invoke the gendered imagery of "good daughters" and "modern women." As daughters, migrants respond to obligations of respect and gratitude owed by all children to their parents; from this perspective migration to Bangkok is an important means for youth to acknowledge their debts to parents by earning money to send home. This is especially significant for young women who, unlike their brothers, cannot take the vows of a Theravada Buddhist monk to earn religious merit for their parents. Spending a few months in the monastic discipline of a Buddhist temple remains among the most important obligations a son has to his mother and father, one that can take precedence over economic contributions. Daughters, however, are raised to express their gratitude and loyalty by caring for the day-to-day needs of household members. They are expected to be more industrious and responsible in such matters than their brothers. According to Nid, whose Bangkok wages as a maid in a tourist guest house paid for the care of a seriously ill father, young men in the village only "play and run around." They may go off, she argued, for days, weeks, or months, sleeping in the temple or at a friend's house; they don't see what the family needs or what they are going without. "Men don't see, they don't pay attention. But women are responsible, they see what's missing; they know when there's not enough rice. Women have to look after the family." Urban wages allow young rural women to fulfill these expectations in a form that is both concrete and highly valued by family at home.

Just as powerful in shaping migration decisions is an explicit desire to be "up-to-date" *(thansamay), to* participate in Thai "modernity." Throughout Thailand images of the beautiful *thansamay* women—on billboards, television ads, serial dramas, and in many other formats—set powerful standards for defining this status. Moreover city life provides a multitude of settings and social institutions—from beauty parlors and shopping malls, to movie theaters and nightclubs—where migrants can observe and pursue "modern" womanhood for themselves.

Part of what draws young rural women into the city is an unspoken but powerful suggestion that there they can be at once beautiful, modern and mobile. With an urban income they can enhance their own beauty and modernity; they can participate in the adventure, excitement and independence of modern city life. Indeed, one of the most valued benefits for migrants is that urban employment allows them to work indoors, away from the skin darkening effects of the sun. White skin is a crucial marker of physical beauty in both urban and rural Thai aesthetic systems. Older villagers often describe women and men moving into Bangkok as "going to get [white] skin" *(pay aw phiw).* While some offered these comments as a disparagement of youthful vanity, migrants on return visits were frequently complimented on their pale skin. At the same time that they acquire such signs of modern attractiveness, young migrants also hope that by sending money back to parents and siblings, they can maintain their standing within the home community as good women and daughters.

In sum, migration decisions involve a fragile convergence between young women's sense of duty and desires for adventure. Working in the city promises a level of personal autonomy unavailable to young women in the village prior to marriage and motherhood, without having to deny their obligations to family. Once in the city, however, the realities of low wages, minimal benefits and often harsh working and living conditions mean that daughterly responsibilities and the pursuit of *thansamay* ideals of autonomy and material display frequently come into conflict. Migrants' hopes to be both modern women and good daughters are not so easily achieved in the face of Bangkok realities.

BEING UP-TO-DATE—MIGRANTS, WORK, AND COMMODITY CONSUMPTION

The young women that I knew both in Bangkok and in rural communities found these images of *thansamay* identity compelling and the prospect of remaining at home dull by comparison. When describing their experiences before coming to the city, many migrants alluded to feelings of boredom: "In the village there's nothing to do." The Bangkok they see on nightly television broadcasts and hear about from friends is, by contrast, a place of boundless novelty and excitement. As one young textile worker explained, "I had to go see for myself." Perhaps more importantly, Bangkok is also where they can earn the money needed to actively enjoy the style and amenities of an "up-to-date" identity. Thip, a textile worker who left her village home at age 19, wanted to work in Bangkok because "at home there was no money and nothing to do, I wanted to have lots of money, money to send home and to buy things for myself as well."

Cash wages, or more particularly what those wages can buy, may be the key attraction of urban employment; however, in some ways young women's desires to be "up-to-date" can be addressed through the work experience itself, especially when they find employment in Bangkok's industrial manufacturing sector. In contrast to the decidedly "old-fashioned" drudgery of family-based rural agriculture (hard, heavy physical labor, largely unmechanized and performed out-of-doors), urban factories in themselves carry an attractive aura of participation in *thansamay* society (performing lighter, even if highly repetitive tasks, involving impressive new technologies, and located indoors out of the sun and rain).

But if factories can project an image of "up-to-date" agency and status to employees, this is not always easy to sustain, especially as migrants struggle to cope with low wages and limited benefits. Employees in large manufacturing companies generally earn the legal minimum (just under US$4.00 per day in 1990, and only rising to about US$6.00 daily by 1996). Lower than minimum wages were reported frequently by the women I interviewed, especially those working in small garment factories or piece-rate sweat shops; particularly low wages were the rule for women employed as domestic servants. In larger industrial companies, where employers were mostly likely to pay workers the legal minimum, many women reported that their wages could be docked for numerous reasons including fines for lateness, failures to make production quotas, or minor infractions of shop floor regulations.

In addition to low wages, young migrants must also learn to cope with new strictures and forms of authority including the rigid time-discipline of urban manufacturing. For example, Bangkok's large garment industry includes thousands of small shops subcontracting for larger companies; these enterprises typically pay employees on a piece-rate basis (e.g., a set amount per finished garment) and work days can last twelve hours or more, especially when an order is due. Larger manufacturing enterprises have standard eight-hour shifts; however, mandatory overtime can be frequent and many involve anywhere from two to eight additional hours of work. Moreover, the largest factories tend to operate in three shifts around the clock. Shifts rotate once a week forcing workers into a new cycle of sleep and eating every seven days. Even without the strains of overtime, this constant upheaval in daily routines frequently results in health problems: disrupted menstruation, headaches and insomnia, intestinal problems and ulcers. In addition, women may confront a variety of other dangers in the workplace such as toxic chemicals and gases, accidents due to improperly maintained machinery or worker fatigue, or respiratory infections from poorly ventilated work areas. Adding to these complaints, young female workers are also potential targets for sexual harassment and other forms of intimidation by male supervisors and other figures of authority at work.

While acknowledging the hardships of long hours and often unpleasant, if not unsafe, working conditions, many of the migrants I interviewed appreciated their relative freedom after working hours. Living conditions in company dormitories or rented rooms in the slums are often crowded, hot, and dirty; still they offer the chance to escape from direct supervision on the shop floor. It is here, at the end of the shift and outside the factory gates, that migrants are best able to explore and absorb images of sophisticated urban lifestyles by watching television and popular movies or going to department stores, entertainment parks and the like. For many young women, these ventures into urban consumer culture are particularly valued aspects of their time in the city.

The young women to whom I spoke were often reluctant to reveal exactly how much they spent in the city, especially on non-essential items; yet any visit to the rooms of young workers reveals the importance given to commodity purchases and display. Ut and Tiw, two sisters, rented a room, one of four tiny partitions on the second floor of an old wooden house. It measured about 2.5 meters across and 4 meters long. One corner was walled off as a tiny bath and toilet area, another was used as a makeshift "kitchen" with a few pots and dishes, an electric rice cooker, and a small gas ring. The rest of the room was furnished with several blankets and cushions along with Ut and Tiw's few other possessions. An electric fan sat in one corner, usually idle unless the sisters were entertaining visitors. On a set of shelves by one wall, a small tape deck stood next to a row of cassettes by well-known Thai vocal performers and pop-rock stars. A half-dozen small photo albums and a camera occupied another shelf, while yet another held a haphazard collection of cosmetics, a bottle or two of deodorants, powders, and lotions along with combs, brushes, and small novelty items, hair clips and ribbons. Not long after I first began to visit Ut and Tiw, I arrived one week to discover a small color television had been added to their belongings, the culmination of nearly three years' effort. The sisters had saved the 7500 baht (US$300) purchase price out of their wages and by taking on occasional piece-rate assembly work given out by Tiw's company for those wanting to earn extra money on their own time.

In addition to acquiring new mass-market commodities, many rural-urban migrants are eager to join in new commodified forms of leisure and entertainment. At home a young village woman is enmeshed in an intense web of social relations that include parents, elders, and neighbors as well as siblings and friends, all of whom can observe, comment upon, and potentially influence her behavior; as factory workers in the city, migrants' primary social interaction is with friends and co-workers, most of whom are of similar age and background. The expectations and interests of their peers play an important role in shaping the consumption behavior of many migrants.

Working side-by-side, sharing a rented room or living in the common quarters of factory dormitories, young women find themselves in an intense world of peer-oriented companionship, far removed from the authority of parents and elders that would frame and intersect such ties in the village setting. Friendly pressures to participate in common activities—such as shared meals and outings—place steady demands upon the cash earnings of young workers. Money, they said, is hard to hang onto, not because of large or flamboyant purchases but because of the everyday demands of urban existence, including their desires to hang out and "have fun" with friends. Almost inevitably these interactions involve some form of consumption: whether gatherings revolve around purchased meals, trips to local markets, or more rarely, spending a day at one of the city's commercial amusement parks (such as "Happyland" or the part-zoo/part-rock concert venue, "The Crocodile Farm").

These peer group "outings" *(pay thiaw)* in search of fun and entertainment are, for many migrants, among the most satisfying experiences of life in Bangkok. Given migrants' limited leisure hours and low wages, a *thiaw is* usually brief—an afternoon's trip to the market, a shopping mall, or a park; but it may also be a much longer excursion, perhaps over a holiday weekend, to the beach or (more commonly) to a friend's home in a distant and unfamiliar province. Such outings offer a dramatic break from the tedium and exhaustion of factory shifts. They are also the best chances for most migrants by their own actions to approximate dominant images of a truly "modern" lifestyle. For example, participating in these peer group activities requires investing in certain kinds of *thansamay* commodity display. Young women dress carefully for these events, usually in blue jeans and colorful blouses or t-shirts. Other commodities like cameras can also be in high demand especially on longer trips.

URBAN DILEMMAS—CONFRONTING AMBIVALENCE AND MARGINALITY

While the acquisition and display of commodities in these ways provide crucial demonstrations of *thansamay* identity and status among migrant peers, within the broader urban setting these claims receive little recognition. Amid Bangkok's exploding consumerism migrants' consumption patterns—restricted as they are by low wages and limited leisure time—offer only a weak approximation of truly "up-to-date" urban living. There are always more and newer commodities to acquire, more places to see, more outings to take. Wearing jeans and cosmetics, taking trips to the Crocodile Farm or an air-conditioned department store are pleasant and attractively *thansamay* activities; nevertheless, surrounded by the city's hypermodernity and intense commercialization, rural women's access to and control over the extensive cultural repertoire of "being up-to-date" is partial at best.

It is not surprising, then, that the women I knew in Bangkok almost universally expressed ambivalence about their experiences in the city. They appreciated the many "conveniences" and "comforts" *(khwaam saduak sabaay)* of city life: easy access to running water, electricity, transportation, markets and entertainment. And central to these advantages was the fact that, "In the city there's money; in the village there's none." Just as recognizable, however, were Bangkok's less pleasant dimensions. They city was polluted, noisy, and congested. Workers lived in crowded dormitories or cheap rented rooms in which, nevertheless, it was very easy to feel alone and isolated. On the job, too, they endured insecure, often unhealthy and oppressive working conditions.

The continuing strength of migrants' identification with rural family and community—i.e., what informs the "good daughter" imagery of Khem's and other migrants' stories—is at least partly rooted in pragmatic assessments of their longer term insecurity as urban laborers. For example, migrants know that few Bangkok factories will hire women over the age of 25 and some restrict new hires to 21 or younger. Women who stay in the city after their mid-twenties are very careful not to lose their current employment lest they find themselves choosing between a premature return home or poorly paid informal sector work such as domestic service or sweatshop subcontracting labor. Similar fears underlie a widespread reluctance among migrant women to marry and start a family in the city. Workers know well that urban employers tend to prefer not only youthful but also unmarried, unencumbered employees. A woman who marries and especially a woman with children to care for is at a significant disadvantage in the labor market. Consequently many rural women believe that a return to the village household remains their most reliable source of economic security as they age, and particularly when they marry.

But this generalized perception of long-term vulnerability in the city does not mean that the prospect of a return home is without problems. If the idea of settling in the city is fraught with difficulty, going home to a future of rice farming and motherhood raises a different set of concerns, ones linked to migrants' ongoing aspirations for *thansamay* forms of success and autonomy. The wages they can earn in Bangkok, limited though they may be, provide a steady and individualized source of cash income, unlike the more irregular, often unpredictable, and collective earnings that characterize household agricultural production. A former textile worker in her mid-twenties, having returned to her village in preparation for marriage to a local man, was quick to identify the unfortunate consequences that this move was going to have. She was happy with her prospective husband, but their union would put an end to her time in Bangkok; from then on she would be "only a mother and housewife." Her sense of loss was shared by many young women as they contemplated when to leave urban work and take up the burdens of raising their own family.

One response among migrant women is to plan for a return home but to do so in a way that will preserve some of their hard-won *thansamay* status and autonomy. A common ambition is to open a small shop or food vending enterprise. Others who are able to marshall their resources and energy during their limited leisure hours choose to invest in further education or vocational training. Maew, an employee in a leather bag factory, at age nineteen decided to drastically reduce both her expenditures in the city and remittances home, in order to pay for a high school education. When I met her she had been taking adult education classes every Sunday for the past two years; she expected to complete her diploma in another two or three years. She was also saving money in a bank account so that when she left Bangkok to go home she would be able to continue her education at the provincial teacher's college. In a similar case, Lek, a textile worker from the same village as Maew, saved her wages until she could pay the 7000 baht (US$280) tuition at a Bangkok beauty school. On her days off from the factory she attended classes and practiced the skills of hairdressing and cosmetic application. Most of the rural-urban migrants that I knew either had less concrete plans for their future or were unable or unwilling to ignore parental expectations so consistently. Nevertheless, they too hoped to be more than just "rice and upland crop farmers" *(chaaw naa chaaw ray)* when they left the city.

All migrant women I knew confronted this dilemma to some degree during their time in the city. Attempts to pursue *thansamay* aspirations are fundamentally at odds with young women's obligations to rural kin. Whatever the purpose of their urban expenditures (personal items, daily needs, entertainment with friends, education or vocational training) every baht spent in Bangkok is, at least in theory, one less available to assist family at home. New patterns of commodity consumption, while necessary for the pursuit of a *thansamay* sense of self, confront migrants both with their own marginal status within the dominant, commodified culture of Bangkok and with their potential (or actual) failure to maintain the ideal image of a "good daughter." Although, among the women I interviewed, the economic hardships of rural households were rarely the primary motivating factor in their migration decisions, all recognized the moral force of family obligations.

The amounts and frequency of migrants' contributions to rural households varied widely among the women I interviewed; self-reporting commonly elicited contributions totaling anywhere from 30% to 80% of monthly income but these initial claims were usually revealed later on to represent much more occasional remittances. There were very few women who would admit to never having sent money but most agreed that they would rather wait and save a particular sum (often 2000 or 3000 baht, US$80–$120) over several months which they could then take home on a visit instead of sending back smaller but more frequent contributions.

In part this allowed the women to exercise greater control over the use of their earnings by saving toward particular consumption projects, the most common being the purchase of materials to use in building their parents a new house. These goals were often supported by rural kin but they could also be frustrated by periodic demands for increased or immediate contributions. Some of these requests come at predictable intervals: calls for help with harvest or transplanting expenses, or younger siblings' school costs at the beginning of term (e.g., uniforms, books, high school tuition, etc.). At other times migrants will be called upon to help out in a household emergency, particularly when a sudden or severe illness strikes. Although young women may complain amongst themselves that people in the village think only about money, most migrants do their best to comply with requests from home. But sometimes daughters find themselves in the position of censoring the consumption demands of their own parents. For example, when Lan's mother asked for a color television to replace the black-and-white set that Lan and a sister (also working in the city) had bought a few years before, Lan responded with some exasperation: "I'm saving now for the cost of building her a new house. [My sister and I] bought the supporting posts last year. Mother will have to wait for the television."

If the demands of urban consumption styles jeopardize the fragile balance of migrants' desires to be both "modern women" and "good daughters," there are moments when migrants can confront these tensions and rework them to their own benefit. Here the importance of maintaining ties to rural kin can be seen as not only a matter of migrants' pragmatic concerns for the future but also because it is through trips home, bringing money, wearing new clothes and accompanied by new friends that migrants can lessen, if only briefly, the strains of urban life and project a solid identity of both *thansamay* success and filial respect and gratitude.

These tensions, and migrants' attempts to resolve them, are an important aspect of one of the most popular activities in which rural-urban migrants engage: organizing (and participating in) elaborate ceremonial trips to make ritual donations to village temples. Although framed within the Buddhist merit-making language of popular Thai religious beliefs, the enthusiasm with which migrants participate in these events often has less to do with desires to add to their store of karmic merit (although such goals are by no means irrelevant) than with the opportunities that these trips provide to resolve (if only temporarily) some of the tensions that arise during the course of their urban experiences. Specifically, these merit-making trips are occasions when migrants' *thansamay* consumption practices parallel and even support their commitment to the village home.

On these occasions, several people, usually from the same village, will plan an excursion, rent a bus and recruit friends in the city to come along. Both women and men migrants participate (indeed the mixed sex format is an added attraction for many young people); however, it is often the women who attend to the time-consuming details. Passengers pay a fare for the bus trip and contribute to a merit fund which will be offered to the community temple.

But organizing a merit-making trip, as the women I knew quickly pointed out, is a lot of work. A successful trip (i.e., one that raises a substantial amount of money) depends on recruiting many participants. Migrants from the same village must coordinate among themselves, not an easy task when they may live and work in opposite ends of Bangkok and seldom have access to private telephone lines which could facilitate contact. A rented bus must be reserved for the occasion, invitations to participants and envelopes for their contributions must be printed, donors must be solicited. This last task is often the most troublesome. One worker in a large cotton factory complained that every year so many ceremonies took place she was reluctant to ask her friends to contribute to yet another one. "If you ask them they try to give something but it may only be 10 baht [US$0.40]."

In the performance of these events participants can enact the close convergence of ongoing ties to kin and community with their claims to *thansamay* autonomy and urban success. On the several merit-making trips I attended, a large passenger bus, packed with people, and decorated on one side with a long banner proclaiming the destination and ceremonial objective of its purpose, left Bangkok in the evening, usually on a Saturday at the end of the afternoon factory shift. We traveled all night, arriving at the host community sometime in the early to mid-morning. Each time the journey began in an atmosphere of celebration and revelry that continued throughout the night, fueled in part by a steady flow of alcohol (consumed mainly but not exclusively by the male passengers), along with soft drinks and other treats purchased by passengers in anticipation of the evening's festivities. Those who tried to rest their heads against seat backs and windows hoping to catch a little sleep were loudly serenaded by their more energetic companions usually with the aid of a microphone hooked into the bus's internal sound system and backed by drums and cymbals brought along by the celebrants. Sometime during the night the organizers of the trip passed through the bus collecting envelopes they had distributed earlier and that passengers had filled with cash contributions. The amounts would later be recorded along with participants' names for the final offering at the temple.

The ceremony itself took place soon after reaching the host community. On one *thoht phaa paa* to a village in the northeastern province of Khon Kaen, we arrived in time to complete the *phaa paa* presentation before the daily offering of the monks' late morning meal, the food for which had been prepared in large quantities by villagers in order that everyone attending could share once the monks had eaten. The presentation of money to the temple was the focus of the ritual but it also includ[ed] offerings of commodity items for the personal use of resident monks: robes, bath and laundry soap, toilet paper, packaged drinks and drink mixes such as Ovaltine. These were presented in elaborate cellophane wrapped bundles, a format that has been standardized by urban stores specializing in such ready-to-go merit packages. The ceremony concluded with speeches by community leaders and the most senior organizers of the *thoht phaa paa,* as well as ritual chants and blessings led by the temple monks. Meanwhile the final amount of money donated had been tallied and was announced for everyone to hear.

When the ritual itself was finished the merit-makers could finally relax. Migrants visited with family and introduced the friends who had accompanied them from Bangkok. Fresh from the successful display of devotion to temple and community concerns, they could enjoy their status (however temporary) as good daughters (and sons) whose successful sojourns as modern wage workers in the nation's capital had made possible their contributions to the prosperity of their community and its temple. The congratulatory atmosphere continued well into the evening with the performance by a folk-opera *(moh lam)* troupe hired by the host community for the occasion. The next morning it was time to get back on the bus and return to the city.

Young people working in Bangkok acknowledge the religious merit that participants earn on these excursions but also emphasize that the trips are fun and entertaining. This combination of spiritual and worldly purposes in merit-making ceremonies is a key part of their power to defuse ongoing conflicts, at least temporarily, between migrants' aspirations for achievement within the dominant culture of urban "modernity" and their continuing attachments to village family and community. *Thoht phaa paa* and other ceremonial trips provide an opportunity to display success and to show off urban friends to people back home, as well as to renew and affirm solidarity with the rural community and its moral focus, the temple. It is one of the few moments when fulfilling one's obligations as a good village daughter (or son) and the pursuit of a *thansamay* identity appear to coincide.

CONCLUSION

By looking carefully at how migrants use their hard-earned wages—for commodity purchases, for entertainment, for merit-making trips, as well as for cash remittances—we can begin to see that consumption offers a range of strategies by which young rural women can pursue their own interests and stretch, if only temporarily, the limits of their subordination within the wider Thai society. Viewing migrants as consumers (and not only as workers) reveals more complex dimensions of women's urban employment and personal agency. In effect, labor migrants' consumption practices are one of the few available avenues through which they can exercise new forms of autonomy and seek to construct socially satisfying and valued identities.

As they move between rural and urban settings, young Thai women must negotiate not only shifts in space but also shifting identities and social relations. In this context, rural-urban mobility must be recognized as more than a strategy for economic survival or accumulation; it is also a vehicle through which migrants struggle over what it means to be "modern" in contemporary Thai society and how to reconcile these aspirations and images with equally compelling concerns for and moral commitments to rural kin and community.

In the midst of these complex demands, it is little wonder that women should experience the movement into urban employment in highly ambivalent ways. Nevertheless, this ambivalence cannot be taken as passivity or a failure to recognize the inequities they encounter. Throughout their time in the city, young women make very real efforts to maintain a sense of meaning and purpose despite the many difficulties they face. Young women in Bangkok are often torn between duty and affection for rural kin on the one hand, and personal desires for autonomy and urban adventure on the other. The choices they make, however, are shaped not only by the structural disparities of Thai society and a globalized economy but also by the cultural resources that are available to them and through which they seek to understand who they are and who they wish to become.

READING 8

The Uses of Poverty: The Poor Pay All

Herbert J. Gans

introduction

Of the several social classes in the United States, sociologists have concentrated their studies on the poor. The super-rich and, for the most part, the ordinarily wealthy are beyond the reach of researchers. Sociologists are not members of the wealthy classes or of the power elite, and members of these groups have the means to insulate themselves from the prying eyes (and questionnaires and tape recorders) of sociologists. When it comes to the middle classes, sociologists are likely to take their members for granted. The middle classes are part of their everyday life, and, like others, sociologists often overlook the things closest to them. The characteristics and situations of the poor, however, are different enough to strike the interests of sociologists. And the poor are accessible. People in poverty are generally willing to be interviewed. They are even a bit flattered that sociologists, for the most part members of the upper middle class, will take the time to talk to them. Hardly anyone else takes them seriously.

A couple of thousand years ago, Jesus said, "The poor you'll always have with you." In this selection, as Herbert Gans places the sociological lens yet again on people in poverty, he uses a functionalist perspective to explain why we always will have people in poverty. Simply put, from a functionalist perspective, we *need* the poor.

Thinking Critically

As you read this selection, ask yourself:

1. What functions (or uses) of poverty does Gans identify?
2. Of the functions of poverty that Gans identifies, which two do you think are the most important? Which two the least important? Why?
3. Do you think that Gans has gone overboard with his analysis? That he has stretched the functionalist perspective beyond reason? Or do you agree with him? Why or why not?

Some years ago Robert K. Merton applied the notion of functional analysis to explain the continuing though maligned existence of the urban political machine: If it continued to exist, perhaps it fulfilled latent—unintended or unrecognized—positive functions. Clearly it did. Merton pointed out how the political machine provided central authority to get things done when a decentralized local government could not act, humanized the services of the impersonal bureaucracy for fearful citizens, offered concrete help (rather than abstract law or justice) to the poor, and otherwise performed services needed or demanded by many people but considered unconventional or even illegal by formal public agencies.

Today, poverty is more maligned than the political machine ever was; yet it, too, is a persistent social phenomenon. Consequently, there may be some merit in applying functional analysis to poverty, in asking whether it also has positive functions that explain its persistence.

Merton defined functions as "those observed consequences [of a phenomenon] which make for the adaptation or adjustment of a given [social] system." I shall use a slightly different definition; instead of identifying functions for an entire social system, I shall identify them for the interest groups, socioeconomic classes, and other population aggregates with shared values that "inhabit" a social system. I suspect that in a modern heterogeneous society, few phenomena are functional or dysfunctional for the society as a whole, and that most result in benefits to some groups and costs to others. Nor are any phenomena indispensable; in most instances, one can suggest what Merton calls "functional alternatives" or equivalents for them, i.e., other social patterns or policies that achieve the same positive functions but avoid the dysfunction. (In the following discussion, positive functions will be abbreviated as functions and negative functions as dysfunctions. Functions and dysfunctions, in the planner's terminology, will be described as benefits and costs.)

Associating poverty with positive functions seems at first glance to be unimaginable. Of course, the slumlord and the loan shark are commonly known to profit from the existence of poverty, but they are viewed as evil men, so their activities are classified among the dysfunctions of poverty. However, what is less often recognized, at least by the conventional wisdom, is that poverty also makes possible the existence or expansion of respectable professions and occupations, for example, penology, criminology, social work, and public health. More recently, the poor have provided jobs for professional and para-professional "poverty warriors," and for journalists and social scientists, this author included, who have supplied the information demanded by the revival of public interest in poverty.

Clearly, then, poverty and the poor may well satisfy a number of positive functions for many nonpoor groups in American society. I shall describe 13 such functions—economic, social and political—that seem to me most significant.

From "The Uses of Poverty: The Poor Pay All," by Herbert J. Gans, *Social Policy,* July/August 1971.

THE FUNCTIONS OF POVERTY

First, the existence of poverty ensures that society's "dirty work" will be done. Every society has such work: physically dirty or dangerous, temporary, dead-end and underpaid, undignified, and menial jobs. Society can fill these jobs by paying higher wages than for "clean" work, or it can force people who have no other choice to do the dirty work—and at low wages. In America, poverty functions to provide a low-wage labor pool that is willing—or rather, unable to be *un*willing—to perform dirty work at low cost. Indeed, this function of the poor is so important that in some Southern states, welfare payments have been cut off during the summer months when the poor are needed to work in the fields. Moreover, much of the debate about the Negative Income Tax and the Family Assistance Plan [welfare programs] has concerned their impact on the work incentive, by which is actually meant the incentive of the poor to do the needed dirty work if the wages therefrom are no larger than the income grant. Many economic activities that involve dirty work depend on the poor for their existence: restaurants, hospitals, parts of the garment industry, and "truck farming," among others, could not persist in their present form without the poor.

Second, because the poor are required to work at low wages, they subsidize a variety of economic activities that benefit the affluent. For example, domestics subsidize the upper-middle and upper classes, making life easier for their employers and freeing affluent women for a variety of professional, cultural, civic, and partying activities. Similarly, because the poor pay a higher proportion of their income in property and sales taxes, among others, they subsidize many state and local governmental services that benefit more affluent groups. In addition, the poor support innovation in medical practice as patients in teaching and research hospitals and as guinea pigs in medical experiments.

Third, poverty creates jobs for a number of occupations and professions that serve or "service" the poor, or protect the rest of society from them. As already noted, penology would be minuscule without the poor, as would the police. Other activities and groups that flourish because of the existence of poverty are the numbers game, the sale of heroin and cheap wines and liquors, Pentecostal ministers, faith healers, prostitutes, pawn shops, and the peacetime army, which recruits its enlisted men mainly from among the poor.

Fourth, the poor buy goods others do not want and thus prolong the economic usefulness of such goods—day-old bread, fruit and vegetables that otherwise would have to be thrown out, secondhand clothes, and deteriorating automobiles and buildings. They also provide incomes for doctors, lawyers, teachers, and others who are too old, poorly trained or incompetent to attract more affluent clients.

In addition to economic functions, the poor perform a number of social functions.

Fifth, the poor can be identified and punished as alleged or real deviants in order to uphold the legitimacy of conventional norms. To justify the desirability of hard work, thrift, honesty, and monogamy, for example, the defenders of these norms must be able to find people who can be accused of being lazy, spendthrift, dishonest, and promiscuous. Although there is some evidence that the poor are about as moral and law-abiding as anyone else, they are more likely than middle-class transgressors to be caught and punished when they participate in deviant acts. Moreover, they lack the political and cultural power to correct the stereotypes that other people hold of them and thus continue to be thought of as lazy, spendthrift, etc., by those who need living proof that moral deviance does not pay.

Sixth, and conversely, the poor offer vicarious participation to the rest of the population in the uninhibited sexual, alcoholic, and narcotic behavior in which they are alleged to participate and which, being freed from the constraints of affluence, they are often thought to enjoy more than the middle classes. Thus many people, some social scientists included, believe that the poor not only are more given to uninhibited behavior (which may be true, although it is often motivated by despair more than by lack of inhibition) but derive more pleasure from it than affluent people (which research by Lee Rainwater, Walter Miller and others shows to be patently untrue). However, whether the poor actually have more sex and enjoy it more is irrelevant; so long as middle-class people believe this to be true, they can participate in it vicariously when instances are reported in factual or fictional form.

Seventh, the poor also serve a direct cultural function when culture created by or for them is adopted by the more affluent. The rich often collect artifacts from extinct folk cultures of poor people; and almost all Americans listen to the blues, Negro spirituals, and country music, which originated among the Southern poor. Recently they have enjoyed the rock styles that were born, like the Beatles, in the slums, and in the last year, poetry written by ghetto children has become popular in literary circles. The poor also serve as culture heroes, particularly, of course, to the left; but the hobo, the cowboy, the hipster, and the mythical prostitute with a heart of gold have performed this function for a variety of groups.

Eighth, poverty helps to guarantee the status of those who are not poor. In every hierarchical society, someone has to be at the bottom; but in American society, in which social mobility is an important goal for many and people need to know where they stand, the poor function as a reliable and relatively permanent measuring rod for status comparisons. This is particularly true for the working class, whose politics is influenced by the need to maintain status distinctions between themselves and the poor, much as the aristocracy must find ways of distinguishing itself from the *nouveaux riches.*

Ninth, the poor also aid the upward mobility of groups just above them in the class hierarchy. Thus a goodly number of Americans have entered the middle class through the profits earned from the provision of goods and services in the slums, including illegal or nonrespectable ones that upper-class and upper-middle-class businessmen shun because of their low prestige. As a result, members of almost every immigrant group have financed their upward mobility by providing slum housing, entertainment, gambling, narcotics, etc., to later arrivals—most recently to blacks and Puerto Ricans.

Tenth, the poor help to keep the aristocracy busy, thus justifying its continued existence. "Society" uses the poor as clients of settlement houses and beneficiaries of charity affairs; indeed, the aristocracy must have the poor to demonstrate its superiority over other elites who devote themselves to earning money.

Eleventh, the poor, being powerless, can be made to absorb the costs of change and growth in American society. During the nineteenth century, they did the backbreaking work that built the cities; today, they are pushed out of their neighborhoods to make room for "progress." Urban renewal projects to hold middle-class taxpayers in the city and expressways to enable suburbanites to commute downtown have typically been located in poor neighborhoods, since no other group will allow itself to be displaced. For the same reason, universities, hospitals, and civic centers also expand into land occupied by the poor. The major costs of the industrialization of agriculture have been borne by the poor, who are pushed off the land without recompense; and they have paid a large share of the human cost of the growth of American power overseas, for they have provided many of the foot soldiers for Vietnam and other wars.

Twelfth, the poor facilitate and stabilize the American political process. Because they vote and participate in politics less than other groups, the political system is often free to ignore them. Moreover, since they can rarely support Republicans, they often provide the Democrats with a captive constituency that has no other place to go. As a result, the Democrats can count on their votes, and be more responsive to voters—for example, the white working class—who might otherwise switch to the Republicans.

Thirteenth, the role of the poor in upholding conventional norms (see the *fifth* point, above) also has a significant political function. An economy based on the ideology of laissez-faire requires a deprived population that is allegedly unwilling to work or that can be considered inferior because it must accept charity or welfare in order to survive. Not only does the alleged moral deviancy of the poor reduce the moral pressure on the present political economy to eliminate poverty but socialist alternatives can be made to look quite unattractive if those who will benefit most from them can be described as lazy, spendthrift, dishonest and promiscuous.

THE ALTERNATIVES

I have described 13 of the more important functions poverty and the poor satisfy in American society, enough to support the functionalist thesis that poverty, like any other social phenomenon, survives in part because it is useful to society or some of its parts. This analysis is not intended to suggest that because it is often functional, poverty *should* exist, or that it *must* exist. For one thing, poverty has many more dysfunctions than functions; for another, it is possible to suggest functional alternatives.

For example, society's dirty work could be done without poverty, either by automation or by paying "dirty workers" decent wages. Nor is it necessary for the poor to subsidize the many activities they support through their low-wage jobs. This would, however, drive up the costs of these activities, which would result in higher prices to their customers and clients. Similarly, many of the professionals who flourish because of the poor could be given other roles. Social workers could provide counseling to the affluent, as they prefer to do anyway; and the police could devote themselves to traffic and organized crime. Other roles would have to be found for badly trained or incompetent professionals now relegated to serving the poor, and someone else would have to pay their salaries. Fewer penologists would be employable, however. And Pentecostal religion could probably not survive without the poor—nor would parts of the second- and third-hand-goods market. And in many cities, "used" housing that no one else wants would then have to be torn down at public expense.

Alternatives for the cultural functions of the poor could be found more easily and cheaply. Indeed, entertainers and adolescents are already serving as the deviants needed to uphold traditional morality and as devotees of orgies to "staff" the fantasies of vicarious participation.

The status functions of the poor are another matter. In a hierarchical society, some people must be defined as inferior to everyone else with respect to a variety of attributes, but they need not be poor in the absolute sense. One could conceive of a society in which the "lower class," though last in the pecking order, received 75 percent of the median income, rather than 15–40 percent, as is now the case. Needless to say, this would require considerable income redistribution.

The contribution the poor make to the upward mobility of the groups that provide them with goods and services could also be maintained without the poor's having such low incomes. However, it is true that if the poor were more affluent, they would have access to enough capital to take over the provider role, thus competing with, and perhaps rejecting, the "outsiders."... Similarly, if the poor were more affluent, they would make less willing clients for upper-class philanthropy, although some would still use settlement houses to achieve upward mobility, as they do now. Thus "Society" could continue to run its philanthropic activities.

The political functions of the poor would be more difficult to replace. With increased affluence the poor would probably obtain more political power and be more active politically. With higher incomes and more political power, the poor would be likely to resist paying the costs of growth and change. Of course, it is possible to imagine urban renewal and highway projects that properly reimbursed the displaced people, but such projects would then become considerably more expensive, and many might never be built. This, in turn, would reduce the comfort and convenience of those who now benefit from urban renewal and expressways.

In sum, then, many of the functions served by the poor could be replaced if poverty were eliminated, but almost always at higher costs to others, particularly more affluent others. Consequently, a functional analysis must conclude that poverty persists not only because it fulfills a number of positive functions but also because many of the functional alternatives to poverty would be quite dysfunctional for the affluent members of society. A functional analysis thus ultimately arrives at much the same conclusion as radical sociology, except that radical thinkers treat as manifest what I describe as latent: that social phenomena that are functional for affluent or powerful groups and dysfunctional for poor or powerless ones persist; that when the elimination of such phenomena through functional alternatives would generate dysfunctions for the affluent or powerful, they will continue to persist; and that phenomena like poverty can be eliminated only when they become dysfunctional for the affluent or powerful, or when the powerless can obtain enough power to change society.

POSTSCRIPT*

Over the years, this article has been interpreted as either a direct attack on functionalism or a tongue-in-cheek satirical comment on it. Neither interpretation is true. I wrote the article for two reasons. First and foremost, I wanted to point out that there are, unfortunately, positive functions of poverty which have to be dealt with by antipoverty policy. Second, I was trying to show that functionalism is not the inherently conservative approach for which it has often been criticized, but that it can be employed in liberal and radical analyses.

*A note from the author to the editor.

READING 9

Showing My Color

Clarence Page

introduction

As you know, the circumstances that we inherit at birth (sometimes called *social capital*) affect what happens to us in life. Some of us are born poor, others rich, and most of us in between. Some of us are born to single mothers, others to married parents; some to parents who are college graduates, others to parents who have not finished high school. Even our geography (South, West, rural, urban) sets up background factors that play a significant role in our orientations to life. Sociologists use the term *life chances* to refer to how the background factors that surround our birth affect our fate in life.

In the United States, race–ethnicity is a major divide. It opens and closes doors of opportunity and privilege. It is a primary source of identity, uniting us with some people, while separating us from others. Although race–ethnicity becomes a vital part of our identity, as with other concepts, we are not born with an awareness of race or ethnicity. These we learn from others around us, which can be a jarring experience. In this selection, Page, a journalist, recounts how he learned that he was a black in a white society. He also shares examples of what this has meant for his life.

Thinking Critically

As you read this selection, ask yourself:

1. Should U.S. institutions be "color blind"? That is, based on what you read in this article, do you think public policy should be made without regard to race–ethnicity?
2. How do your experiences with race and ethnicity compare with those that Page reports? Why do they differ in these ways?
3. How did you become aware of your race–ethnicity? How did you develop your current race–ethnicity identity?

Race has long had a rude presence in my life. While visiting relatives in Alabama as a child in the 1950s, I first saw water fountains marked "white" and "colored." I vaguely recall being excited. I rushed over to the one marked "colored" and turned it on, only to find, to my deep disappointment, that the water came out clear, just like the water back home in Ohio.

"Segregation," my dad said. I'd never heard the word before. My southern-born parents explained that it was something the white folks "down home" practiced. Some "home." Yet unpleasant experiences in the North already had taught me a more genteel, yet no less limiting, version.

"There are places white people don't want colored to go," my elders told me in their soft southern accents, "and white people make the rules."

We had plenty of segregation like that in the North. We just didn't have the signs, which made it cheaper and easier to deny. We could look out of my schoolhouse window to see a public swimming pool closed to nonwhites. We had to go across town to the separate-but-equal "pool for colored." The steel mill that was our town's biggest employer held separate picnics for colored and white employees, which seemed to be just fine with the employees. Everyone had a good time, separately and unequally. I think the colored folks, who today would be called the "black community," were just happy to have something to call their own.

When I was about six years old, I saw a television commercial for an amusement park near the southern Ohio factory town where I grew up.

I chose to go. I told my parents. They looked at each other sadly and informed me that "little colored kids can't go there." I was crushed.

"I wish I was white," I told my parents.

"No, you don't!" Mom snapped. She gave me a look terrible enough to persuade me instantly that no, I didn't.

"Well, maybe for a few minutes, anyway?" I asked. "Just long enough for me to get past the front gates?" Then I could show them, I thought. I remember I wanted to show them what a terrific kid I was. I felt sorry for the little white children who would be deprived of getting to know me.

Throughout our childhood years, my friendships with white schoolchildren (and with Pancho from the only Latino family in the neighborhood) proceeded without interruption. Except for the occasional tiff over some injudicious use of the N-word or some other slur we had picked up from our elders, we played in each other's backyards as congenially as Spanky, Buckwheat, and the rest of the gang on the old Hal Roach *Our Gang* comedies we used to watch on television.

Yet it quickly became apparent to me that my white friends were growing up in a different reality from the one to which I was accustomed. I could tell from the way one white friend happily discussed his weekend at LeSourdesville Lake that he did not have a clue of my reality.

"Have you been?" he asked.

"Colored can't go there," I said, somewhat astonished that he had not noticed.

"Oh, that can't be," he said.

For a moment, I perked up, wondering if the park's policy had changed. "Have you seen any colored people there?" I asked.

My white friend thought for a moment, then realized that he had not. He expressed surprise. I was surprised that he was surprised.

By the time I reached high school in the early 1960s, LeSourdesville Lake would relax its racial prohibitions. But the lessons of it stuck with me. It taught me how easily white people could ignore the segregation problem because, from their vantage point, it was not necessarily a problem. It was not necessarily an advantage to them, either, although some undoubtedly thought so. White people of low income, high insecurity, or fragile ego could always say that, no matter how badly off they felt, at least they were not black. Segregation helped them uphold and maintain this illusion of superiority. Even those white people who considered themselves to have a well-developed sense of social conscience could easily rationalize segregation as something that was good for both races. We played unwittingly into this illusion, I thought, when my friends and I began junior high school and, suddenly thrust into the edgy, high hormonal world of adolescence, quickly gravitated into social cliques according to tastes and race.

It became even more apparent to me that my white friends and I were growing up in *parallel realities,* not unlike the parallel universes described in the science fiction novels and comic books I adored—or the "parallel realities" experienced by Serbs, Bosnians, and Croatians as described years later by feminist writer Slavenka Drakulic in *The Balkan Express.* Even as the evil walls of legal segregation were tumbling down, thanks to the hard-fought struggles of the civil rights movement, it occurred to me that my reality might never be quite the same as that experienced by my white friends. We were doomed, I felt, to dwell in our parallel realities. Separated by thick walls of prejudice, we would view each other through windows of stained-glass perceptions, colored by our personal experiences. My parents had taught me well.

"Don't be showin' yo' color," my parents would admonish me in my youth, before we would go out in public, especially among white folks. The phrase had special meaning in Negro conversations. Imbued with many subtle meanings and nuances, the showing of one's "color" could be an expression of chastisement or warning, admonishment or adulation, satire or self-hatred, anger or celebration. It could mean acting out or showing anger in a loud and uncivilized way.

Its cultural origins could be traced to the Africa-rooted tradition of "signifying," a form of witty, deliberately provocative, occasionally combative word play. The thrill of the game comes from taking one's opponent close to the edge of tolerable insult. Few subjects—except perhaps sex itself—could be a more sensitive matter between black people than talk about someone else's "color." The showing of one's "color," then, connoted the display of the very worst stereotypes anyone ever dreamed up about how black people behaved. "White people are not really white," James Baldwin wrote in 1961, "but colored people can sometimes be extremely colored."

Sometimes you can still hear black people say in the heat of frustration, "I almost showed my color today," which is a way of saying they almost lost their "cool," "dropped the mask," or "went off." Losing one's cool can be a capital offense by black standards, for it shows weakness in a world in which spiritual rigor is one of the few things we can call our own. Those who keep their cool repress their "color." It is cool, in other words, to be colorless.

Showing My Color (the title of the book from which this reading is taken) emerged from my fuming discontent with the current fashions of *racial denial,* steadfast repudiations of the difference race continues to make in American life. Old liberals, particularly white liberals who have become new conservatives, charge that racial pride and color consciousness threaten to "Balkanize" American life, as if it ever was a model of unity. Many demand that we "get past race." But denials of a cancer, no matter how vigorous they may be, will not make the malignancy go away.

No less august a voice than the Supreme Court's conservative majority has taken to arguing in the 1990s for a "color-blind" approach to civil rights law, the area of American society in which color and gender consciousness have made the most dramatic improvement in equalizing opportunities.

The words of the Reverend Martin Luther King, Jr., have been perverted to support this view. Most frequently quoted is his oft-stated dream of the day when everyone would "not be judged by the color of their skin but by the content of their character." I would argue that King never intended for us to forget *all* about color. Even in his historic "I Have a Dream" speech, from which this line most often is lifted, he also pressed the less-often quoted but piquantly salient point about "the promissory note" America gave freed slaves, which, when they presented it, was returned to them marked "insufficient funds."...

I would argue that too much has been made of the virtue of "color blindness." I don't want Americans to be blind to my color as long as color continues to make a profound difference in determining life chances and opportunities. Nor do I wish to see so significant a part of my identity denied. "Ethnic differences are the very essence of cultural diversity and national creativity," black social critic Albert Murray wrote in *The Omni-Americans* (1970). "The problem is not the existence of ethnic differences, as is so often assumed, but the intrusion of such differences into areas where they do not belong."

Where, then, *do* they belong? Diversity is enriching, but race intrudes rudely on the individual's attempts to define his or her own identity. I used to be "colored." Then I was "Negro." Then I became "black." Then I became "African-American." Today I am a "person of color." In three decades, I have been transformed from a "colored person" to a "person of color." Are you keeping up with me?

Changes in what we black people call ourselves are quite annoying to some white people, which is its own reward to some black people. But if white people are confused, so are quite a few black people. There is no one way to be black. We are a diverse people amid a nation of diverse people. Some black people are nationalists who don't want anything to do with white people. Some black people are assimilationists who don't want anything to do with other black people. Some black people are integrationists who move in and out of various groups with remarkable ease. Some of us can be any of the three at any given time, depending on when you happen to run into us.

Growing up as part of a minority can expose the individual to horrible bouts of identity confusion. I used to think of myself as something of a *transracial man,* a figure no less frustrated than a transsexual who feels trapped in the body of something unfamiliar and inappropriate to his or her inner self.

These bouts were most torturous during adolescence, the period of life when, trembling with the shock of nascent independence from the ways of one's elders, the budding individual stitches together the fragile garments of an identity to be worn into adulthood. Stuttering and uncooperative motor skills left me severely challenged in dancing, basket shooting, and various social applications; I felt woefully inadequate to the task of being "popular" in the hot centers of black social activity at my integrated high school and college. "Are you black?" an arbiter of campus militancy demanded one day, when he "caught" me dining too many times with white friends. I had the skin pass, sure enough, but my inclinations fell well short of his standards. But I was not satisfied with the standards of his counterparts in the white world, either. If I was not "black" enough to please some blacks, I would never be "white" enough to please all whites.

Times have changed. Choices abound for black people, if we can afford them. Black people can now go anywhere they choose, as long as they can pay the bill when they get there. If anyone tries to stop them or any other minorities just because of their color, the full weight of the federal government will step in on the side of the minorities. I thank God and the hard-won gains of the civil rights revolution for my ability to have more choices. But the old rules of race have been replaced in many ways by new ones. . . .

Today, I live a well-integrated life in the suburbs [of Montgomery County, Maryland, outside Washington, D.C.]. Black folks still tell me how to be "black" when I stray from the racial party lines, while white folks tell me how to be "colorblind." I still feel as frustrated in my attempts to transcend race as a reluctant lemming must feel while being rushed over the brink by its herd. But I find I have plenty of company in my frustration. Integration has not been a simple task for upwardly mobile African-Americans, especially for those of us who happen also to be parents.

A few years ago, after talking to black friends who were raising teenage boys, I realized that I was about to face dilemmas not unlike those my parents faced. My son was turning three years old. Everyone was telling me that he was quite cute, and because he was the spitting image of his dad, I was the last to argue.

But it occurred to me that in another decade he would be not three but thirteen. If all goes well, somewhere along the way he is going to turn almost overnight from someone who is perceived as cute and innocent into someone who is perceived as a menace, the most feared creature on America's urban streets today, a *young black male*. Before he, like me when I was barred from a childhood amusement park, would have a chance to let others get to know him, he would be judged not by the content of his character, but by the color of his skin. . . .

My mom is gone now, after helping set me up with the sort of education that has freed me to make choices. I have chosen to move my father to a nice, predominantly white, antiseptically tidy retirement village near me in Maryland with large golf courses and swimming pools. It is the sort of place he might have scrubbed floors in but certainly not have lived in back in the old days. It has taken him a while to get used to having so many well-off white people behaving so nicely and neighborly to him, but he has made the adjustment well.

Still the ugly specter of racism does not easily vanish. He and the other hundred or so African-American residents decided to form a social club like the other ethnically or religiously based social clubs in the village. One night during their meeting in the main social room, someone scrawled *KKK* on little sheets of paper and slipped them under the windshields of some of their cars in the parking lot. "We think maybe some of the white people wanted the blacks to socialize with the whites, not in a separate group," one lady of the club told me. If so, they showed an unusual method for extending the arms of brotherhood.

I live in a community that worships diversity like a state religion, although individuals sometimes get tripped up by it. The excellent Spanish "immersion" program that one of the county's "magnet" schools installed to encourage middle-class parents to stay put has itself become a cover for "white flight" by disgruntled white parents. Many of them, despite a lack of empirical evidence, perceive the school's regular English program as inferior, simply because it is 90 percent minority and mostly composed of children who come from a less-fortunate socioeconomic background. So the Spanish immersion classes designed to encourage diversity have become almost exclusively white and Asian America[n], while the English classes have become almost exclusively—irony of ironies—black and Latino, with many of the children learning English as a second language. Statistically, the school is "diverse" and "integrated." In reality, its student body is divided by an indelible wall, separate but supposedly equal. . . .

Despite all these color-conscious efforts to educate the country's children in a color-blind ideal of racial equality, many of our children seem to be catching on to race codes anyway, although with a twist suitable to the hip-hop generation. One local junior high school teacher, when he heard his black students referring to themselves as "bad," had the facts of racial life explained to him like this: They were not talking about the "bad means good" slang popularized by Michael Jackson's *Bad* album. They meant "bad" in the sense of misbehaving and poorly motivated. The black kids are "bad," the students explained, and the white kids are "good." The Asian kids are "like white," and the Latino kids "try to be bad, like the blacks." Anyone who tried to break out of those stereotypes was trying to break the code, meaning that a black or Latino who tried to make good grades was "trying to be white."

It is enough, as Marvin Gaye famously sang, to make you want to holler and throw up both your hands. Yet my neighbors and I hate to complain too loudly because, unlike other critics you may read or hear about, we happen to be a liberal community that not only believes in the dream of integration and true diversity, but actually is trying to live it. . . .

We see icons of black success—Colin Powell, Douglas Wilder, Bill Cosby, Oprah Winfrey, Bryant Gumbel, the two Michaels: Jordan and Jackson—not only accepted but adored by whites in ways far removed from the arm's-length way white America regarded Jackie Robinson, Willie Mays, Lena Horne, and Marian Anderson.

Yet, although the media show happy images of blacks, whites, Asians, and Hispanics getting along, amicably consuming the good life, a fog of false contentment conceals menacing fissures cracking the national racial landscape.

Despite the growth of the black middle class, most blacks and whites live largely separate lives. School integration actually peaked in 1967, according to a Harvard study, and has declined ever since. Economic segregation has proceeded without interruption, distancing poor blacks not only from whites but also from upwardly mobile blacks, making the isolation and misery of poor blacks worse. One out of every two black children lives below the poverty line, compared to one out of every seven white children. Black infants in America die at twice the rate of white infants. A record-setting million inmates crowd the nation's prisons, half of them black. The black out-of-wedlock birth rate has grown from about 25 percent in 1965 to more than 60 percent (more than 90 percent in the South Bronx and other areas of concentrated black poverty). . . .

The decline of industrial America, along with low-skill, high-pay jobs, has left much of black America split in two along lines of class, culture, opportunity and hope. The "prepared" join the new black middle class, which grew rapidly in the 1970s and early 1980s. The unprepared populate a new culture, directly opposed not only to the predominantly white mainstream, but also to any blacks who aspire to practice the values of hard work, good English, and family loyalty that would help them to join the white mainstream. The results of this spiritual decline, along with economic decline, have been devastating. Although more black women go to college than ever before, it has become a commonplace to refer to young black males as an endangered species. New anti-black stereotypes replace the old. Prosperous, well-dressed African Americans still complain of suffering indignities when they try to hail a taxicab. The fact that the taxi that just passed them by was driven by a black cabby, native born or immigrant, makes no difference. . . .

Behind our questions of race lurk larger questions of identity, our sense of who we are, where we belong, and where we are going. Our sense of place and peoplehood within groups is a perpetual challenge in some lives, particularly lives in America, a land where identity bubbles quite often out of nothing more than a weird alchemy of history and choice. "When I discover who I am, I'll be free," Ralph Ellison once wrote.

I reject the melting pot metaphor. People don't melt. Americans prove it on their ethnic holidays, in the ways they dance, in the ways they sing, in the culturally connected ways they worship. Displaced people long to celebrate their ethnic roots many generations and intermarriages after their ancestors arrived in their new land. Irish-American celebrations of St. Patrick's Day in Boston, Chicago, and New York City are far more lavish than anything seen on that day in Dublin or Belfast. Mexican-American celebrations of Cinco de Mayo, the Fifth of May, are far more lavish in Los Angeles and San Antonio than anything seen that day in Mexico City. It is as if holidays give us permission to expose our former selves as we imagine them to be. Americans of European descent love to show their ethnic cultural backgrounds. Why do they get nervous only when black people show their love for theirs? Is it that black people on such occasions suddenly remind white people of vulnerabilities black people feel quite routinely as a minority in a majority white society? Is it that white people, by and large, do not like this feeling, that they want nothing more than to cleanse themselves of it and make sure that it does not come bubbling up again? Attempts by Americans to claim some ephemeral, all-inclusive "all-American" identity reminds me of Samuel Johnson's observation: "Sir, a man may be so much of everything, that he is nothing of anything."

Instead of the melting pot metaphor, I prefer the mulligan stew, a concoction my parents tell me they used to fix during the Great Depression, when there was not a lot of food around the house and they "made do" with whatever meats, vegetables, and spices they had on hand. Everything went into the pot and was stirred up, but the pieces didn't melt. Peas were easily distinguished from carrots or potatoes. Each maintained its distinctive character. Yet each loaned its special flavor to the whole, and each absorbed some of the flavor from the others. That flavor, always unique, always changing, is the beauty of America to me, even when the pot occasionally boils over. . . .

African Americans are as diverse as other Americans. Some become nationalistic and ethnocentric. Others become pluralistic or multicultural, fitting their black identity into a comfortable niche among other aspects of themselves and their daily lives. Whichever they choose, a comfortable identity serves to provide not only a sense of belonging and protection for the individual against the abuses of racism, but also, ultimately, a sturdy foundation from which the individual can interact effectively with other people, cultures, and situations beyond the world of blackness.

"Identity would seem to be the garment with which one covers the nakedness of the self," James Baldwin wrote in *The Devil Finds Work,* "in which case, it is best that the garment be loose, a little like the robes of the desert, through which one's nakedness can always be felt, and, sometimes, discerned. This trust in one's nakedness is all that gives one the power to change one's robes."

The cloak of proud black identity has provided a therapeutical warmth for my naked self after the chilly cocoon of inferiority imposed early in my life by a white-exalting society. But it is best worn loosely, lest it become as constricting and isolating for the famished individual soul as the garment it replaced.

The ancestral desire of my ethnic people to be "just American" resonates in me. But I cannot forget how persistently the rudeness of race continues to intrude between me and that dream. I can defy it, but I cannot deny it. . . .

READING 10

Sick Societies

Robert B. Edgerton

introduction

All human groups develop a system to rank their members. In each group, people also attempt to display the status they have achieved. We are familiar with some of these: wearing clothing with labels deemed prestigious, driving a Rolls Royce, sporting a Rolex watch, getting admitted to a "name" school. In New York City, many reputable businesses have managed to get Park Avenue addresses, even though they are not located on Park Avenue. People who do business by mail with these firms aren't aware that the company's location is actually on an adjoining side street.

Although such matters are of interest, in their studies of social stratification sociologists probe much more deeply than this. Of special interest to sociologists is power, especially the means by which more powerful groups oppress groups with less power. Around the world, gender is a basis for sorting people into groups, with men the group in power. And around the world, men have developed practices to keep women submissive. In some instances, such as those documented by Robert Edgerton in this selection, the means men use to maintain dominance are severely oppressive. Both the practices described here and their acceptance by the oppressed group—which can be termed the *internalization of oppression*—may surprise you.

Thinking Critically

As you read this selection, ask yourself:

1. Why have men as a group dominated women as a group in every society of the world?
2. Why can practices that are painful and disfiguring persist for centuries?
3. What right do the people of one culture (such as one in the West) have to judge (or to force changes in) the customs of another culture (such as one in the East)?

How people feel about the established customs and institutions of their society can be a powerful indicator of how adequately that society and its culture serve their needs. But between blissful contentment and open rebellion lie many complexities and contradictions of human emotion and behavior. For example, women and men alike have gone to remarkable lengths to beautify themselves. They tattoo themselves over their entire bodies, cover themselves with scars, mutilate their genitals, and blacken their teeth, file them into points, and knock some of them out, among other things. These are only a few examples of painful practices that have been, and in some quarters still are, eagerly pursued in the quest for beauty. As painful as these practices are, few things done in the quest for beauty were more extreme than the Chinese practice of binding the feet of women. Young girls, some still in infancy, suffered excruciating pain because their feet were bandaged so tightly that normal growth could not occur. So tightly, in fact, were the toes folded under the foot that the bones were often broken. Accounts of the anguish these children suffered during the process of replacing blood- and pus-soaked bandages with new and still tighter ones are truly harrowing. The pain was so severe that the girls could not walk or even sleep, and they were too young to understand why they were being made to suffer. Eventually, the acute pain subsided, but for the rest of their lives these women were barely able to hobble, and some were carried everywhere in a sedan chair.

Chinese men have admired small feet in women since before Confucian times, but the practice of footbinding apparently did not begin until around 1100 A.D. It was at first confined to the Chinese elite, but it eventually spread throughout society, even including some peasants and the urban poor. The reasons for the origin and spread of footbinding were complex, but in addition to aesthetic considerations, Chinese men said that they saw the practice as an effective way to control the sexual liaisons of their increasingly bold wives. Once women's feet were bound, they could no longer "run around," so to speak, because they could not even leave their houses without assistance. What is more, a woman with bound feet could not work; so her husband achieved prestige by demonstrating that he could afford to have a wife who did not need to work. Men also saw the practice as a clear and necessary expression of their dominance over women. Before long, men also saw fit to praise the erotic advantages of footbinding, saying that the tottering style of walking it produced created more beautiful buttocks and tightened the vagina. The naked bound foot itself—"the golden lotus"—became as much a focus of erotic desire for Chinese men as women's breasts were for Westerners.

The Manchu conquerors outlawed footbinding, but to such little effect that some members of the Manchu court adopted a modified version of the practice themselves. Footbinding endured for over a thousand years without any widespread social protest by women. For one thing, Chinese women lacked political power, but at the same time they could appreciate the advantages of footbinding. It could give them beauty and sensuality, lead to a good marriage, and offer a life of leisure. Of at least equal importance, parents who imposed the practice on their young daughters were not thinking only of their daughters' futures. A daughter's marriage to a wealthy man was of obvious benefit to the entire family.

With these benefits in mind, it is perhaps less surprising that footbinding lasted so long than that it ended as suddenly as it did. Opposed by Christian missionaries, the expansionist Japanese, and Westerners of all sorts, the reform-minded revolutionary governments of early twentieth-century China were able to eradicate footbinding in a decade or so among their urban population although it lasted until the 1930s in some traditional rural areas. That a practice so painful and disfiguring to women can nonetheless persist should not be surprising. In Victorian times, the same Western women (some of whom were the wives of missionaries in China) who deplored footbinding as a "barbaric" custom willingly had themselves cinched into steel- and whalebone-reinforced canvas corsets so tightly that they had difficulty breathing and their internal organs were sometimes damaged. Girls as young as three were corseted, and over time their corsets became progressively tighter. By adolescence many girls' back muscles had atrophied to such an extent that they could neither sit nor walk for more than a few minutes without someone's support. The pursuit of beauty may be directed by men, even imposed by them, but women can find it to their advantage to acquiesce. With the controversy about silicone breast implants so freshly in mind, we need hardly be reminded that many American women (and some men) today endure painful and expensive cosmetic surgery in an effort to "beautify" their faces or bodies.

These cautionary examples alert us to the need to proceed judiciously in evaluating how dissatisfied people may be with their culture. For example, the practice of sending widows or household slaves to the grave with their deceased husbands or masters was known in many parts of the world, including China, Africa, ancient Greece, Scandinavia, and Russia. The reasons for putting a man's wives or slaves to death varied. Sometimes it was said that the deceased would need his wives or slaves to provide him with earthly comforts in the hereafter. Sometimes it was said (more cynically) that this practice would encourage wives or slaves to do everything in their power to keep their husbands or masters alive as long as possible. There were other reasons, too, ranging from jealousy about the sexual activities of surviving wives to elaborate religious justifications. Nowhere did the practice become as widespread or take on such profound metaphysical meaning as in Hindu India, where a widow could achieve virtual divinity by voluntarily immolating herself on her husband's funeral pyre.

Known as *sati* in Sanskrit and Anglicized as "suttee," this practice was observed as early as the fourth century B.C. when Alexander the Great recorded it, and despite heated controversy it has continued to occur now and then in contemporary India. Originally practiced by the wives of kings and great warriors, sati spread first to Brahmins, then to members of lower castes. Although Hindu scriptural justifications for the practice (or practices, since a widow could choose to be buried alive instead of being burned to death) were contradictory, many indicated that by choosing sati she could reduce the pollution that endangered her husband's surviving relatives, absolve herself of sin (wives were thought to bear responsibility for their husbands' death), and rejoin her husband in a cycle of future rebirths. As Richard Shweder has commented, sati can be a heroic act that represents and confirms the "deepest properties of Hinduism's moral world."

Much like a wedding, the sati ceremony required elaborate ritual preparations. Priests, mourners, and an excited crowd followed the ornately dressed widow and her husband's corpse to the funeral pyre. After circling the fire, the widow distributed her jewels and money and looked into a mirror where she saw the past and the future; then a priest quoted scriptural passages that likened the pyre to a marriage bed. After the necessary ritual acts had been completed and the widow had joined her husband's corpse on the pyre, it was set alight by her son (who sometimes collapsed in grief after doing so). After the ceremony, the spot where the sati died became a shrine, and she was revered as a heroine and goddess.

As improbable as the spectacle of a woman willingly, even eagerly, burning herself to death may seem, there are numerous eyewitness reports to the effect that sometimes, at least, that is exactly what took place. William Carey witnessed a sati in 1798 in which the widow actually danced on the pyre to show her contempt for death before lying down next to the corpse of her husband and being consumed by flames. In 1829 a British magistrate named Halliday attempted to convince a widow not to become a sati. "At length she showed some impatience and asked to be allowed to proceed to the site." Horrified, Halliday tried once again to dissuade her by asking if she understood how much pain she was about to suffer. The woman looked scornfully at the Englishman, then demanded that a lamp be brought to her and lighted. "Then steadfastly looking at me with an air of grave defiance she rested her right elbow on the ground and put her finger in the flame of the lamp. The finger scorched, blistered, and blackened and finally twisted up...this lasted for some time, during which she never moved her hand, uttered a sound, or altered the expression of her countenance." Halliday gave permission for the ceremony to proceed.

Over the centuries, many Hindu widows must have chosen sati deaths sublimely and reverently. But there was another reality to sati, one that falls well short of sublimity. First, it will not have escaped the reader's attention that sati was for women only; widowers had no duty to join their deceased wives in the divine devotion of a fiery death. Second, despite great pressure, very few widows actually chose sati. Even in Bengal where sati was most common, only a small minority of widows—less than 10 percent—chose sati although the prospect of widowhood was a dismal one at best. Widows were not only forbidden to remarry but were compelled to live in socially isolated asceticism—praying, fasting, reading holy books, and avoiding any hint of worldly pleasure. Because widows were thought to endanger others and often were accused of being witches, they were also scorned and feared. Despite the wretched conditions of widowhood, the promised rewards of sati, and the often relentless pressure exerted by the deceased husband's relatives on the widow to choose this supreme act of devotion, the great majority of widows preferred to live. Sometimes, however, they were given no choice. Because many women were married as infants, they became widows and "chose" sati while still children. One wife burned with the corpse of her adult husband was only four years old; others were scarcely older.

Sometimes the pressures imposed on a widow to choose sati were anything but subtle; indeed, they amounted to murder. In 1827 a British observer witnessed a sati ceremony in which the fire had no sooner been lighted than the widow leapt off the pyre and tried to flee; several men seized her and flung her back into the blaze. Once again the widow fled, and although badly burned she managed to outdistance her pursuers and throw herself into a nearby stream where she lay "weeping bitterly." She swore that she would not go through with the ceremony. Seeming to take pity on her, a man promised that if she would sit on a large cloth he had spread on the ground, he would carry her home. When she did so, she was once again seized, sewn into the cloth, and thrown back into the inferno. The cloth was immediately consumed by the flames, and the wretched victim once again tried to flee. This time she was beheaded with a sword, and her body was thrown back onto the pyre. Not exactly a serene act of wifely devotion.

It was not just tormented widows who frequently wanted no part of sati; some Hindu scriptures sharply criticized the custom. In *Mahamivantantra* (verses 79 and 80) it is said that a woman who accepts sati will go to hell. And there was a vigorous anti-sati movement in India even before the British attempted to abolish the practice (the movement was not led by women but by a Brahmin man). It was also observed that there were economic reasons for sati. It was most common in Bengal, and it was only in Bengal that a widow without a son had the same rights to the family property formerly possessed by her deceased husband. Surviving family members therefore attempted to protect family property by convincing the widow that it was her duty to join her husband in death (thereby conveniently leaving the property to her husband's family).

In recent years opposition to sati in India has grown, but the ceremony has not been abandoned. In 1987 Roop Kanwar, a beautiful eighteen-year-old, college-educated woman, immolated herself with her dead husband's head on her lap while a crowd estimated at 300,000 watched in admiration. But many Indians were outraged at the death of this young woman, partly because it was reported that she had been injected with morphine before the ceremony, which raised questions about undue influence on the part of her husband's relatives. Following Kanwar's death the government of Rajasthan, where the sati took place, made it a crime punishable by seven years in prison to "glorify" sati by collecting funds, building a temple, or performing a ceremony to preserve the memory of a person who committed sati; it also decreed that any attempt made to abet an act of sati was punishable by death. Many Indians were indignant about this criminalization of the ritual, arguing that a widow's immolation was a courageous, inspirational tradition that reaffirmed marital devotion and belief in rebirth.

The point of this example, perhaps overlong in the telling even though greatly oversimplified, is that people in a society can take quite different views of their customs and institutions. It is not only we outsiders who have differing views of sati; so have Indians themselves. A similar disagreement has existed, and indeed still does, in many parts of Africa with regard to the practice of female genital mutilation, generally known as female infibulation, circumcision, or clitoral excision. In parts of the Sudan, for example, the genitalia of young Nubian girls are still almost completely cut away, and the vaginal opening is sutured closed except for an opening the size of a matchstick for the passage of urine and menstrual blood. Done without anesthesia, the operation is excruciatingly painful, there can be dangerous complications, and some girls die. Nubian men are sometimes squeamish about the practice, but women have continued to support infibulation despite governmental efforts to abolish it. Farther south, in East Africa, the operation does not involve closing the vaginal opening, but it does require excision of the clitoris and both sets of labia—as in Nubia, the pain is terrible. There the operation does not take place until the girls are adolescents, and not every girl is able to stand the pain. Some have to be excised while they are held down by men. For many years, educated East Africans have deplored the practice, and it has been illegal in Kenya for some years. It nevertheless still takes place both in Kenya and elsewhere in Africa....

The extent to which women accept and value their culturally prescribed roles varies from society to society, but in a good many of them, women have been quite unhappy and have (not without justification, I might add) blamed men for their plight. Women have launched spirited verbal and even physical assaults against their husbands in various parts of the world, but with rare exceptions men physically dominate women, and they are often far from gentle about it. As a result, when women protest, they usually do so indirectly. Sometimes women consciously adopt a sick role, as in *susto* (or fright sickness, common in Latin America), to escape, if only temporarily, from the burdens of their lives. Writing about the Zapotec of Oaxaca, Douglas Uzzell concluded that women who claimed to suffer from *susto* were able to withdraw from ordinary relationships—including beatings from their husbands—because the illness was thought to be fatal unless the patient was indulged....

Another form of indirect protest was practiced by women among the Awald' Ali Bedouin in Egypt's western desert. Distressed by the cultural constraints of arranged marriage and enforced segregation, these women indulged in various kinds of irreverent discourse about men and masculinity, including oral lyric poetry that discreetly but pointedly ridiculed, chided, and sometimes excoriated men.

Women have also taken aggressive action against what they have perceived as intolerable behavior on the part of men. From Ulithi Atoll in Micronesia to the Inuit of the far north, aggrieved women sometimes gathered together to direct obscene and abusive taunts and songs against men. Women among the Andean people who were first incorporated into the Inca Empire and later subjugated to Spanish colonial rule protested against the misery of their lives in a number of ways. Sometimes they became so desperate that they preferred suicide to a tormented life. Other Andean women preferred killing their own children to allowing a new generation to suffer under the rule of colonial officials. Those who did so killed their sons rather than their daughters to protest the manifold ways in which men had betrayed them. Still other women fled with their children to inaccessible regions where they established an underground culture of resistance to colonial rule.

Among the Samburu [of Africa]...bands of twenty or so women would sing ribaldly abusive and threatening songs outside the house of an elder who, for instance, was unusually harsh with his wives. In other parts of Africa women's protests could become particularly overt and even painful. When women among the Igbo of Nigeria were offended by something a man did (such as mistreating his wife or infringing on women's economic rights), they would gather at his household where they danced and sang abusive songs that detailed his offenses (and not infrequently questioned his masculinity). They would also pound on the walls of his house, and if he came outside to object, they would even rough him up a bit. All this would continue until the man apologized and promised not to repeat his offenses. Among the Bakweri of West Cameroon, if a woman was offended by a man, she might call out all the women of the village, who then descended on the culprit and demanded an apology and recompense. A similar phenomenon occurred among the Kamba of Kenya, whose women were ordinarily quite subservient to their harshly domineering husbands. However, when Kamba women felt that something had taken place to endanger their crops or their general well-being and that the all-male council of elders had failed to remedy the problem, they would gather together and take direct action. Beating large drums and flailing thorny boughs about them, they would march on the offender to make their demands. Any man who was incautious enough to get in their way would become the target of verbal abuse, and some were even assaulted physically. In apparent recognition of the legitimacy of the women's indignation, the usually dominant Kamba men meekly acquiesced.

Like the Kamba, men among the Pokot of Kenya thoroughly dominated women during the course of everyday life; indeed, a husband rarely hesitated to beat his wife, sometimes severely, and it was considered his right to do so. Pokot women often expressed their anger to one another but typically seemed resigned to a life of subservience. It was common for them to remark, with as much fatalism as anger, that "we cannot rule men; we can only hate them." But sometimes when a man's abuse of his wife went beyond the very generous bounds of husbandly rights, the wife could and did organize other women to "shame" her husband, as the Pokot put it. If, for example, a man beat his wife excessively or failed to have sexual intercourse with her, she and the other women could tie him up while he slept; they then not only ridiculed and reviled him with every imaginable obscenity, but one woman after another showed their genitals to him—something that was ordinarily unthinkable among the Pokot—then urinated and even defecated on him before beating his testicles with small sticks. Finally, they would cut larger sticks and threaten to beat him even more severely. It was not until his wife intervened to halt the beating (no doubt with crocodile tears in her eyes) and the now thoroughly chastened man agreed to allow the women to slaughter and eat his favorite ox (something else that was ordinarily unthinkable) that the women would finally agree to release the man. Throughout this public event, men would make no attempt to intervene. Instead, they found that they were needed elsewhere....

CONCLUSION*

[Throughout history, the subjugation of women by men has taken many forms. In control of society, males have set the standards of beauty and loyalty that women have had to meet in order to achieve social status. We reviewed footbinding as an

*Conclusion by the editor.

example of how the male idea of beauty was forced upon women, female circumcision as a way of enforcing male standards of sexuality, and sati as a final act of male dominance. For some women, the consequence has been extreme pain; for others, death. We also reviewed examples of societies in which women banded together to rebel against their subjugation.]

PART

IV Social Institutions

From the previous parts, you have seen many of the social forces that influence our lives, that twist and turn us in one direction or another. You have read about culture and socialization, social control and deviance, and various forms of social stratification. In this part, we turn our focus onto *social institutions,* the standard ways that society sets up to meet its basic needs.

To exist, every society must solve certain problems. Babies must be nourished and children given direction. The sex drive must also be held within bounds. To help accomplish these things, every society has set up some form of marriage and family, the first social institution we meet on the stage of life. Social order—keeping people from robbing and killing one another—also has to be established. To accomplish this, each social group sets up some form of what we call politics. Goods and services also have to be produced and distributed. This leads to what is called the economy. The new generation also has to be taught how to view the world in the established, accepted, "correct" way, as well as to have the skills to participate in the economy. For this, we have some form of education. Then there are views of the spiritual world, of God and morality, perhaps of an afterlife. For this, we have religion.

We are immersed in social institutions, and we never escape from them. We are born into one (the family), we attend school in another (education), and we make our living in still another (economy). Even if we don't vote, the political institution surrounds us with the demands of its laws. Even if we don't worship at a church, synagogue, or mosque, we can't avoid religion, for religious principles are the foundation of law. Even closing most offices, schools, and factories on Sunday is based on religion.

Social institutions, then, are another way that society nudges us to fit in. As a curb or median is to an automobile, so social institutions are to us. They set boundaries around us, directing us to feel, think, and act along certain avenues, to turn one way instead of another.

Social institutions are so significant that some sociologists specialize in a single social institution. Some focus on marriage and family, others study politics or the economy, whereas still others do research on religion or education. After this introductory course, which is sort of a survey of sociology, students usually can take courses on specific social institutions. Often, for example, departments of sociology teach a course on marriage and family. In large departments, there may be a course on each social institution, one on the sociology of religion, another on the sociology of education, and so on. In very large departments, the social institutions may be broken down into smaller components, and there may be several courses on the sociology of politics, education, and so on.

To focus on social institutions, we open this part with an article that has become a classic in sociology. C. Wright Mills analyzes the ruling elite of the United States. What he calls the *power elite* is the group that makes the major decisions that affect our lives. Arlie Hochschild then analyzes a major change that is taking place in some work and family settings, where work becomes more enjoyable than family life. We conclude this part with a research report by Peter and Patricia Adler on the role of athletics in education—or perhaps we should say, the lack of education in athletes.

READING 11

The Power Elite

C. Wright Mills

introduction

A theme that has run through many of the preceding selections is how groups influence us—how in some instances they even control our behavior. Our membership in some of these groups (as with gender in the immediately preceding selection) comes with birth and is involuntary. Other groups, we join because we desire the membership. All groups—whether our membership is voluntary or involuntary—try to control our behavior. The broad, overarching groups, which lay the general boundaries for our actions and even our thinking, are the *social institutions* of our society. We are born and we die within social institutions. And between birth and death, we live within them—from family and school to politics and religion.

A central question that sociologists ask concerns power. Who has it, and how is it exercised? In this selection, C. Wright Mills says that power in U.S. society has become concentrated in our political, military, and economic institutions. Not only have these three grown larger, but also they have become more centralized and interconnected. As a result, their power has outstripped those of our other social institutions. Together, these three form a "triangle of power." The interests of the top political, military, and business leaders have coalesced, says Mills, and in his term, they now form a *power elite.* It is this power elite that makes the major decisions that so vitally affect our welfare—and, increasingly, with the dominance of the United States in global affairs, the welfare of the world.

Thinking Critically

As you read this selection, ask yourself:

1. If the members of the power elite don't meet together as a group, how can they be considered the primary source of power in the United States?
2. Mills identifies the top leaders of the top corporations as the pinnacle of power. Why doesn't he identify the top military or political leaders as this pinnacle?
3. Use Mills' analysis to explain why in *Essentials* war is classified as an aspect of politics. Why do you think that the power elite often calls the waging of war by the United States by terms other than war, such as "interventions," "helping a people or government," even—and my favorites—"establishing democracy" or "establishing peace"?

The powers of ordinary men* are circumscribed by the everyday worlds in which they live, yet even in these rounds of job, family, and neighborhood they often seem driven by forces they can neither understand nor govern. "Great changes" are beyond their control, but affect their conduct and outlook nonetheless. The very framework of modern society confines them to projects not their own, but from every side, such changes now press upon the men and women of the mass society, who accordingly feel that they are without purpose in an epoch in which they are without power.

But not all men are in this sense ordinary. As the means of information and of power are centralized, some men come to occupy positions in American society from which they can look down upon, so to speak, and by their decisions mightily affect, the everyday worlds of ordinary men and women. They are not made by their jobs; they set up and break down jobs for thousands of others; they are not confined by simple family responsibilities; they can escape. They may live in many hotels and houses, but they are bound by no one community. They need not merely "meet the demands of the day and hour"; in some part, they create these demands, and cause others to meet them. Whether or not they profess their power, their technical and political experience of it far transcends that of the underlying population. What Jacob Burckhardt said of "great men," most Americans might well say of their elite: "They are all that we are not."

The power elite is composed of men whose positions enable them to transcend the ordinary environments of ordinary men and women; they are in positions to make decisions having major consequences. Whether they do or do not make such decisions is less important than the fact that they do occupy such pivotal positions: Their failure to act, their failure to make decisions, is itself an act that is often of greater consequence than the decisions they do make. For they are in command of the major hierarchies and organizations of modern society. They rule the big corporations. They run the machinery of the state and claim its prerogatives. They direct the military establishment. They occupy the strategic command posts of the social structure, in which are now centered the effective means of the power and the wealth and the celebrity which they enjoy.

The power elite are not solitary rulers. Advisers and consultants, spokesmen and opinion-makers are often the captains of their higher thought and decision. Immediately below the elite are the professional politicians of the middle levels of power, in the Congress and in the pressure groups, as well as among the new and old upper classes of town and city and region. Mingling with them, in curious ways which we shall explore, are those professional celebrities who live by being continually displayed but are never, so long as they remain celebrities, displayed enough. If such celebrities are not at the head of any dominating hierarchy, they do often have the power to distract the attention of the public or afford sensations to the masses,

*As with the first article in this anthology, when Mills wrote, "men" was used to refer to both men and women and "his" to both hers and his. Although the writing style has changed, the sociological ideas are as significant as ever.

or, more directly, to gain the ear of those who do occupy positions of direct power. More or less unattached, as critics of morality and technicians of power, as spokesmen of God and creators of mass sensibility, such celebrities and consultants are part of the immediate scene in which the drama of the elite is enacted. But that drama itself is centered in the command posts of the major institutional hierarchies.

The truth about the nature and the power of the elite is not some secret which men of affairs know but will not tell. Such men hold quite various theories about their own roles in the sequence of event and decision. Often they are uncertain about their roles, and even more often they allow their fears and their hopes to affect their assessment of their own power. No matter how great their actual power, they tend to be less acutely aware of it than of the resistances of others to its use. Moreover, most American men of affairs have learned well the rhetoric of public relations, in some cases even to the point of using it when they are alone, and thus coming to believe it. The personal awareness of the actors is only one of the several sources one must examine in order to understand the higher circles. Yet many who believe that there is no elite, or at any rate none of any consequence, rest their argument upon what men of affairs believe about themselves, or at least assert in public.

There is, however, another view: those who feel, even if vaguely, that a compact and powerful elite of great importance does now prevail in America often base that feeling upon the historical trend of our time. They have felt, for example, the domination of the military event, and from this they infer that generals and admirals, as well as other men of decision influenced by them, must be enormously powerful. They hear that the Congress has again abdicated to a handful of men decisions clearly related to the issue of war or peace. They know that the bomb was dropped over Japan in the name of the United States of America, although they were at no time consulted about the matter. They feel that they live in a time of big decisions; they know that they are not making any. Accordingly, as they consider the present as history, they infer that at its center, making decisions or failing to make them, there must be an elite of power.

On the one hand, those who share this feeling about big historical events assume that there is an elite and that its power is great. On the other hand, those who listen carefully to the reports of men apparently involved in the great decisions often do not believe that there is an elite whose powers are of decisive consequence.

Both views must be taken into account, but neither is adequate. The way to understand the power of the American elite lies neither solely in recognizing the historic scale of events nor in accepting the personal awareness reported by men of apparent decision. Behind such men and behind the events of history, linking the two, are the major institutions of modern society. *These hierarchies of state [politics] and corporation [business] and army [military] constitute the means of power* [italics added]; as such they are now of a consequence not before equaled in human history—and at their summits, there are now those command posts of modern society which offer us the sociological key to an understanding of the role of the higher circles in America.

Within American society, major national power now resides in the economic, the political, and the military domains. Other institutions seem off to the side of modern history, and, on occasion, duly subordinated to these. No family is as directly powerful in national affairs as any major corporation; no church is as directly powerful in the external biographies of young men in America today as the military establishment; no college is as powerful in the shaping of momentous events as the National Security Council. Religious, educational, and family institutions are not autonomous centers of national power; on the contrary, these decentralized areas are increasingly shaped by the big three, in which developments of decisive and immediate consequence now occur.

Families and churches and schools adapt to modern life; governments and armies and corporations shape it; and, as they do so, they turn these lesser institutions into means for their ends. Religious institutions provide chaplains to the armed forces where they are used as a means of increasing the effectiveness of its morale to kill. Schools select and train men for their jobs in corporations and their specialized tasks in the armed forces. The extended family has, of course, long been broken up by the industrial revolution, and now the son and the father are removed from the family, by compulsion if need be, whenever the army of the state sends out the call. And the symbols of all these lesser institutions are used to legitimate the power and the decisions of the big three.

The life-fate of the modern individual depends not only upon the family into which he was born or which he enters by marriage, but increasingly upon the corporation in which he spends the most alert hours of his best years; not only upon the school where he is educated as a child and adolescent, but also upon the state which touches him throughout his life; not only upon the church in which on occasion he hears the word of God, but also upon the army in which he is disciplined.

If the centralized state could not rely upon the inculcation of nationalist loyalties in public and private schools, its leaders would promptly seek to modify the decentralized educational system. If the bankruptcy rate among the top five hundred corporations were as high as the general divorce rate among the [57] million married couples, there would be economic catastrophe on an international scale. If members of armies gave to them no more of their lives than do believers to the churches to which they belong, there would be a military crisis.

Within each of the big three, the typical institutional unit has become enlarged, has become administrative, and, in the power of its decisions, has become centralized. Behind these developments there is a fabulous technology, for as institutions, they have incorporated this technology and guide it, even as it shapes and paces their developments.

The economy—once a great scatter of small productive units in autonomous balance—has become dominated by two or three hundred giant corporations, administratively and politically interrelated, which together hold the keys to economic decisions.

The political order, once a decentralized set of several dozen states with a weak spinal cord, has become a centralized, executive establishment which has taken up into itself many powers previously scattered, and now enters into each and every crany of the social structure.

The military order, once a slim establishment in a context of distrust fed by state militia, has become the largest and most expensive feature of government, and, although well versed in smiling public relations, now has all the grim and clumsy efficiency of a sprawling bureaucratic domain.

In each of these institutional areas, the means of power at the disposal of decision makers have increased enormously; their central executive powers have been enhanced; within each of them modern administrative routines have been elaborated and tightened up.

As each of these domains becomes enlarged and centralized, the consequences of its activities become greater, and its traffic with the others increases. The decisions of a handful of corporations bear upon military and political as well as upon economic developments around the world. The decisions of the military establishment rest upon and grievously affect political life as well as the very level of economic activity. The decisions made within the political domain determine economic activities and military programs. There is no longer, on the one hand, an economy, and, on the other hand, a political order containing a military establishment unimportant to politics and to money-making. There is a political economy linked, in a thousand ways, with military institutions and decisions. On each side of the world-split running through central Europe and around the Asiatic rimlands, there is an ever-increasing inter-locking of economic, military, and political structures. If there is government intervention in the corporate economy, so is there corporate intervention in the governmental process. In the structural sense, this triangle of power is the source of the interlocking directorate that is most important for the historical structure of the present.

The fact of the interlocking is clearly revealed at each of the points of crisis of modern capitalist society—slump, war, and boom. In each, men of decision are led to an awareness of the interdependence of the major institutional orders. In the nineteenth century, when the scale of all institutions was smaller, their liberal integration was achieved in the automatic economy, by an autonomous play of market forces, and in the automatic political domain, by the bargain and the vote. It was then assumed that out of the imbalance and friction that followed the limited decisions then possible a new equilibrium would in due course emerge. That can no longer be assumed, and it is not assumed by the men at the top of each of the three dominant hierarchies.

For given the scope of their consequences, decisions—and indecisions—any one of these ramify into the others, and hence top decisions tend either to become coordinated or to lead to a commanding indecision. It has not always been like this. When numerous small entrepreneurs made up the economy, for example, many of them could fail and the consequences still remain local; political and military authorities did not intervene. But now, given political expectations and military commitments, can they afford to allow key units of the private corporate economy to break down in slump? Increasingly, they do intervene in economic affairs, and as they do so, the controlling decisions in each order are inspected by agents of the other two, and economic, military, and political structures are interlocked.

At the pinnacle of each of the three enlarged and centralized domains, there have arisen those higher circles which make up the economic, the political, and the military elites. At the top of the economy, among the corporate rich, there are the chief executives; at the top of the political order, the members of the political directorate; at the top of the military establishment, the elite of soldier-statesmen clustered in and around the Joint Chiefs of Staff and the upper echelon. As each of these domains has coincided with the others, as decisions tend to become total in their consequence, the leading men in each of the three domains of power—the warlords, the corporation chieftains, the political directorate—tend to come together, to form the power elite of America.

The higher circles in and around these command posts are often thought of in terms of what their members possess: They have a greater share than other people of the things and experiences that are most highly valued. From this point of view, the elite are simply those who have the most of what there is to have, which is generally held to include money, power, and prestige—as well as all the ways of life to which these lead. But the elite are not simply those who have the most, for they could not "have the most" were it not for their positions in the great institutions. For such institutions are the necessary bases of power, of wealth, and of prestige, and at the same time, the chief means of exercising power, of acquiring and retaining wealth, and of cashing in the higher claims for prestige.

By the powerful we mean, of course, those who are able to realize their will, even if others resist it. No one, accordingly, can be truly powerful unless he has access to the command of major institutions, for it is over these institutional means of power that the truly powerful are, in the first instance, powerful. Higher politicians and key officials of government command such institutional power; so do admirals and generals, and so do the major owners and executives of the larger corporations. Not all power, it is true, is anchored in and exercised by means of such institutions, but only within and through them can power be more or less continuous and important.

Wealth also is acquired and held in and through institutions. The pyramid of wealth cannot be understood merely in terms of the very rich; for the great inheriting families, as we shall see, are now supplemented by the corporate institutions of modern society: Every one of the very rich families has been and is closely connected—always legally and frequently managerially as well—with one of the multimillion-dollar corporations.

The modern corporation is the prime source of wealth, but, in latter-day capitalism, the political apparatus also opens and closes many avenues to wealth. The amount as well as the source of income, the power over consumers' goods as well as over productive capital, are determined by position within the political economy. If our interest in the very rich goes beyond their lavish or their miserly consumption, we must examine their relations to modern forms of corporate property as well as to the state; for such relations now determine the chances of men to secure big property and to receive high income.

Great prestige increasingly follows the major institutional units of the social structure. It is obvious that prestige depends, often quite decisively, upon access to the publicity machines that are now a central and normal feature of all the big institutions of modern America. Moreover, one feature of these hierarchies of corporation, state, and military establishment is that their top positions are increasingly interchangeable. One result of this is the accumulative nature of prestige. Claims for prestige, for example, may be initially based on military roles, then expressed in and augmented by an educational institution run by corporate executives; and cashed in, finally, in the political order, where, for [top military leaders who become president, such as] General Eisenhower and those [they represent], power and prestige finally meet at the very peak. Like wealth and power, prestige tends to be cumulative: The more of it you have, the more you can get. These values also tend to be translatable into one another: The wealthy find it easier than the poor to gain power; those with status find it easier than those without it to control opportunities for wealth.

If we took the one-hundred most powerful men in America, the one-hundred wealthiest, and the one-hundred most celebrated away from the institutional positions they now occupy, away from their resources of men and women and money, away from the media of mass communication that are now focused upon them—then they would be powerless and poor and uncelebrated. For power is not of a man. Wealth does not center in the person of the wealthy. Celebrity is not inherent in any personality. To be celebrated, to be wealthy, to have power requires access to major institutions, for the institutional positions men occupy determine in large part their chances to have and to hold these valued experiences.

The people of the higher circles may also be conceived as members of a top social stratum, as a set of groups whose members know one another, see one another socially and at business, and so, in making decisions, take one another into account. The elite, according to this conception, feel themselves to be, and are felt by others to be, the inner circle of "the upper social classes." They form a more or less compact social and psychological entity; they have become self-conscious members of a social class. People are either accepted into this class or they are not, and there is a qualitative split, rather than merely a numerical scale, separating them from those who are not elite. They are more or less aware of themselves as a social class and they behave toward one another differently from the way they do toward members of other classes. They accept one another, understand one another, marry one another, tend to work and to think if not together at least alike.

Now, we do not want by our definition to prejudge whether the elite of the command posts are conscious members of such a socially recognized class, or whether considerable proportions of the elite derive from such a clear and distinct class. These are matters to be investigated. Yet in order to be able to recognize what we intend to investigate, we must note something that all biographies and memoirs of the wealthy and the powerful and the eminent make clear: No matter what else they may be, the people of these higher circles are involved in a set of overlapping "crowds" and intricately connected "cliques." There is a kind of mutual attraction among those who "sit on the same terrace"—although this often becomes clear to them, as well as to others, only at the point at which they feel the need to draw the line; only when, in their common defense, they come to understand what they have in common, and so close their ranks against outsiders.

The idea of such ruling stratum implies that most of its members have similar social origins, that throughout their lives they maintain a network of internal connections, and that to some degree there is an interchangeability of position between the various hierarchies of money and power and celebrity. We must, of course, note at once that if such an elite stratum does exist, its social visibility and its form, for very solid historical reasons, are quite different from those of the noble cousinhoods that once ruled various European nations.

That American society has never passed through a feudal epoch is of decisive importance to the nature of the American elite, as well as to American society as a historic whole. For it means that no nobility or aristocracy, established before the capitalist era, has stood in tense opposition to the higher bourgeoisie. It means that this bourgeoisie has monopolized not only wealth but prestige and power as well. It means that no set of noble families has commanded the top positions and monopolized the values that are generally held in high esteem; and certainly that no set has done so explicitly by inherited right. It means that no high church dignitaries or court nobilities, no entrenched landlords with honorific accouterments, no monopolists of high army posts have opposed the enriched bourgeoisie and in the name of birth and prerogative successfully resisted its self-making.

But this does *not* mean that there are no upper strata in the United States. That they emerged from a "middle class" that had no recognized aristocratic superiors does not mean they remained middle class when enormous increases in wealth made their own superiority possible. Their origins and their newness may have made the upper strata less visible in America than elsewhere. But in America today there are in fact tiers and ranges of wealth and power of which people in the middle and lower ranks know very little and may not even dream. There are families who, in their well-being, are quite insulated from the economic jolts and lurches felt by the merely prosperous and those farther down the scale. There are also men of power who in quite small groups make decisions of enormous consequence for the underlying population....

READING 12

When Work Becomes Home and Home Becomes Work

Arlie Russell Hochschild

introduction

The social institution that introduces us to society is the family. The family is our great socializer and is considered by most sociologists to be the basic building block of society. Within the family, we learn our basic orientations to social life. Here we learn our language, the norms of proper behavior, basic etiquette, even how much self-centeredness we are allowed to display in our interactions. Our family also introduces us to its acceptable ways of viewing gender, race-ethnicity, social class, religion, people with disabilities, the elderly—even our own body. With such far-reaching implications for what we become in life, it is difficult to overstate the influence of the family.

Like our other social institutions, U.S. families are changing. They have become smaller, they have more disposable income, parental authority has decreased, wives have more power, and divorce has made families fragile. (Some sociologists point out that because parents used to die at a much earlier age, today's children have about the same chance as children of two hundred years ago of living through childhood with both their parents.) Sociologists have uncovered another change, one that has just begun to appear. As we have moved away from factory work and vast numbers of women have joined the white-collar workforce, more emphasis is being placed on social relationships at work. This has made work more pleasant and satisfying. At the same time, the emotional demands of the family seem to have become greater. One result, as Arlie Hochschild found in her study of a company she calls Amerco, is a reversal of conditions: Some parents find work to be a refuge from home, rather than their family being a refuge from work.

Thinking Critically

As you read this selection, ask yourself:

1. Do you think you will prefer work to family life? Why or why not?
2. Hochschild says that because of a "time bind" there are two sides of the same family: the rushed family that they actually are and the relaxed family they imagine they might be if only they had time. How does this apply to your own family life?
3. What does Hochschild mean when she says that the corporate world is creating a sense of "neighborhood" and a "feminine culture"? How does this development pertain to family life?

It's 7:40 A.M. when Cassie Bell, 4, arrives at the Spotted Deer Child-Care Center, her hair half-combed, a blanket in one hand, a fudge bar in the other. "I'm late," her mother, Gwen, a sturdy young woman whose short-cropped hair frames a pleasant face, explains to the child-care worker in charge. "Cassie wanted the fudge bar so bad, I gave it to her," she adds apologetically.

"*Please,* can't you take me with you?" Cassie pleads.

"You know I can't take you to work," Gwen replies in a tone that suggests that she has been expecting this request. Cassie's shoulders droop. But she has struck a hard bargain—the morning fudge bar—aware of her mother's anxiety about the long day that lies ahead at the center. As Gwen explains later, she continually feels that she owes Cassie more time than she gives her—she has a "time debt."

Arriving at her office just before 8, Gwen finds on her desk a cup of coffee in her personal mug, milk no sugar (exactly as she likes it), prepared by a co-worker who managed to get in ahead of her. As the assistant to the head of public relations at a company I will call Amerco, Gwen has to handle responses to any reports that may appear about the company in the press—a challenging job, but one that gives her satisfaction. As she prepares for her first meeting of the day, she misses her daughter, but she also feels relief; there's a lot to get done at Amerco.

Gwen used to work a straight eight-hour day. But over the last three years, her workday has gradually stretched to eight and a half or nine hours, not counting the e-mail messages and faxes she answers from home. She complains about her hours to her co-workers and listens to their complaints—but she loves her job. Gwen picks up Cassie at 5:45 and gives her a long, affectionate hug.

At home, Gwen's husband, John, a computer programmer, plays with their daughter while Gwen prepares dinner. To protect the dinner "hour"—8:00–8:30—Gwen checks that the phone machine is on, hears the phone ring during dinner but resists the urge to answer. After Cassie's bath, Gwen and Cassie have "quality time," or "Q.T.," as John affectionately calls it. Half an hour later, at 9:30, Gwen tucks Cassie into bed.

There are, in a sense, two Bell households: the rushed family they actually are and the relaxed family they imagine they might be if only they had time. Gwen and John complain that they are in a time bind. What they say they want seems so modest—time to throw a ball, to read to Cassie, to witness the small dramas of her development, not to speak of having a little fun and romance themselves. Yet even these modest wishes seem strangely out of reach. Before going to bed, Gwen has to e-mail messages to her colleagues in preparation for the next day's meeting; John goes to bed early, exhausted—he's out the door by 7 every morning.

Nationwide, many working parents are in the same boat. More mothers of small children than ever now work outside the home. American men average 48.8 hours of work a week, and women 41.7 hours, including overtime and commuting. All in all, more women are on the economic train, and for many—men and women alike—that train is going faster.

But Amerco has "family-friendly" policies. If your division head and supervisor agree, you can work part time, share a job with another worker, work some hours at home, take parental leave or use "flex time." But hardly anyone uses these policies. In seven years, only two Amerco fathers have taken formal parental leave. Fewer than 1 percent have taken advantage of the opportunity to work part time. Of all such policies, only flex time—which rearranges but does not shorten work time—has had a significant number of takers (perhaps a third of working parents at Amerco).

Forgoing family-friendly policies is not exclusive to Amerco workers. A study of 188 companies conducted by the Families and Work Institute found that while a majority offered part-time shifts, fewer than 5 percent of employees made use of them. Thirty-five percent offered "flex place"—work from home—and fewer than 3 percent of their employees took advantage of it. And a Bureau of Labor Statistics survey asked workers whether they preferred a shorter workweek, a longer one or their present schedule. About 62 percent preferred their present schedule; 28 percent would have preferred longer hours. Fewer than 10 percent said they wanted a cut in hours.

Still, I found it hard to believe that people didn't protest their long hours at work. So I contacted Bright Horizons, a company that runs 136 company-based child-care centers associated with corporations, hospitals and Federal agencies in 25 states. Bright Horizons allowed me to add questions to a questionnaire they sent out to 3,000 parents whose children attended the centers. The respondents, mainly middle-class parents in their early 30s, largely confirmed the picture I'd found at Amerco. A third of fathers and a fifth of mothers described themselves as "workaholic," and 1 out of 3 said their partners were.

To be sure, some parents have tried to shorten their hours. Twenty-one percent of the nation's women voluntarily work part time, as do 7 percent of men. A number of others make under-the-table arrangements that don't show up on surveys. But while working parents say they need more time at home, the main story of their lives does not center on a struggle to get it. Why? Given the hours parents are working these days, why aren't they taking advantage of an opportunity to reduce their time at work?

The most widely held explanation is that working parents cannot afford to work shorter hours. Certainly this is true for many. But if money is the whole explanation, why would it be that at places like Amerco, the best-paid employees—upper-level managers and professionals—were the least interested in part-time work or job sharing, while clerical workers who earned less were more interested?

Similarly, if money were the answer, we would expect poorer new mothers to return to work more quickly after giving birth than rich mothers. But among working women nationwide, well-to-do new mothers are not much more likely to stay home after 13 weeks with a new baby than low-income new mothers. When asked what they look for in a job, only a third of respondents in a recent study said salary came first. Money is important, but by itself, money does not explain why many people don't want to cut back hours at work.

Were workers uninformed about the company's family-friendly policies? No. Some even mentioned that they were proud to work for a company that offered such enlightened policies. Were rigid middle managers standing in the way of workers using these policies? Sometimes. But when I compared Amerco employees who worked for flexible managers with those who worked for rigid managers, I found that the flexible managers reported only a few more applicants than the rigid ones. The evidence, however counterintuitive, pointed to a paradox: workers at the company I studied weren't protesting the time bind. They were accommodating to it.

Why? I did not anticipate the conclusion I found myself coming to: namely, that work has become a form of "home" and home has become "work." The worlds of home and work have not begun to blur, as the conventional wisdom goes, but to reverse places. We are used to thinking that home is where most people feel the most appreciated, the most truly "themselves," the most secure, the most relaxed. We are used to thinking that work is where most people feel like "just a number" or "a cog in a machine." It is where they have to be "on," have to "act," where they are least secure and most harried.

But new management techniques so pervasive in corporate life have helped transform the workplace into a more appreciative, personal sort of social world. Meanwhile, at home the divorce rate has risen, and the emotional demands have become more baffling and complex. In addition to teething, tantrums and the normal developments of growing children, the needs of elderly parents are creating more tasks for the modern family—as are the blending, unblending, reblending of new stepparents, stepchildren, exes and former in-laws.

This idea began to dawn on me during one of my first interviews with an Amerco worker. Linda Avery, a friendly, 38-year-old mother, is a shift supervisor at an Amerco plant. When I meet her in the factory's coffee-break room over a couple of Cokes, she is wearing blue jeans and a pink jersey, her hair pulled back in a long, blond ponytail. Linda's husband, Bill, is a technician in the same plant. By working different shifts, they manage to share the care of their 2-year-old son and Linda's 16-year-old daughter from a previous marriage. "Bill works the 7 A.M. to 3 P.M. shift while I watch the baby," she explains. "Then I work the 3 P.M. to 11 P.M. shift and he watches the baby. My daughter works at Walgreen's after school."

Linda is working overtime, and so I begin by asking whether Amerco required the overtime or whether she volunteered for it. "Oh, I put in for it," she replies. I ask her whether, if finances and company policy permitted, she'd be interested in cutting back on the overtime. She takes off her safety glasses, rubs her face and, without answering my question, explains: "I get home, and the minute I turn the key, my daughter is right there. Granted, she needs somebody to talk to about her day.... The baby is still up. He should have been in bed two hours ago, and that upsets me. The dishes are piled in the sink. My daughter comes right up to the door and complains about anything her stepfather said or did, and she wants to talk about her job. My husband is in the other room hollering to my daughter, 'Tracy, I don't ever get any time to talk to your mother, because you're always monopolizing her time before I even get a chance!' They all come at me at once."

Linda's description of the urgency of demands and the unarbitrated quarrels that await her homecoming contrast with her account of arriving at her job as a shift supervisor: "I usually come to work early, just to get away from the house. When I arrive, people are there waiting. We sit, we talk, we joke. I let them know what's going on, who has to be where, what changes I've made for the shift that day. We sit and chitchat for 5 or 10 minutes. There's laughing, joking, fun."

For Linda, home has come to feel like work and work has come to feel a bit like home. Indeed, she feels she can get relief from the "work" of being at home only by going to the "home" of work. Why has her life at home come to seem like this? Linda explains it this way: "My husband's a great help watching our baby. But as far as doing housework or even taking the baby when I'm at home, no. He figures he works five days a week; he's not going to come home and clean. But he doesn't stop to think that I work seven days a week. Why should I have to come home and do the housework without help from anybody else? My husband and I have been through this over and over again. Even if he would just pick up from the kitchen table and stack the dishes for me, that would make a big difference. He does nothing. On his weekends off, he goes fishing. If I want any time off, I have to get a sitter. He'll help out if I'm not here, but the minute I am, all the work at home is mine."

With a light laugh, she continues: "So I take a lot of overtime. The more I get out of the house, the better I am. It's a terrible thing to say, but that's the way I feel."

When Bill feels the need for time off, to relax, to have fun, to feel free, he climbs in his truck and takes his free time without his family. Largely in response, Linda grabs what she also calls "free time"—at work. Neither Linda nor Bill Avery wants more time together at home, not as things are arranged now.

How do Linda and Bill Avery fit into the broader picture of American family and work life? Current research suggests that however hectic their lives, women who do paid work feel less depressed, think better of themselves and are more satisfied than women who stay at home. One study reported that women who work outside the home feel more valued at home than housewives do. Meanwhile, work is where many women feel like "good mothers." As Linda reflects: "I'm a good mom at home, but I'm a better mom at work. At home, I get into fights with Tracy. I want her to apply to a junior college, but she's not interested. At work, I think I'm better at seeing the other person's point of view."

Many workers feel more confident they could "get the job done" at work than at home. One study found that only 59 percent of workers feel their "performance" in the family is "good or unusually good," while 86 percent rank their performance on the job this way.

Forces at work and at home are simultaneously reinforcing this "reversal." This lure of work has been enhanced in recent years by the rise of company cultural engineering—in particular, the shift from Frederick Taylor's principles of scientific management to the Total Quality principles originally set out by W. Edwards Deming. Under the influence of a Taylorist world view, the manager's job was to coerce the worker's mind and body, not to appeal to the worker's heart. The Taylorized worker was de-skilled, replaceable and cheap, and as a consequence felt bored, demeaned and unappreciated.

Using modern participative management techniques, many companies now train workers to make their own work decisions, and then set before their newly "empowered" employees moral as well as financial incentives. At Amerco, the Total

Quality worker is invited to feel recognized for job accomplishments. Amerco regularly strengthens the familylike ties of co-workers by holding "recognition ceremonies" honoring particular workers or self-managed production teams. Amerco employees speak of "belonging to the Amerco family" and proudly wear their "Total Quality" pins or "High Performance Team" T-shirts, symbols of their loyalty to the company and of its loyalty to them.

The company occasionally decorates a section of the factory and serves refreshments. The production teams, too, have regular get-togethers. In a New Age recasting of an old business slogan—"The Customer Is Always Right"—Amerco proposes that its workers "Value the Internal Customer." This means: Be as polite and considerate to co-workers inside the company as you would be to customers outside it. How many recognition ceremonies for competent performance are being offered at home? Who is valuing the internal customer there?

Amerco also tries to take on the role of a helpful relative with regard to employee problems at work and at home. The education-and-training division offers employees free courses (on company time) in "Dealing With Anger," "How to Give and Accept Criticism," "How to Cope With Difficult People."

At home, of course, people seldom receive anything like this much help on issues basic to family life. There, no courses are being offered on "Dealing With Your Child's Disappointment in You" or "How to Treat Your Spouse Like an Internal Customer."

If Total Quality calls for "re-skilling" the worker in an "enriched" job environment, technological developments have long been de-skilling parents at home. Over the centuries, store-bought goods have replaced homespun cloth, homemade soup and home-baked foods. Day care for children, retirement homes for the elderly, even psychotherapy are, in a way, commercial substitutes for jobs that a mother once did at home. Even family-generated entertainment has, to some extent, been replaced by television, video games and the VCR. I sometimes watched Amerco families sitting together after their dinners, mute but cozy, watching sitcoms in which television mothers, fathers and children related in an animated way to one another while the viewing family engaged in relational loafing.

The one "skill" still required of family members is the hardest one of all—the emotional work of forging, deepening or repairing family relationships. It takes time to develop this skill, and even then things can go awry. Family ties are complicated. People get hurt. Yet as broken homes become more common—and as the sense of belonging to a geographical community grows less and less secure in an age of mobility—the corporate world has created a sense of "neighborhood," of "feminine culture," of family at work. Life at work can be insecure; the company can fire workers. But workers aren't so secure at home, either. Many employees have been working for Amerco for 20 years but are on their second or third marriages or relationships. The shifting balance between these two "divorce rates" may be the most powerful reason why tired parents flee a world of unresolved quarrels and unwashed laundry for the orderliness, harmony and managed cheer of work. People are getting their "pink slips" at home.

Amerco workers have not only turned their offices into "home" and their homes into workplaces; many have also begun to "Taylorize" time at home, where families are succumbing to a cult of efficiency previously associated mainly with the office and factory. Meanwhile, work time, with its ever longer hours, has become more hospitable to sociability—periods of talking with friends on e-mail, patching up quarrels, gossiping. Within the long workday of many Amerco employees are great hidden pockets of inefficiency while, in the far smaller number of waking weekday hours at home, they are, despite themselves, forced to act increasingly time-conscious and efficient.

The Averys respond to their time bind at home by trying to value and protect "quality time." A concept unknown to their parents and grandparents, "quality time" has become a powerful symbol of the struggle against the growing pressures at home. It reflects the extent to which modern parents feel the flow of time to be running against them. The premise behind "quality time" is that the time we devote to relationships can somehow be separated from ordinary time. Relationships go on during quantity time, of course, but then we are only passively, not actively, wholeheartedly, specializing in our emotional ties. We aren't "on." Quality time at home becomes like an office appointment. You don't want to be caught "goofing off around the water cooler" when you are "at work."

Quality time holds out the hope that scheduling intense periods of togetherness can compensate for an overall loss of time in such a way that a relationship will suffer no loss of quality. But this is just another way of transferring the cult of efficiency from office to home. We must now get our relationships in good repair in less time. Instead of nine hours a day with a child, we declare ourselves capable of getting "the same result" with one intensely focused hour.

Parents now more commonly speak of time as if it is a threatened form of personal capital they have no choice but to manage and invest. What's new here is the spread into the home of a financial manager's attitude toward time. Working parents at Amerco owe what they think of as time debts at home. This is because they are, in a sense, inadvertently "Taylorizing" the house—speeding up the pace of home life as Taylor once tried to "scientifically" speed up the pace of factory life.

Advertisers of products aimed at women have recognized that this new reality provides an opportunity to sell products, and have turned the very pressure that threatens to explode the home into a positive attribute. Take, for example, an ad promoting Instant Quaker Oatmeal: it shows a smiling mother ready for the office in her square-shouldered suit, hugging her happy son. A caption reads: "Nicky is a very picky eater. With Instant Quaker Oatmeal, I can give him a terrific hot breakfast in just 90 seconds. And I don't have to spend any time coaxing him to eat it!" Here, the modern mother seems to have absorbed the lessons of Frederick Taylor as she presses for efficiency at home because she is in a hurry to get to work.

Part of modern parenthood seems to include coping with the resistance of real children who are not so eager to get their cereal so fast. Some parents try desperately not to appease their children with special gifts or smooth-talking promises about the future. But when time is scarce, even the best parents find themselves passing a system-wide familial speed-up along to the most vulnerable workers on the line. Parents are then obliged to try to control the damage done by a reversal of worlds. They monitor mealtime, homework time, bedtime, trying to cut out "wasted" time.

In response, children often protest the pace, the deadlines, the grand irrationality of "efficient" family life. Children dawdle. They refuse to leave places when it's time to leave. They insist on leaving places when it's not time to leave. Surely, this is part of the usual stop-and-go of childhood itself, but perhaps, too, it is the plea of children for more family time and more control over what time there is. This only adds to the feeling that life at home has become hard work.

Instead of trying to arrange shorter or more flexible work schedules, Amerco parents often avoid confronting the reality of the time bind. Some minimize their ideas about how much care a child, a partner or they themselves "really need." They make do with less time, less attention, less understanding and less support at home than they once imagined possible. They *emotionally downsize* life. In essence, they deny the needs of family members, and they themselves become emotional ascetics. If they once "needed" time with each other, they are now increasingly "fine" without it.

Another way that working parents try to evade the time bind is to buy themselves out of it—an approach that puts women in particular at the heart of a contradiction. Like men, women absorb the work-family speed-up far more than they resist it; but unlike men, they still shoulder most of the workload at home. And women still represent in people's minds the heart and soul of family life. They're the ones—especially women of the urban middle and upper-middle classes—who feel most acutely the need to save time, who are the most tempted by the new "time saving" goods and services—and who wind up feeling the most guilty about it. For example, Playgroup Connections, a Washington-area business started by a former executive recruiter, matches playmates to one another. One mother hired the service to find her child a French-speaking playmate.

In several cities, children home alone can call a number for "Grandma, Please!" and reach an adult who has the time to talk with them, sing to them or help them with their homework. An ad for Kindercare Learning Centers, a for-profit child-care chain, pitches its appeal this way: "You want your child to be active, tolerant, smart, loved, emotionally stable, self-aware, artistic and get a two-hour nap. Anything else?" It goes on to note that Kindercare accepts children 6 weeks to 12 years old and provides a number to call for the Kindercare nearest you. Another typical service organizes children's birthday parties, making out invitations ("sure hope you can come") and providing party favors, entertainment, a decorated cake and balloons. Creative Memories is a service that puts ancestral photos into family albums for you.

An overwhelming majority of the working mothers I spoke with recoiled from the idea of buying themselves out of parental duties. A bought birthday party was "too impersonal," a 90-second breakfast "too fast." Yet a surprising amount of lunchtime conversation between female friends at Amerco was devoted to expressing complex, conflicting feelings about the lure of trading time for one service or another. The temptation to order flash-frozen dinners or to call a local number for a homework helper did not come up because such services had not yet appeared at Spotted Deer Child-Care Center. But many women dwelled on the question of how to decide where a mother's job began and ended, especially with regard to babysitters and television. One mother said to another in the breakroom of an Amerco plant: "Damon doesn't settle down until 10 at night, so he hates me to wake him up in the morning and I hate to do it. He's cranky. He pulls the covers up. I put on cartoons. That way I can dress him and he doesn't object. I don't like to use TV that way. It's like a drug. But I do it."

The other mother countered: "Well, Todd is up before we are, so that's not a problem. It's after dinner, when I feel like watching a little television, that I feel guilty, because he gets too much TV at the sitter's."

As task after task falls into the realm of time-saving goods and services, questions rise about the moral meanings attached to doing or not doing such tasks. Is it being a good mother to bake a child's birthday cake (alone or together with one's partner)? Or can we gratefully save time by ordering it, and be good mothers by planning the party? Can we save more time by hiring a planning service, and be good mothers simply by watching our children have a good time? "Wouldn't that be nice!" one Amerco mother exclaimed. As the idea of the "good mother" retreats before the pressures of work and the expansion of motherly services, mothers are in fact continually reinventing themselves.

The final way working parents tried to evade the time bind was to develop what I call "potential selves." The potential selves that I discovered in my Amerco interviews were fantasy creations of time-poor parents who dreamed of living as time millionaires.

One man, a gifted 55-year-old engineer in research and development at Amerco, told how he had dreamed of taking his daughters on a camping trip in the Sierra Mountains: "I bought all the gear three years ago when they were 5 and 7, the tent, the sleeping bags, the air mattresses, the backpacks, the ponchos. I got a map of the area. I even got the freeze-dried food. Since then the kids and I have talked about it a lot, and gone over what we're going to do. They've been on me to do it for a long time. I feel bad about it. I keep putting it off, but we'll do it, I just don't know when."

Banished to garages and attics of many Amerco workers were expensive electric saws, cameras, skis and musical instruments, all bought with wages it took time to earn. These items were to their owners what Cassie's fudge bar was to her—a substitute for time, a talisman, a reminder of the potential self.

Obviously, not everyone, not even a majority of Americans, is making a home out of work and a workplace out of home. But in the working world, it is a growing reality, and one we need to face. Increasing numbers of women are discovering a great male secret—that work can be an escape from the pressures of home, pressures that the changing nature of work itself are only intensifying. Neither men nor women are going to take up "family-friendly" policies, whether corporate or governmental, as long as the current realities of work and home remain as they are. For a substantial number of time-bound parents, the stripped-down home and the neighborhood devoid of community are simply losing out to the pull of the workplace.

There are several broader, historical causes of this reversal of realms. The last 30 years have witnessed the rapid rise of women in the workplace. At the same time, job mobility has taken families farther from relatives who might lend a hand, and made it harder to make close friends of neighbors who could help out. Moreover, as women have acquired more education and have joined men at work, they have absorbed the views of an older, male-oriented work world, its views of a "real career," far more than men have taken up their share of the work at home. One reason women have changed more than men is the world of "male" work seems more honorable and valuable than the "female" world of home and children.

So where do we go from here? There is surely no going back to the mythical 1950s family that confined women to the home. Most women don't wish to return to a full-time role at home—and couldn't afford it even if they did. But equally troubling is a workaholic culture that strands both men and women outside the home.

For a while now, scholars on work-family issues have pointed to Sweden, Norway and Denmark as better models of work-family balance. Today, for example, almost all Swedish fathers take two paid weeks off from work at the birth of their children, and about half of fathers and most mothers take additional "parental leave" during the child's first or second year. Research shows that men who take family leave when their children are very young are more likely to be involved with their children as they grow older. When I mentioned this Swedish record of paternity leave to a focus group of American male managers, one of them replied, "Right, we've already heard about Sweden." To this executive, paternity leave was a good idea not for the U.S. today, but for some "potential society" in another place and time.

Meanwhile, children are paying the price. In her book *When the Bough Breaks: The Cost of Neglecting Our Children,* the economist Sylvia Hewlett claims that "compared with the previous generation, young people today are more likely to underperform at school; commit suicide; need psychiatric help; suffer a severe eating disorder; bear a child out of wedlock; take drugs; be the victim of a violent crime." But we needn't dwell on sledgehammer problems like heroin and suicide to realize that children like those at Spotted Deer need more of our time. If other advanced nations with two-job families can give children the time they need, why can't we?

READING 13

College Athletes and Role Conflict

Peter Adler and Patricia A. Adler

introduction

In earlier societies, there was no separate social institution called education. There were no special buildings called schools, and no people who earned their living as teachers. Instead, as an integral part of growing up, children learned what was necessary to get along in life. If hunting and cooking were the skills required for survival and taking on adult roles in their group, then people who already possessed those skills taught them to children. Socialization into adult roles by family and friends was education.

No longer is an informal system of passing on knowledge and skills adequate, and today a formal social institution known as education has become highly significant in social life. With each generation, the amount of education that young people are expected to attain has increased. A hundred years ago, graduating from the eighth grade was considered sufficient education for almost everyone—except for the few who went on to *higher* education in a place called *high* school. Today, in contrast, most young people are asked, "Where are you going to college?" This question is also asked of every top high school athlete, whom everyone presumes will be awarded a scholarship to college. Of the athletes who do get scholarships, many fail to graduate from college. Peter and Patricia Adler, a husband and wife team of sociologists, explore reasons for this.

Thinking Critically

As you read this selection, ask yourself:

1. Why is it common for athletes who receive college scholarships to fail to graduate from college? What part does the athlete subculture play in this?
2. What role conflict do college athletes experience? Why?
3. If you were the president of a Top 10 college and you wanted to dramatically increase the college graduation rate of your athletes, based on the findings in this selection, what would you do?

Athletes attend colleges and universities for the ostensible purpose of getting an education while they exercise and refine their athletic skills, but recent studies note that this ideal has become increasingly corrupted. Reports by journalists, former athletes, and social scientists note the commercialization of big-time college athletics, where the money and prestige available to universities have turned their athletic programs into business enterprises that emphasize winning at all costs, often neglecting the education goals of their institutions. The equality of the exchange between college athletes and their educational institutions has therefore been sharply questioned, with many critics leveling charges that universities have exploited their athletes by making excessive demands of them and failing to fulfill their educational promises to them. Several studies have suggested that these factors...result in [athletes] having lower grades and less chance of graduating than other students.... Drawing on four years of intensive participant observation with a major college basketball team, this article examines college athletes' academic experiences....

METHODS AND SETTING

For four years the authors studied a major college basketball program via participant-observation.... The research was conducted at a medium-size private university with a predominantly white, suburban, and middle-class student body. The university's academic standards were demanding as it was striving to enhance its academic reputation. The athletic department, as a whole, had a recent history of success. Players were generally recruited from the region, were 70% black, and ranged from the lower to the middle classes. The basketball program fit what Coakley and Frey termed *big-time college athletics*. Although it could not compare to the really large universities, its recent success had compensated for its size and lack of historical tradition. The national ranking and past success of the basketball team and other teams in sending graduating members into the professional leagues imbued the entire athletic milieu with a sense of seriousness and purpose.

The basketball players' circle of significant others was largely predetermined by athletic environment. The role-set members fell into three main categories: athletic, academic, and social. Within the athletic realm, in addition to their teammates, athletes related primarily to the coaching staff, trainers, team managers, secretaries, and athletic administrators. Secondary role-set members included boosters, fans, and the news media. Within the academic realm, athletes' role-set members consisted of professors, tutors, classmates, and, to a lesser extent, academic counselors and administrators. Within the social realm, athletes related to girlfriends, local friends, and students (non-athletes), but most especially to their college athlete peers: the teammates and dormmates who were members of their subculture.

ROLE EXPECTATIONS

Most incoming college athletes observed approached their academic role with initial feelings of idealism. They were surrounded by family and cultural messages that college would enhance their upward mobility and benefit their lives in many ways. They never doubted this assertion. Because of their academic experiences in high school, few athletes questioned their ability to succeed in college ("I graduated high school, didn't I?"). Athletes' idealism about their impending academic experience was further strengthened by the positive tone coaches had taken toward academics during the recruiting process. Entering freshmen commonly held the following set of prior expectations about their academic role: (1) they would go to classes and do the work (phrased as "putting the time in"); (2) they would graduate and get a degree, and (3) there would be no problems.

Approximately 47% ($N = 8$) of the entering athletes observed showed their initially high academic aspirations and expectations by requesting to be placed in a preprofessional major in the colleges of business, engineering, or arts and sciences. Despite warnings from coaches and older teammates about how difficult it would be to complete this coursework and play ball, they felt they could easily handle the demands. These individuals planned to use college athletics as a stepping-stone to career opportunities. As one freshman stated:

> I goin' to use basketball to get an education. Sure I'd like to make the NBA someday, but right now I've got to have something to fall back on if I don't.

Another group of freshmen, who had already accorded academics a less salient role (45%, $N = 17$), were enrolled by coaches in more "manageable" majors, such as physical education or recreation. Most of these individuals, though, believed that they too would get a degree. They had few prior expectations about academics, but assumed that they would make it through satisfactorily. Someone had taken care of these matters in high school, and they felt that college would be no different. Only a few individuals from the sample (8%, $N = 3$) entered college expecting to turn professional shortly thereafter. From the beginning these individuals disdained the academic role.

Much of this initial idealism was based on an inaccurate picture of college. Athletes did not anticipate the focus on analytical thinking and writing they would encounter, expecting that college courses would be an extension of their high school experiences. One sophomore reflected back on his expectations:

> I didn't think about it much, but when I did, I thought it'd be more or less the same here as it be back in high school, no big change. I be passin' all my courses there, but I still be goin' out every night.

In their first weeks on campus during their summer program, this early idealism was once again bolstered. Repeatedly the head coach stressed the importance of earning a degree. He cared about his players as people and wanted them to build a future out of their college experience. In fact, one of the main reasons athletes' parents encouraged their sons to attend this university was because of the head coach's integrity and good values. Once the school year began, athletes attended required nightly study halls, were told that tutors were available, and were constantly reminded by the coach to go to class. One freshman, interviewed during the preseason period, showed his idealism through his expectations and impressions:

> I'm here for two reasons: to get my degree and play basketball. I don't think it's goin' to be no problem to get my degree. I want to graduate in four years and I think I will. I think that's really important to Coach, too, because in practice he always mentions how important the degree is and everything.

Contrary to popular sentiment, most of the athletes observed began their college careers with a positive attitude toward academics. While their athletic role was unquestionably the most salient and their social role secondary, the academic role was still a critical dimension of their self-identity. Their behavior in the academic realm reflected this; they missed few classes, and turned in assignments regularly. For most this period lasted anywhere from one semester to two years.

ROLE CONFLICT

After two semesters in school and a full basketball season, athletes began to realize that their academic expectations had not been entirely accurate. Their early naive idealism gave way to disappointment and cynicism.... A major change athletes encountered in shifting from high school to college basketball lay in their athletic role. In large part this was due to the professionalization process they underwent. As one junior remarked:

> In high school, basketball was fun and games, but now it's a job. We get to the gym, we gotta work. You gotta put your all into it no matter how you feelin' that day. 'Cause this is big business. There's a lotta money ridin' on us.

Compounding the professionalization was a dramatic increase in pressure. The basketball players were all public figures in the local area who received intense news coverage. They clearly knew how important winning was to the coaches, boosters, and fans.

The players' athletic role often encroached on their academic role. They soon discovered that handling both roles was not always possible. A primary reason was the time conflict: some courses they wanted or needed for their majors were only offered in the afternoons during practice time; road trips caused them to miss key lectures, examinations, or review sessions, and banquets and other booster functions (which occurred at least once a week) cut into their studying time. At some point during this freshman year, most athletes realized that they did not have the time to perform as well as they had originally hoped in the academic role....

Athletes' perceptions of their athletic–academic role conflict was also influenced by the role model of their coaches. While the coaches sincerely cared about their players' academic responsibilities and achievements, they had their own priorities. Once the season began, they were too busy with their athletic work to pay much attention to academics. The pressures of recruiting, funding, and winning absorbed their energy. Despite their best preseason intentions, once practice officially began in October, the coaches became predominantly concerned with their players as athletes and ended up passing on the pressures of their organizational demands and constraints. Like their players, they were faced with a complex situation to which they often reacted, rather than acted. While they verbally stressed the importance of academics, they accorded athletic and team functions higher salience than school obligations: players' athletic time was strictly regulated, but their academic time was not. Players' behavior in practice, at games, at booster events, and on road trips was carefully monitored, yet their performance in class was not. Despite the coaches' concern about academics, the predominant message that athletes received was that, in contrast to academics, athletics had to be strictly adhered to because a powerful role-set member was always present.

ACADEMIC ROLE

During the school year, players began to notice other characteristics of their academic role that undercut their coaches' verbal emphasis on scholarship. One of the first was their lack of autonomy over their course (and sometimes major) selection. An assistant coach picked out classes and registered the athletes without consulting them. Assistant coaches bought their books, added and dropped courses for them, and contacted their professors if they had to be absent or were doing poorly in their work. By taking care of these academic matters for them, the coaches served as intermediaries between players and the academic realm. Consequently, most athletes failed to develop the knowledge, initiative, or the interest to handle these academic matters themselves, or to develop significant relationships with their professors or other academic role-set members. Thus, when the coaches were too busy to attend to these details, the players were unable to manage for themselves. As one senior remarked:

> Most of those guys don't even know how to fill out an add-drop card, so when they want to switch classes they just do it, and they tell the coaches to switch them. They figure it's not their job. But a lot of guys get Fs because the coaches never got around to it. The only reason I got through is that my girlfriend did it for me. I don't even know how to read a schedule of classes or where to get one.

Despite their occasional lapses, the fact that coaches managed these administrative matters gave athletes a false sense of security, a feeling that someone was always looking out for them academically and would make sure that they were given another chance. The athletes believed that they could fail to perform academically and not have to pay the consequences. They developed the perception that...they would be taken care of academically, and that they need not overly involve themselves in this arena....

Concomitant with this lack of autonomy came a new freedom. Unlike high school, their attendance at classes was not compulsory. Being able to skip classes placed a greater responsibility for self-motivation on them. When their motivation waned, athletes developed a pattern of slipping behind in their attendance and classwork until their problems compounded. When athletes did attend class, they often encountered another set of difficulties or disillusionments. In the classroom athletes thought that many professors labeled them as jocks. This image was fostered by the fact that they were surrounded in their classes by other athletes (also placed there by assistant coaches), and that they were identified early in the semester to their professor as athletes (because assistant coaches called or sent out reports to monitor their academic progress). They therefore encountered different expectations and treatment than the general student body. Whether they were given greater tolerance (extra tutoring sessions, relaxed deadlines, relaxed academic standards) or less tolerance ("Those guys think they're entitled to special treatment because they're athletes, and I'm going to show them they're wrong"), they were treated as less than full adults. This special treatment reinforced the differentiation between these two roles and their perceptions of themselves as athletes more than students. When they returned to the dormitory rooms at night, exhausted and sore from practicing, it became easier for them to rationalize, procrastinate, and fritter away their time instead of studying.

Athletes also became disinterested in their academic role because of the content of their classes. The level of disinterest varied between the athletes enrolled in arts and sciences, business, or engineering courses, and those taking physical education or recreation courses. Many of those in the latter category had wanted and expected to take courses in college that were either entertaining, vocational, or in some way relevant to their everyday lives. This was not what they found. Instead, they were enrolled in courses that they considered comical and demeaning. One sophomore articulated the commonly held view:

> How could I get into this stuff? They got me taking nutrition, mental retardation, square dancing, and camp counseling. I thought I was goin' to learn something here. It's a bunch o' BS.

Players enrolled in more rigorous academic courses were often unequipped for the demanding calibre of the work. Many did not have the knowledge, interests, skills, or study habits to compete with other students. With their inadequate training, tight schedules, and waning motivation, athletes became frustrated, bored, and disinterested. Players often stopped going to classes they did not like, yet never officially withdrew from them. When they did poorly on the first test, they gave up on the course, figuring "to hell with it, I'm not gonna try." The positive feedback from their academic role that the athletes anticipated often was replaced by a series of disappointments. As a result they often spent their days lying around the dormitory rooms, watching television, and convincing each other not to go to class. Athletes' academic failures then brought them feelings of inadequacy and uncertainty, as one player described:

> When I first came here I thought I'd be goin' to class all the time and I'd study and that'd be it. But I sure didn't think it meant studyin' all the time. Back in high school you just be memorizin' things, but that's not what they want here. Back in high school I thought I be a pretty good student, but now I don't know.

Players' experiences in the classroom were very different from their preconceptions. The work was harder and they were not taken care of to the extent they had imagined. The intense competition of the athletic arena led them to be obsessed with success. Their frequent academic failures (or at best mediocre grades) led athletes to distance themselves from self-involvement in the academic role. It was better not to try than to try and fail. And they derived plenty of support for this tack within the peer subculture.

SOCIAL ROLE

Athletes' social experiences at the university were predominantly with other athletes. Initially they had expected to derive both friendship and status recognition from other students as they had in high school. Instead they found themselves socially isolated. Geographically they were isolated by being housed in an athletic dormitory on a remote side of the campus. Temporally they were cut off by the demands of their practices, games, study halls, and booster functions. Culturally they were racially, socially, and economically different from the rest of the student body. Physically, they were different from other students in size and build, and many students, especially women, found them imposing or occasionally intimidating.

These factors left other athletes as their primary outlets for social relations. Housed together in a dormitory reserved almost exclusively for male athletes (primarily football and basketball players), they bonded together into a reference group and peer subculture. Relations within this group were made especially cohesive by the intensity of their living, playing, and traveling together. A junior described this living situation:

> Living in the jock dorm the privacy is limited. Everybody knows everythin' 'bout what you doin' and who you seein'. You got to live with these same faces twelve months out of the year, they like your brothers, and we all one big family, like it or not. You just got to fit in.

Within the dormitory, athletes briefed each other about what to expect from and think about various individuals, and how to handle certain situations. They formed generalized attitudes and beliefs about what things were important and what things were not. The peer subculture provided them with a set of norms that guided their interpretations of and actions within their various roles.

One of the peer subculture's strongest influences lay in its anti-intellectual and anti-academic character. Typically, dormitory conversation centered on athletic and social dimensions of their lives with little reference to academic, cultural, or intellectual pursuits. In fact, individuals who displayed too much interest, effort, or success in academics were often ridiculed, as one player described:

> When most of the other guys are making Ds or Fs, if I work hard and I get a B on a test, if I go back to the dorm and they all see I got a B, then they goin' "snap on" [make fun of] me. So most of the guys, they don't try. They all act like it's a big joke.

The athletes' peer subculture conflicted with their academic role in five ways: (1) by discouraging them from exerting effort in academics; (2) by providing them with distractions that made it harder for them to study; (3) by providing them with role models who appeared to be getting through college while according their academic role negligible identity salience; (4) by discouraging them from seeking out and associating with other students who could have provided greater academic role modeling; and (5) by providing excuses and justifications that legitimated their academic failures.

The conflict between their athletic, academic, and social roles pulled the athletes in too many directions. One junior expressed his continuing distress over this role conflict:

> When I think about it I get tense and frustrated, you just can't be everything they expect you to be and what you want to be. Something's gotta give. It's either cut off my social life, or flunk out of school, or not do the things I have to do to be able to make pro.

ROLE CONFLICT RESOLUTIONS

Athletes' expectations for their academic role were gradually replaced by feelings of anomie as they came to perceive the disparity between the recruiting and cultural rhetoric they had encountered and the reality of college life. In order to successfully negotiate their college experience they had to find some way to resolve this role conflict, which they did by realigning the expectations, priorities, and identity salience [the significance of a role, or how much one identifies with it] of their roles.

The biggest change in their core identity salience lay in the growth of their athletic role. While athletics had always been the first priority for most, it now engulfed them. This shift was brought about by the demands and expectations of their athletic role set and by their own desire to cling to their dreams of making it in the NBA. First, the head coach overwhelmed athletes by the intensity of his power and role demands. He expected them to place basketball before everything else. He influenced their view of their present and future life chances by framing these for them based on athletic priorities. He heard about everything they did and reprimanded them for violations of his behavior code. Yet it was the intensity of the athletic experience itself that ensured their self-immersion in this role. The glamour and excitement of playing for a big-time athletic program offered even the most marginal players their most fulfilling gratification and rewards. One player described the impossibility of maintaining any balance between his athletic and other roles:

> When I go to sleep at night what do you think I be thinking? History? Sociology? No way. I hear coach yelling in my ear, "Run, run, get on the ball, play defense, Robinson. Damn, Robinson, can you move your feet, son?" During the season I sleep, eat, and breathe basketball.

In addition, the athletic role pervaded and dominated the identity of their other roles in social and academic situations. On campus they were recognized as athletes first and students second. Off campus and even out of uniform, they were constantly responsible for "representing the program." Their appearance and demeanor reflected on their teammates, their coaches, their basketball program, and the entire university. They therefore had to relinquish a great deal of privacy and freedom.

The growth of the athletic role's identity salience was further endorsed by their peer subculture. Most of the athletes in their dormitory had reprioritized their roles and become engulfed by athletics. These significant others offered them a model of role conflict resolution that adopted the coach's perspective on the predominance of athletics, maintained the secondary importance of having a social life, and reshuffled academics to an even lower identity salience. All of the athletes realigned the identity salience of these roles in this manner, progressively detaching themselves from academics.

These changes in athletes' identities led to a series of pragmatic adjustments in their academic goals. Of the individuals who began with preprofessional majors, only one-fourth of them stayed with these all the way through college and graduated. They did so primarily without the academic care and concern they had originally anticipated. They ceased attending classes regularly, diminished their efforts to get to know professors, did not bother to get class notes or reading assignments until just before tests, and exerted the minimum amount of effort necessary to get by. More commonly, these individuals reassessed their academic goals and found that some adjustment was necessary. A second group (the remaining three-fourths of this original group) adjusted by both shifting their behavior and by changing from their preprofessional program to a more manageable major. While this shift meant that they had abandoned both their academic idealism and their earlier career goals, they still held to the goal of graduating. The predominant attitude changed to getting a diploma regardless of the major. As one player commented, "When you apply for a job all that matters is if you have that piece of paper. They don't care what you majored in." Many of the athletes in this group managed to graduate or keep on a steady course toward graduation. Much like Merton's innovators, they retained the socially approved goal but replaced their earlier means with a creative alternative.

Athletes who began their college careers with lower initial academic aspirations and who majored in physical education or recreation from the start made corresponding adjustments. Approximately one-fifth of these in this group originally held on to their initial goal and managed to graduate in one of these fields. Like the preprofessional majors, they did so with less concern than they had displayed on entering. The other four-fifths came to the realization, usually relatively late, that their chances for graduating from college were unrealistic. They therefore shifted their orientation toward maintaining their athletic eligibility. A junior's remarks illustrated how this shift to maintaining eligibility affected his attitude toward his academic role:

> I used to done thought I was goin' to school, but now I know it's not for real.... I don't have no academic goals. A player a coach is counting on, that's all he think about is ball. That's what he signed to do. So what you gotta do is show up, show your smilin' face. Try as hard as you can. Don't just lay over in the room. That's all the coach can ask. Or else you may not find yourself playing the next year. Or even that year.

By their senior year, when they had met their final eligibility requirements, many members of this last group abandoned the academic role entirely. They either anticipated going to one of the professional leagues, or they knew that their scholarships would soon expire and they would have to look for a job. In either case, wasting their time in class no longer seemed necessary.

DISCUSSION

...In their academic role, many college athletes received poor or marginal grades and had to relinquish or readjust the academic goals they held on entering college. This perception awakened them to the conflict between their expectations that college would be much like high school and their realizations that the academic demands at the university were greater than they could achieve. Their emphasis on competition and winning, derived from their athletic role, made the failure especially difficult to accept.

When faced with extreme role conflict, individuals doing very poorly in their classes engaged in role distance, diminishing the importance of this role to their self-identity. Individuals from stronger academic backgrounds fared slightly better, however, and did not as greatly diminish their [identity with the] academic role.... As individuals assessed their relative strengths and weaknesses within given roles, they accorded higher salience to those in which they were evaluated positively and lower salience to those in which they were negatively evaluated....

Most athletes' initial commitment to the academic role was induced by cultural expectations and by the encouragement of others, but that commitment was not firmly embedded in their self-conceptions. Once they got to college, their commitment to work hard academically was easily dislodged by their first few adverse experiences and by the peer culture's devaluation of academics. In contrast, their commitment to the athletic role was entrenched, because this was their dream since childhood. No matter how little playing time they received or how much the coach criticized them, they clung to the primary self-identification as athletes....

As college athletes learned the nature of their new status they learned that they were seen as basketball players by nearly everyone they encountered. Their athletic identity pervaded and dominated the identity of their other roles in almost all other situations. This designation was true in their academic and social lives both on campus and off, and it grew more pervasive as they progressed through their playing careers and advanced to more visible team positions.... When people are constantly identified by one role to the near total exclusion of their others, they become increasingly committed to that role and it is likely to take precedence in influencing their self-conceptions....

Athletes' position at the university was characterized by "institutional powerlessness," as their coaches had the ability to control all aspects of their lives. By influencing their personal time, academic schedules, and playing role on the team, coaches could dominate not only their athletic role, but their social and academic roles as well. Regardless of the players' own goals, expectations, or desires, they had to take into consideration the wishes and demands of the coach. Players also believed...that the coach could...keep them eligible to play if he wanted, even if they got into academic difficulty. The omnipotence of their athletic over their academic role influenced them to shift greater identity salience to the role where the apparent power lay....

PART V Social Change

Like it or not, we are destined to live in the midst of rapid social change. Social change is one of the chief characteristics of our society. It is so extensive that little remains the same from one generation to the next. Social change is so swift that it can be difficult to keep up with it. We have to learn new skills—and relearn old ones. Although U.S. physicians receive a top notch education and are familiar with the latest developments in their profession, if they fail to continue reading journals and taking courses in their specialties, in a short time they fall woefully behind.

Some changes are small and of little consequence for our lives. A fast food outlet opens where a gas station used to be. The new models of cars sprout new lines—ever so slightly. Computers appear in new colors or shapes, or add functions. Our college adds a course and drops another. A band, singer, author, or actor becomes an overnight sensation, then quickly drops from sight.

Other changes are more significant and have greater impact on us. Cities grow so greatly that they expand into one another, and no longer can you tell where one ends and the other leaves off. Increasingly, these megacities affect U.S. culture, changing the way we view life. Latinos migrate to the United States in such vast numbers that they become the largest U.S. minority group. Upset about some social condition, people band together in social movements, their protests echoing through the culture.

Some changes are more significant and affect the lives of even more people. The *globalization of capitalism* both sweeps jobs away from us, transplanting them into other parts of the world, and brings other ones in their place, transforming our own economic future, those of our children, and those of people across the globe. The mass media becomes more powerful, increasingly shaping public opinion, and with it, the affairs of the nation. Computers change the way we work, get educated, and even how we get medical treatment and fight wars. They even change the way we think, although this fundamental impact is so recent—and so subtle—that we currently have little understanding of it.

To conclude this book, then, we shall consider social change. Elijah Anderson opens this final part by focusing on the changing city, analyzing how social class and racial–ethnic groups coexist—uneasily—within the same city space. George Ritzer examines a fundamental change that is affecting us all, the rationalization of our lives, which he calls the McDonaldization of society. The selection that closes this part, written by a team of researchers, examines changes in the sex life of Americans.

READING 14

Streetwise

Elijah Anderson

introduction

The city can be a dangerous place, and all of us avoid certain areas of the city. Those areas make us uncomfortable. They seem threatening, foreboding places where we can expect the worst. We help control our lives by sticking to areas with which we are familiar and comfortable. Part of the discomfort that we feel in some areas is because we don't know the norms of interaction. We know that different things are expected there, but we don't know exactly what.

In this reading, Elijah Anderson analyzes interaction on city streets. For 14 years, he did participant observation in a changing neighborhood of Philadelphia that he refers to as the Village-Northton. The Village has undergone *gentrification*, a process by which the relatively affluent move into an urban area inhabited by the poor and renovate the buildings. Next to the Village is a ghetto, from where high crime spills over into the Village. Consequently, for the relatively affluent African Americans and whites who live in the Village, the presence of strangers makes even walking down the street a problem, and the middle class interacts uneasily with the poor. This selection examines public interaction when distrust and the threat of violence enshroud people's relationships.

Thinking Critically

As you read this selection, ask yourself:

1. Are there areas of the city (or entire cities, perhaps) that you avoid? Apply ideas in this article to explain why you avoid those areas.
2. If you lived in the Village-Northton, how would your interactions be different from what they now are? Exactly what behaviors would you change?
3. If you lived in the Village-Northton, how could you tell a mugger from a regular person?

An overwhelming number of young black males in the Village are committed to civility and law-abiding behavior. They often have a hard time convincing others of this, however, because of the stigma attached to their skin color, age, gender, appearance, and general style of self-presentation. Moreover, most residents ascribe criminality, incivility, toughness, and street smartness to the anonymous black male, who must work hard to make others trust his common decency.

This state of affairs is worth exploring [because]...the situation of young black men as a group encapsulates the stigmatizing effect of "negative" status-determining characteristics, in this case gender and race. Because public encounters between strangers on the streets of urban America are by nature brief, the participants must draw conclusions about each other quickly, and they generally rely on a small number of cues. This process is universal, and it unavoidably involves some prejudging—prejudice—but its working out is especially prominent in the public spaces of the Village-Northton....

The residents of the area, including black men themselves, are likely to defer to unknown black males, who move convincingly through the area as though they "run it," exuding a sense of ownership. They are easily perceived as symbolically inserting themselves into any available social space, pressing against those who might challenge them. The young black males, the "big winners" of these little competitions, seem to feel very comfortable as they swagger confidently along. Their looks, their easy smiles, and their spontaneous laughter, singing, cursing, and talk about the intimate details of their lives, which can be followed from across the street, all convey the impression of little concern for other pedestrians. The other pedestrians, however, are very concerned about them....

People, black or white, who are more familiar with the black street culture are less troubled by sharing the streets with young black males. Older black men, for instance, frequently adopt a refined set of criteria. In negotiating the streets, they watch out particularly for a certain *kind* of young black male: "jitterbugs" or those who might belong to "wolf packs," small bands of black teenage boys believed to travel about the urban areas accosting and robbing people.

Many members of the Village community, however, both black and white, lack these more sophisticated insights. Incapable of making distinctions between law-abiding black males and others, they rely for protection on broad stereotypes based on color and gender, if not outright racism. They are likely to misread many of the signs displayed by law-abiding black men, thus becoming apprehensive of almost any black male they spot in public.... The "master status-determining characteristic" of race (Hughes 1945) is at work in the most casual street encounter. Becker's application of Hughes's conception of the contradictions and dilemmas of status has special relevance:

> Some statuses, in our society as in others, override all other statuses and have a certain priority. Race is one of these. Membership in the Negro race, as socially defined, will override most other status considerations in most situations; the fact that one is a physician or middle class or female will not protect one from being treated as a Negro first and any of these other things second. The status of deviant (depending on the kind of deviance) is this kind of master status. One receives the status as a result of breaking a

> rule, and the identification proves to be more important than most others. One will be identified as a deviant first, before other identifications are made. The question raised: "What kind of person would break such an important rule?" And the answer given: "One who is different from the rest of us, who cannot or will not act as a moral human being and therefore might break other important rules." The deviant identification becomes the controlling one.
>
> Treating a person as though he were generally rather than specifically deviant produces a self-fulfilling prophecy. It sets in motion several mechanisms which conspire to shape the person in the image people have of him. (Becker 1963: 33, 34)

In the minds of many Village residents, black and white, the master status of the young black male is determined by his youth, his blackness, his maleness, and what these attributes have come to stand for in the shadow of the ghetto....

Because public interactions generally matter for only a few crucial seconds, people are conditioned to rapid scrutiny of the looks, speech, public behavior, gender, and color of those sharing the environment.... The central strategy in maintaining safety on the streets is to avoid strange black males. The public awareness is color-coded: white skin denotes civility, law abidingness, and trustworthiness, while black skin is strongly associated with poverty, crime, incivility, and distrust. Thus an unknown young black male is readily deferred to. If he asks for anything, he must be handled quickly and summarily. If he is persistent, help must be summoned.

This simplistic racial interpretation of crime creates a "we/they" dichotomy between whites and blacks. Yet here again the underlying issue is class.... Middle-income blacks in the Village, who also are among the "haves," often share a victim mentality with middle-income whites and appear just as distrustful of black strangers. Believing they are immune to the charge of racism, Village blacks make some of the same remarks as whites do, sometimes voicing even more incisive observations concerning "street blacks" and black criminality....

STREET ETIQUETTE

A set of informal rules has emerged among residents and other users of the public spaces of the Village. These rules allow members of diverse groups orderly passage with the promise of security, or at least a minimum of trouble and conflict.... The process begins something like this. One person sees another walking down the street alone, with another person, or perhaps with a few others. Those seen might be getting out of an unusual car, riding a ten-speed bicycle, walking a dog, strolling on the grounds of a dwelling in the neighborhood, or simply crossing the street at the light or leaving a store carrying groceries. The sight of people engaging in such everyday activities helps to convey what may be interpreted as the usual picture of public life—what residents take for granted.

Skin color, gender, age, dress, and comportment are important markers that characterize and define the area. Depending on the observer's biases, such specific markers can become the most important characteristics determining the status of those being watched, superseding other meaningful attributes. However, the most important aspect of the situation is simply that the observer takes mental note of the other person: a significant social contact, though usually not a reciprocal one, is made. The person seen, and the category he or she is believed to represent, comes to be considered an ordinary part of the environment.

Although the initial observation is important, it is not the crucial element in "knowing about" others and feeling comfortable. Rather, it helps determine the social context for any other meaningful interactions, whether unilateral or bilateral. It gives users of the streets a sense of whom to expect where and when, and it allows them to adjust their plans accordingly.

The significance of the initial encounter is contingent upon subsequent meetings and interactions. If the person is never seen again, the encounter gradually loses significance. But if the observer sees the person again or meets others who are similar, the initial impression may become stronger and might develop into a theory about the category of people, a working conception of a social type. The strength of such impressions—nurtured and supported through repeated encounters, observations, and talk with other residents—gradually builds.

Background information and knowledge may provide a basis for social connection. A stranger may be seen in one context, then in another, then in a third. In time the observer might say to himself, "I know that person." Certainly he does know the person, if only by sight. He has noticed him many times in various neighborhood contexts, and with each successive encounter he has become increasingly familiar with him and the class he has come to represent. Probably the two are not yet speaking, though they may have exchanged looks that establish the minimal basis for trust. If asked directly, the observer might say, "Yeah, I've seen him around." In this way strangers may know each other and obtain a degree of territorial communion without ever speaking a word. It is quite possible that they will never reach speaking terms.

But there are circumstances where the social gap between visual and verbal interaction in public is pressed and the relationship between incomplete strangers is required to go further. People sometimes feel silly continually passing others they know well by sight without speaking to them. They may resolve their discomfort by greeting them or by contrived avoidance. If they choose to speak, they may commit themselves to a series of obligatory greetings.

Introductions may also occur when two people who have seen each other in the neighborhood for some time happen to meet in a different part of town; there, despite some awkwardness, they may feel constrained to greet each other like long-lost friends. Perhaps they had not yet reached the point of speaking but had only warily acknowledged one another with knowing looks, or even with the customary offensive/defensive scowl used on the street for keeping strangers at a distance. After this meeting, previously distant villagers may begin to speak regularly on the neighborhood streets. In this way trust can be established between strangers, who may then come to know each other in limited ways or very well.

Just the fact of their regular presence offers a sense of security, or at least continuity, to their neighbors. Thus, many people walk the streets with a confidence that belies their serious concerns. They use those they "know" as buffers against danger. Although they may still be strangers, they feel they can call on each other as allies when neighborhood crises emerge, when they would otherwise be seriously short of help, or when they must protect themselves or their loved ones. For example, during emergencies such as house fires, street crimes in which someone clearly needs help, or some other event where partial strangers have an opportunity to gather and compare notes with neighbors who seemed out of reach before, they may first provide help and only then reach out a hand and introduce themselves, saying, "Hello, my name is...."

Eyework

Many blacks perceive whites as tense or hostile to them in public. They pay attention to the amount of eye contact given. In general, black males get far less time in this regard than do white males. Whites tend not to "hold" the eyes of a black person. It is more common for black and white strangers to meet each other's eyes for only a few seconds, and then to avert their gaze abruptly. Such behavior seems to say, "I am aware of your presence," and no more. Women especially feel that eye contact invites unwanted advances, but some white men feel the same and want to be clear about what they intend. This eye work is a way to maintain distance, mainly for safety and social purposes....

Many people, particularly those who see themselves as more economically privileged than others in the community, are careful not to let their eyes stray, in order to avoid an uncomfortable situation. As they walk down the street they pretend not to see other pedestrians, or they look right at them without speaking, a behavior many blacks find offensive.

Moreover, whites of the Village often scowl to keep young blacks at a social and physical distance. As they venture out on the streets of the Village and, to a lesser extent, of Northton, they may plant this look on their faces to ward off others who might mean them harm. Scowling by whites may be compared to gritting by blacks as a coping strategy. At times members of either group make such faces with little regard for circumstances, as if they were dressing for inclement weather. But on the Village streets it does not always storm, and such overcoats repel the sunshine as well as the rain, frustrating many attempts at spontaneous human communication.

Money

Naturally, given two adjacent neighborhoods representing "haves" and "have-nots," there is tremendous anxiety about money: how much to carry, how to hold it, how to use it safely in public. As in other aspects of Village life, shared anecdotes and group discussions help newcomers recognize the underlying rules of comportment.

Perhaps the most important point of etiquette with regard to money in public places is to be discreet. For example, at the checkout counter one looks into one's wallet or purse and takes out only enough to cover the charge, being careful that the remaining contents are not on display. Further, one attempts to use only small bills so as not to suggest that one has large ones.

When walking on the streets at night, it is wise to keep some money in a wallet or purse and hide the rest in other parts of one's clothing—some in a jacket pocket, some in the back pocket of one's jeans, maybe even some in a sock. In this way one would not lose everything in a mugging, yet the mugger would get something to appease him.

A final rule, perhaps the most critical, is that in a potentially violent situation it is better to lose one's money than one's life. Thus the person who plans to travel at dangerous times or in dangerous areas should have some money on hand in case of an assault:

> It was 9:00 P.M., and the Christmas party had ended. I was among the last to leave. John [a forty-five-year-old professional], the host, had to run an errand and asked if I wanted to go with him. I agreed. While I was waiting, Marsha, John's wife, said in a perfectly serious voice, "Now, John, before you go, do you have $10 just in case you get mugged?" "No, I don't have it, do you?"
>
> Marsha fetched $10 and gave it to John as what was in effect protection money, a kind of consolation prize designed to cool out a prospective mugger. As we walked the three blocks or so on the errand, John said, "We've come two blocks, and it's not so bad." His tone was that of a nervous joke, as though he really half expected to encounter muggers.

The reality of the Village is that residents can make their lives safer by "expecting" certain problems and making plans to cope with them. The mental preparation involved—imagining a bad situation and coming up with the best possible solution, acting it out in one's mind—may well be a valuable tool in learning to behave safely on the streets....

Other Safety Rules and Strategies

Dress is an important consideration when walling the Village streets, day or night. Women wear clothing that negates stereotypical "female frailty" and symbolizes aggressiveness. Unisex jackets, blue jeans, and sneakers are all part of the urban female costume. "Sexy" dresses are worn only when women are in a group, accompanied by a man, or traveling by car.

Village men also stick to practical, nonshowy clothing. Most times this means blue jeans or a sweat suit. More expensive clothing is relegated to day-time work hours or, as for females, travel by car.

The safety of cars and things in them is a major worry. Newcomers learn to park on the east-west streets to avoid nighttime vandalism and theft. They buy "crime locks" and hood locks for their cars. They learn, sometimes through painful error, to remove attractive items like tape decks and expensive briefcases, or anything that looks valuable, before they lock up and leave.

Their homes may be similarly barricaded. They sometimes have chains for their bicycles, bars for their first-floor windows, and dead bolts for their back doors. Some install elaborate and expensive burglar alarms or keep dogs for the same purpose. They may build high fences to supplement the quaint waist-high wrought-iron fences from the early 1900s when the wealthy still claimed hegemony in the area.

Watching from the car as companions go into their houses is a standard precaution for city dwellers. The driver idles the motor out front and keeps an eye on the street until the resident has unlocked the door and is safely inside. This common practice has become ritualized in many instances, perhaps more important as a sign of a caring bond between people than as a deterrent of assault. It helps to make people feel secure, and residents understand it as a polite and intelligent action.

But some people are given to overreaction and to overelaboration of "mug-proofing" behaviors and are likely to see a potential mugger in almost anyone with certain attributes, most noticeably black skin, maleness, and youth. A middle-aged white woman told me this story:

> I had a white taxi driver drive me home once, and he was horrified at the neighborhood I lived in. It was night, and he told me what a horrible neighborhood I lived in, speaking of how dangerous it was here. He said, "This neighborhood is full of blacks. You'll get raped; you'll get murdered, or robbed." I replied, "I've lived here for a long time. I really like this neighborhood." He let me out on the opposite side of Thirty-fourth Street. He said, "OK, you go straight in your door, and I'll cover you." And he pulled out a gun. I said, "Please put it away." But he wouldn't. I was scared to death he was going to shoot me or something as I walked toward the house. It was so offensive to me that this man [did this], whom I trusted less than I trusted any of my neighbors, even those I knew only by sight. I felt sick for days.

The woman surmised that the taxi driver "must have been from a white ethnic and working-class background." It is commonly assumed among local blacks that such men feel especially threatened by blacks. But some middle- and upper-middle-class whites within the Village are susceptible to similar situational behavior.

STREET WISDOM

...Street wisdom and street etiquette are comparable to a scalpel and a hatchet. One is capable of cutting extremely fine lines between vitally different organs; the other can only make broader, more brutal strokes....

The streetwise individual thus becomes interested in a host of signs, emblems, and symbols that others exhibit in everyday life. Besides learning the "safety signals" a person might display—conservative clothing, a tie, books, a newspaper—he also absorbs the vocabulary and expressions of the street. If he is white, he may learn for the first time to make distinctions among different kinds of black people. He may learn the meaning of certain styles of hats, sweaters, jackets, shoes, and other emblems of the subculture, thus rendering the local environment "safer" and more manageable....

A primary motivation for acquiring street wisdom is the desire to have the upper hand. It is generally believed that this will ensure safe passage, allowing one to outwit a potential assailant. In this regard a social game may be discerned. Yet it is a serious game, for failing could mean loss of property, injury, or even death. To prevail means simply to get safely to one's destination, and the ones who are most successful are those who are "streetwise." Street wisdom is really street etiquette wisely enacted....

Typically, those generally regarded as streetwise are veterans of the public spaces. They know how to get along with strangers, and they understand how to negotiate the streets. They know whom to trust, whom not to trust, what to say through body language or words. They have learned how to behave effectively in public. Probably the most important consideration is the experience they have gained through encounters with "every kind of stranger." Although one may know about situations through the reports of friends or relatives, this pales in comparison with actual experience. It is often sheer proximity to the dangerous streets that allows a person to gain street wisdom, and formulate some effective theory of the public spaces. As one navigates there is a certain edge to one's demeanor, for the streetwise person is both wary of others and sensitive to the subtleties that could salvage safety out of danger.

The longer people live in this locale, having to confront problems on the streets and public spaces every day, the greater chance they have to develop a sense of what to do without seriously compromising themselves. Further, the longer they are in the area, the more likely they are to develop contacts who might come to their aid, allowing them to move boldly.

This self-consciousness makes people likely to be alert and sensitive to the nuances of the environment. More important, they will project their ease and self-assurance to those they meet, giving them the chance to affect the interaction positively. For example, the person who is "streetdumb," relying for guidance on the most superficial signs, may pay too much attention to skin color and become needlessly tense just because the person approaching is black. A streetwise white who meets a black person will probably just go about his or her business. In both cases the black person will pick up the "vibe" being projected—in the first instance fear and hostility, in the second case comfort and a sense of commonality. There are obviously times when the "vibe" itself could tip the balance in creating the subsequent interaction.

Crisis and Adaptation

Sometimes the balance tips severely, and the whole neighborhood reacts with shock and alarm. A wave of fear surges through the community when violent crimes are reported by the media or are spread by word of mouth through the usually peaceful Village. One February a young woman, a new mother, was stabbed and left for dead in her home on one of the well-traveled north-south streets. Her month-old baby was unharmed, but it was weeks before the mother, recuperating in the hospital, remembered she had recently given birth. Word of how the stabbing occurred spread up and down the blocks of the Village. Neighbors said the woman often went out her back door to take out the garbage or call in the dog. But to uninitiated newcomers, the brick streets and large yards seem deceptively peaceful. Crises like these leave in their wake a deeper understanding of the "openness" that characterizes this quaint area of the city.

They also separate those who survive by brittle etiquette from those who—despite increased temporary precautions—can continue to see strangers as individuals. Less than half a block away from the scene of the attack, in a building facing an east-west street, a friend of the young mother was overcome with fear. Her husband was scheduled to go out of town the week after the vicious attack on her friend. She was so frightened that he had to arrange for a neighbor to "baby-sit" with his wife and children at night while he was away.

Security all over the Village was tightened for a time. People who used to go in and out, feeding the birds, shoveling walks, visiting their neighbors and friends, no longer came and went so carelessly. As the news traveled, fear rippled out from the young victim's immediate neighbors to affect behavior in other parts of the Village. One young black man reported that after the attack he was greeted with suspicious stares on his way to Mr. Chow's. "Everyone's looking over their shoulder suddenly," he said. "All black people are suspects."

"It makes you stop and wonder about living here," said one young mother shortly after the stabbing became the main item of conversation. "I've never lived in such a dangerous neighborhood. I run upstairs and leave my back door open sometimes. Like today, I got both kids and took them upstairs, and all of a sudden I said, "Oh, no! I left the door unlocked!" and I just stopped what I was doing and ran downstairs to lock it." This kind of fear-induced behavior occurs as neighbors work out their group perspective on what is possible, if not probable, in the aftermath of such a crime.

Violence causes residents to tense up and begin taking defensive action again. They may feel uncomfortable around strangers on the streets, particularly after dark. They become especially suspicious of black males. An interview with a young black man from the area sheds some light on how residents react to neighborhood blacks shortly after a violent incident:

> People come out of the door and they're scared. So when they see blacks on the streets they try to get away. Even ones who live right next door. All of a sudden they change attitudes toward each other. They're very suspicious. The guy that killed that lady and her husband down on Thirty-fourth in the Village, he from the Empire [gang]. He tried to rape the lady right in front of the husband—he stabbed the husband and killed him. He'll get the electric chair now; they gave him the death penalty. They caught him comin' out. Wouldn't been so bad, the cops got another call to next door where he did it at. She was screamin' and the cops heard and came around to the door.
>
> After that happened, you could feel the vibes from the whites. When things like that happen, things get very tense between blacks and whites. And you can feel it in the way they look at you, 'cause they think you might be the one who might do the crime. Every time they see a black they don't trust 'em. Should stay in their own neighborhood.
>
> That's the Village. They paranoid.

In time the fear recedes. Through successive documentations and neighborhood gossip, Villagers slowly return to some level of complacency, an acceptance of the risks of living in the city. Familiar people on the streets are "mapped" and associated with their old places, much as veteran Villagers have mapped them before. Streets, parks, and playgrounds are again made theirs. When these mental notations remain reliable and undisturbed for a time, a kind of "peace" returns. More and more can be taken for granted. Night excursions become more common. Children may be given a longer tether. Villagers gather and talk about the more pleasant aspects of neighborhood life. But they know, and are often reminded, that the peace is precarious....

REFERENCES

Becker, Howard S. 1963. *Outsiders: Studies in the sociology of deviance.* New York: Macmillan.

Hughes, Everett C. 1945. Dilemmas and contradictions of status. *American Journal of Sociology 50*:353–59.

READING 15

The McDonaldization of Society

George Ritzer

introduction

A key term in sociology is *rationalization.* This term refers to choosing the most efficient means to accomplish tasks. In business it refers to the bottom line, calculating costs to produce the most gain. With rationalization, profit becomes king, while people, evaluated according to what they bring to the bottom line, become expendable.

The rationalization of society, said Max Weber, the sociologist who first analyzed this process, is extremely significant, for it tends to ensnare us all. The traditional ways of doing things—which may be inefficient but which are also the source of satisfactions that come from personal relationships—are passing. In their place come bureaucracies with time and motion studies, cold analyses of every act, with profits placed higher than the people who make up the work setting. Weber didn't know how far reaching and accurate his analysis would prove. Rationalization threatens to engulf all of society, locking us all in what Weber called an iron cage of rationality. College administrators, for example, want to evaluate instructors not by how they challenge students to think or by how they open their minds to new perceptions, but, rather, by the sheer number of students they turn out each semester. Even traditional, routine, everyday aspects of family life are not impervious to this change, as becomes evident in Ritzer's analysis.

Thinking Critically

As you read this selection, ask yourself:

1. How is your own life being rationalized?
2. What further rationalizations of everyday life do you think the future will bring?
3. In what ways is the rationalization of life good? Bad? Indifferent?

McDonald's has sought to construct highly efficient systems, and *McDonaldization* implies the search for maximum efficiency in increasingly numerous and diverse social settings. *Efficiency* means the choice of the optimum means to a given end, but this definition requires some clarification. Although we use the term *optimum,* it is rare that the truly optimum means to an end is ever found. Rather, there is a search for a...far better means to an end than would be employed under ordinary circumstances....

WIRELESS KEYBOARDS AND SELF-SERVICE SLURPEES

The emphasis of McDonaldization on efficiency implies that contrasting, nonrational systems are less efficient, or even inefficient. The fast-food restaurant grew as a result of its greater efficiency in comparison to alternative methods of obtaining a meal. In the early 1950s, at the dawning of the era of the fast-food restaurant, the major alternative was the home-cooked meal made largely from ingredients previously purchased at various markets....

But the home-cooked meal was, and still is, a relatively inefficient way of obtaining a meal. The restaurant has long been a more efficient alternative. But restaurants can be inefficient in that it may take several hours to go to the restaurant, consume a meal, and then return home. The desire for more efficient restaurants led to the rise of some of the ancestors of the fast-food restaurant—diners, cafeterias, and early drive-through or drive-in restaurants. The modern fast-food restaurant can be seen as being built on the latter models and as a further step in the direction of more efficient food consumption....

Above all else, it was the efficiency of the McDonald brothers' operation that impressed Ray Kroc [the individual behind the franchising of McDonald's], as well as the enormous profit potential of such a system if it were applied in a large number of sites. Here is how Kroc described his initial reactions to the McDonald's system:

> I was fascinated by the simplicity and effectiveness of the system.... Each step in producing the limited menu was stripped down to its essence and accomplished with a minimum of effort. They sold hamburgers and cheeseburgers only. The burgers were...all fried the same way.

Kroc and his associates looked at each component of the hamburger in order to increase the efficiency with which it could be produced and served. For example, they started with only partially sliced buns that were attached to one another. However, it was found that buns could be used more efficiently if they were sliced all the way through and separated from one another. At first, the buns arrived in cardboard boxes and the griddle workers had to spend time opening the boxes, separating the buns, slicing them, and discarding the leftover paper and cardboard. In addition to separating and preslicing them, buns were made efficient to use by having them shipped in reusable boxes. Similar attention was devoted to the meat patty. For example, the paper between the patties had to have just the right amount of wax so that the patties would readily slide off the paper and onto the grill.

Kroc makes it clear that the goal of these kinds of refinements was greater efficiency:

> The purpose of all these refinements, and we never lost sight of it, was to make our griddle man's job easier to do quickly and well. And the other considerations of cost cutting, inventory control, and so forth were important to be sure, but they were secondary to the critical detail of what happened there at the smoking griddle. This was the vital passage of our *assembly-line*, and the product had to flow through it smoothly or the whole plant would falter. (Italics added.)

...Once diners enter the fast-food restaurant, the process continues to appear to be efficient. Parking lots are adjacent to the restaurant and parking spots are readily available. It's a short walk to the counter, and although there is sometimes a line, food is usually quickly ordered, obtained, and paid for. The highly limited menu makes the choice of a meal's components quite easy. This contrasts to the many choices available in many of the alternatives to the fast-food restaurant. With the food obtained, it is but a few steps to a table and the beginning of the "dining experience." The fare almost always involves an array of finger foods (for example, Chicken McNuggets and french fries) that can be popped into the diner's mouth with the result that the entire meal is ordinarily consumed in a few minutes. Because there is little inducement to linger, the diners generally gather the leftover paper, styrofoam, and plastic, discard them in a nearby trash receptacle, and are back in their car and on their way to the next (often McDonaldized) activity.

Not too many years ago, those in charge of fast-food restaurants discovered that there was a way—the drive-through window—to make this whole process far more efficient for both themselves and the consumer. Instead of the "laborious" and "inefficient" process of parking the car, walking to the counter, waiting in line, ordering, paying, carrying the food to the table, eating, and disposing of the remnants, the drive-through window offered diners the choice of driving to the window (perhaps waiting in a line of cars), ordering, paying, and driving off with the meal. It was even possible to engage in the highly efficient act of eating while driving, thereby eliminating the need to devote a separate time period to dining. The drive-through window is also efficient from the perspective of the fast-food restaurant. As more and more people use the drive-through window, fewer parking spaces, tables, and employees are needed. Further, consumers take their debris with them as they drive away, thereby eliminating the need for additional trash receptacles and employees to periodically empty those receptacles....

"HOME-MADE" FAST FOOD AND THE STAIRMASTER

Given the efficiency of the fast-food restaurant, the home kitchen has had to grow more efficient or it might have faced total extinction. Had the kitchen not grown more efficient, a comedian could have envisioned a time when the kitchen would have been replaced by a large, comfortable telephone lounge used for calling Domino's for pizza delivery. The key to the salvation of the kitchen was the development and widespread adoption of the microwave oven. The microwave is simply a far more efficient means than its major alternative, the convection oven, for preparing a meal. It is usually faster than the old oven and one can prepare a wider array of foods in it than the old-fashioned oven. Perhaps most importantly from the point of view of this chapter, it spawned the development of a number of microwavable foods (including soup, pizza, hamburgers, fried chicken, french fries, and popcorn) that permit the efficient preparation of the fare one usually finds in the fast-food restaurants. For example, one of the first microwavable foods produced by Hormel was an array of biscuit-based breakfast sandwiches "popularized in recent years by many of the fast-food chains," most notably McDonald's and its Egg McMuffin. Banquet rushed to market with microwavable chicken breast nuggets. In fact, many food companies now employ people who continually scout fast-food restaurants for new ideas for foods that can be marketed for the home. As one executive put it, "Instead of having a breakfast sandwich at McDonald's, you can pick one up from the freezer of your grocery store." As a result, one can now, in effect, enjoy fast food at home without venturing out to the fast-food restaurant....

Another factor in the continued success of the fast-food restaurant is that it has many advantages over the "home-cooked" microwave dinner. For example, a trip to the fast-food restaurant offers people a dinner out rather than just another meal at home. For another, as Stan Luxenberg has pointed out in *Roadside Empires,* McDonald's offers more than an efficient meal, it offers fun—brightly lit, colorful, and attractive settings, garish packaging, special inducements to children, give-aways, contests—in short, it offers a kind of carnival-like atmosphere in which to buy and consume fast food. Thus, faced with the choice of an efficient meal at home or one in a fast-food restaurant, many people are still likely to choose the fast-food restaurant because it not only offers efficiency but a range of other rewards.

The microwave oven (as well as the range of products it spawned) is but one of many contributors to the increasing efficiency of home cooking. Among other obvious technological advances are the replacement of the hand beater by the electric beater; slicers, dicers, and even knives by the Cuisinart; and the presence of either stand-alone freezers or those that are an integral part of the refrigerator.

The large freezer has permitted a range of efficiencies, such as a few trips to the market for enormous purchases rather than many trips for small purchases. It has permitted the storage of a wide range of ingredients that can be readily extracted when needed for food preparation. It has allowed for the cooking of large portions which can then be divided up, frozen, and defrosted periodically for dinner. The widespread availability of the home freezer led to the expansion of the production of frozen foods of all types. The most notable frozen food from the point of view of efficiency is the "TV dinner." People can stock their freezers with an array of such dinners (for example, Chinese, Italian, and Mexican dinners as well as a wide variety of "American" cooking) and quite readily bring them out and pop them into the oven, sometimes even the microwave....

The McDonaldization of food preparation and consumption has been extended to the booming diet industry. Diet books promising all sorts of efficient shortcuts to weight loss are often at the top of the best-seller lists. Losing weight is normally difficult and time-consuming, hence the lure of various diet books that promise to make weight loss easier and quicker, that is, more efficient.

For those on a diet, and many people are on more or less perpetual diets, the preparation of low-calorie food has been made more efficient. Instead of needing to cook diet foods from scratch, they may now purchase an array of prepared foods in frozen and/or microwavable form. For those who do not wish to go through the inefficient process of eating those diet meals, there are the diet shakes, like Slim•Fast, that can be mixed and consumed in a matter of seconds.

A fairly recent development is the growth of diet centers like Nutri/System and Jenny Craig. Nutri/System sells dieters, at substantial cost, prepackaged freeze-dried food. All the dieter need do is add water when it is time for the next meal. Freeze-dried foods are not only efficient for the dieter but also for Nutri/System, because they can be efficiently packaged, transported, and stored. Furthermore, the dieter's periodic visit to a Nutri/System center is efficiently organized. A counselor is allotted ten minutes with each client. During that brief time the counselor takes the client's weight, blood pressure, and measurements, asks routine questions, fills out a chart, and devotes some time to "problem-solving." If the session extends beyond the allotted ten minutes and other clients are waiting, the receptionist will buzz the counselor's room. Counselors learn their techniques at Nutri/System University where, after a week of training (no inefficient years of matriculation here), they earn certification and an NSU diploma.

There is a strong emphasis on efficiency in modern health clubs, including such chains as Holiday Spas. These clubs often offer, under one roof, virtually everything needed to lose weight and stay in shape, including a wide array of exercise machines, as well as a running track and a swimming pool. The exercise machines are highly specialized so that one may efficiently increase fitness in specific areas of the body. Thus, working out on running machines and the StairMaster—one kind of exercise machine—increases cardiovascular fitness, whereas using various weightlifting machines increases strength and muscularity in targeted areas of the body. Another efficiency associated with many of these machines is that one can do other things while exercising. Thus, many clubs have television sets throughout the gym allowing people to both watch television and exercise. The exerciser can also read, listen to music, or even listen to a book-on-tape while working out. The exercise machines also offer a high degree of calculability, with many of them registering miles run, level of difficulty, and calories burned. All of this in the kind of clean, sterile environment we have come to associate with McDonaldization.

"SELLING MACHINES" AND L. L. BEAN

Shopping has also grown more efficient. The department store obviously is a more efficient place in which to shop than a series of specialty shops dispersed throughout the city or suburbs. The shopping mall increases efficiency by bringing a wide range of department stores and specialty shops under one roof. Kowinsky describes the mall as "an extremely efficient and effective selling machine." It is cost-efficient for retailers because it is the collection of shops and department stores ("mall synergy") that brings in throngs of people. And it is efficient for consumers because in one stop they can visit numerous shops, have lunch at a "food court" (likely populated by many fast-food chains), see a movie, have a drink, and go to an exercise or diet center.

The drive for shopping efficiency did not end with the malls. In recent years, there has been a great increase in catalogue sales (via L. L. Bean, Lands' End, and other mail-order companies), which enables people to shop while never leaving the comfort of their homes. Still more efficient, although it may require many hours in front of the tube, is home television shopping. A range of products is paraded in front of viewers who may simply phone each time a product catches their eye and conveniently charge their purchase to their credit card accounts. The latest advance in home shopping is the "scan-fone," an at-home phone machine that includes "a pen-sized bar-code scanner, a credit card magnetic-strip reader, and a key pad." The customer merely "scans items from a bar-coded catalogue and also scans delivery dates and payment methods. The orders are then electronically relayed to the various stores, businesses, and banks involved." Some mall operators fear that they will ultimately be put out of business because of the greater efficiency of shopping at home.

VIDEO RENTALS AND PACKAGE TOURS

With the advent of videotapes and video rental stores, many people no longer deem it efficient to drive to their local theater to see a movie. Movies can now be viewed, often more than one at a sitting, in one's own den. For those who wish even greater efficiency, viewers can buy one of the new television sets that enable viewers to see a movie while also watching a favorite television program on an inset on the television screen.

The largest video rental franchise in the United States is Blockbuster, which, predictably, "considers itself the McDonald's of the video business." Blockbuster has more than 2,000 outlets.... However, there may already be signs that Blockbuster is in danger of being replaced by even more efficient alternatives. One is pay-per-view movies offered by many cable companies. Instead of trekking to the video store, all one need do is turn to the proper channel and phone the cable company. Another experimental alternative is an effort by GTE to deliver movies to one's home through fiber-optic cables. Just as the video store replaced many movie theaters, video stores themselves may soon be displaced by even more efficient alternatives.

...[T]ravel to exotic efficient locales has also grown more efficient. The best example of this is the package tour. Let us take, for example, a thirty-day tour of Europe. To make these efficient, only the major locales in Europe are visited. Within each of these locales, the tourist is directed toward the major sights. (In Paris, the tour would definitely stop at the Louvre, but perhaps not at the Rodin Museum.) Because the goal is to see as many of the major sights as possible in a short period of time, the emphasis is on the efficient transportation of people to, through, and from each of them. Buses hurtle to and through the city, allowing the tourist to glimpse the maximum number of sights in the time allowed. At particularly interesting or important sights, the bus may slow down or even stop to permit some picture-taking. At the most important locales, a brief stopover is planned; there the visitor can hurry through the site, take a few pictures, buy a souvenir, and then hop back on the bus to head to the next attraction.

There is no question that this is a highly efficient way of seeing the major tourist attractions of Europe. Indeed, the package tour can be seen as a vast people-moving mechanism that permits the efficient transport of people from one locale to another. If tourists attempted to see the major sights of Europe on their own, it would take more time to see the same things and the expense would be greater. There are, of course, costs associated with the package tour (for example, does the tourist ever really have time to experience Europe?), as there are with every other highly rational system, but we will reserve a discussion of them for later....

CUSTOMIZED TEXTBOOKS, BOOKS-ON-TAPE, "NEWS McNUGGETS," AND DRIVE-IN CHURCHES

Turning to the educational system, specifically the university, one manifestation of the pressure for greater efficiency is the machine-graded, multiple-choice examination. In a much earlier era, students were examined on a one-to-one basis by their professors. This may have been a very good way of finding out what students know, but it was (and is) highly labor intensive and inefficient. Later, the essay examination became very popular. While grading a set of essays was more efficient from the professor's perspective than giving individual oral examinations, it was still relatively inefficient and time-consuming. Enter the multiple-choice examination, the grading of which was a snap in comparison to giving oral tests or reading essays. In fact, the grading could be passed on to graduate assistants, an act that was very efficient for the professor. Now we have computer-graded examinations that maximize efficiency for both professors and graduate students.

The multiple-choice examinations still left the professor saddled with the inefficient task of composing the necessary sets of questions. Furthermore, at least some of the questions had to be changed each semester because new students were likely to gain possession of old exams. The solution: Textbook companies provided professors with books (free of charge) full of multiple-choice questions to go along with the textbooks required for use in large classes. Professors no longer had to make up their own questions, they could use those previously provided by the publisher. However, the professor still had to retype the questions or to have them retyped by the office staff. Recently, however, publishers have been kind enough to provide their sets of questions on computer disks. Now all the professor needs to do is select the desired questions and let the printer do the rest.*...

*Some publishers also offer a "call-in testing service." A professor can call a toll-free number, specify the desired questions, and the publisher e-mails the test to the professor—all free.——Editor.

Publishers have provided other services to make teaching more efficient for those professors who adopt their textbooks. With the adoption of a textbook, a professor may receive many materials with which to fill class hours—lecture outlines, computer simulations, discussion questions, videotapes, movies, even ideas for guest lecturers and student projects. With luck, professors can use all of these devices and do little or nothing on their own for their classes. Needless to say, this is a highly efficient means of teaching from a professor's perspective, and it frees up valuable time for the much more valued activities (by professors, but not students) of writing and research....

Another example of efficiency in publishing is the advent of books-on-tape. There is a number of companies that now rent or sell books recorded on audiotape. The availability of such tapes permits greater efficiency in "reading" books. Instead of doing nothing but reading, one can now engage in other activities (driving, walking, jogging, watching TV with the sound off) while listening to a book. Greater efficiency is also provided by many of these books-on-tape being available in abridged form so that they can be devoured far more quickly. Gone are the "wasted" hours listening to "insignificant" parts of novels. With liberal cutting, a book such as *War and Peace* can now be listened to in a sitting.

Most "serious," nontabloid newspapers (for example, *The New York Times* and *The Washington Post*) are relatively inefficient to read. This is especially true of stories that begin on page one and then carry over to one or more additional pages. Stories that carry over to additional pages are said to have "jumped," and many readers are resistant to "jumping" with the stories. *USA Today* eliminated this inefficient way of presenting and reading stories by starting and finishing most of them on the same page, in other words, by offering "News McNuggets." This was accomplished by ruthlessly editing stories so that narrative was dramatically reduced (and no words wasted), leaving a series of relatively bare facts....

In the realm of religion, McDonaldization is manifest, among other places, in drive-in churches. Another is the widespread development of televised religious programs whereby people can get their religion in the comfort of their living rooms. A particularly noteworthy example of such religious rationalization occurred in 1985 when the Vatican announced that Catholics could receive indulgences through the Pope's annual Christmas benediction on TV or radio. ("Indulgences are a release by way of devotional practices from certain forms of punishment resulting from sin.") Before this development Catholics had to engage in the far less efficient activity of going to Rome for the Christmas benediction and manifesting the "proper intention and attitude" in order to receive their indulgences in person....

[DESTROYING RELATIONSHIPS]

The fast-food restaurant offers its employees a dehumanizing setting within which to work. Few skills are required on the job. Said Burger King workers, "A moron could learn this job, it's so easy" and "Any trained monkey could do this job." Thus workers are asked to use only a minute proportion of all their skills and abilities.

Employees are not only not using all of their skills, but they are also not being allowed to think and to be creative on the job. This leads to a high level of resentment, job dissatisfaction, alienation, absenteeism, and turnover among those who work in fast-food restaurants. In fact, the fast-food industry has the highest turnover rate—approximately 100 percent a year—of any industry in the United States. That means that the average worker lasts only about four months at a fast-food restaurant; the entire workforce of the fast-food industry turns over three times a year....

The fast-food restaurant is also dehumanizing as far as the customer is concerned. Instead of a human dining experience, what is offered is eating on a sort of moving conveyor belt or assembly line. The diner is reduced to a kind of overwound automaton who is made to rush through the meal. Little gratification is derived from the dining experience or from the food itself. The best that can usually be said is that it is efficient and it is over quickly.

Some customers might even feel as if they are being fed like livestock in a highly rationalized manner. This point was made a number of years ago on television in a *Saturday Night Live* skit entitled "Trough and Brew," a take-off on a small fast-food chain called Burger and Brew. In the skit, some young executives learn that a new fast-food restaurant called Trough and Brew has opened and they decide to try it for lunch. They are next seen entering the restaurant and having bibs tied around their necks. After that, they discover a long trough, resembling a pig trough. The trough is filled with chili and is periodically refilled by a waiter scooping new supplies from a bucket. The customers bend over, stick their heads into the trough, and begin lapping up the chili as they move along the length of the trough making high-level business decisions. Every so often they come up for air and lap some beer from the communal "brew basin." After they have finished their "meal," they pay their bills, "by the head." Since their faces are smeared with chili, they are literally "hosed off" before they leave the restaurant. The young executives are last seen being herded out of the restaurant, which is being closed for a half-hour so that it can be "hosed down." *Saturday Night Live* was clearly pointing out, and ridiculing, the fact that fast-food restaurants tend to treat their customers like lower animals.

"GET LOST" AND *WHEEL OF FORTUNE*

Another dehumanizing aspect of fast-food restaurants is that they minimize contact among human beings. Let us take, for example, the issue of how customers and employees relate. The nature of the fast-food restaurant turns these into fleeting relationships. Because the average employee stays only a few months, and even then only works on a part-time basis, the customer, even the regular customer, is rarely able to develop a long-term personal relationship with a counterperson. Gone are the days when one got to know well a waitress at a diner or the short-order cook at a local greasy spoon. Gone are the days when an employee knows who you are and knows what you are likely to order.

Not only are the relationships with a McDonald's employee fleeting (because the worker remains on the job only a short period of time), but each contact between worker and customer is of a very short duration. It takes little time at the counter to order, receive one's food, and pay for it. Both employees and customers are likely to feel rushed and to want to move on, customers to their dinner and employees to the next order. There is virtually no time for customer and counterperson to interact in such a context. This is even more true of the drive-through window, where thanks to the speedy service and the physical barriers, the server is but a dim and distant image.

The highly impersonal and anonymous relationship between customer and counterperson is heightened by the employees having been trained to interact in a staged and limited manner with customers. Thus, the customers may feel that they are dealing with automatons who have been taught to utter a few phrases rather than with fellow human beings. For their part, the customers are supposed to be, and often are, in a hurry, so they have little to say to the McDonald's employee. Indeed, it could be argued that one of the reasons for the success of fast-food restaurants is that they are in tune with our fast-paced and impersonal society. People in the modern world want to get on with their business without unnecessary personal relationships. The fast-food restaurant gives them precisely what they want.

Not only are the relationships between employee and customer limited greatly, but also other potential relationships. Because employees remain on the job for only a few months, satisfying personal relationships among employees are unlikely to develop....

Relationships among customers are largely curtailed as well. Although some McDonald's ads would have us believe otherwise, gone are the days when people met in the diner or cafeteria for coffee, breakfast, lunch, or dinner and lingered to socialize with one another. Fast-food restaurants are clearly not conducive to such socializing. If nothing else, the chairs are designed to make people uncomfortable and interested in moving on to something else. The drive-through windows are a further step toward McDonaldization, by completely eliminating the possibility of interacting with other customers....

Fast-food restaurants also tend to have negative effects on other human relationships. There is, for example, the effect on the so-called "family meal." The fast-food restaurant is not conducive to a long, leisurely, conversation-filled dinnertime. The family is unlikely to linger long over a meal at McDonald's. Furthermore, as the children grow into their teens, the nature of fast-food restaurants leads to separate meals as the teens go at one time with their friends, and the parents go at another time. Of course, the drive-through window only serves to reduce the possibility of a family meal. The family that gobbles its food while driving on to its next stop can hardly be seen as having what is called these days "quality time" with each other. Here is the way one journalist describes what is happening to the family meal:

> Do families who eat their suppers at the Colonel's, swinging on plastic seats, or however the restaurant is arranged, say grace before picking up a crispy brown chicken leg? Does dad ask junior what he did today as he remembers he forgot the piccalilli and trots through the crowds over to the counter to get some? Does mom find the atmosphere conducive to asking little Mildred about the problems she was having with third-conjugation French verbs, or would it matter since otherwise the family might

> have been at home chomping down precooked frozen food, warmed in the microwave oven, and watching *Hollywood Squares?*

There is much talk these days about the disintegration of the family, and the fast-food restaurants may well be a crucial contributor to that disintegration.

In fact, as implied above, dinners at home may now not be much different from meals at the fast-food restaurant. Families tended to stop having lunch together by the 1940s and breakfast altogether by the 1950s. Today, the family dinner is following the same route. Even when they eat dinner at home, the meal will probably not be what it once was. Following the fast-food model, people are growing more likely to "graze," "refuel," nibble on this, or snack on that, than they are to sit down to a formal meal. Also, because it is now deemed inefficient to do nothing but just eat, families are likely to watch television while they are eating, thereby efficiently combining two activities. However, the din, to say nothing of the lure, of dinnertime TV programs such as *Wheel of Fortune* is likely to make it difficult for family members to interact with one another.

A key technology in the destruction of the family meal is the microwave oven and the vast array of microwavable foods it helped generate. It is striking to learn that more than 70 percent of American households have a microwave oven. A recent *Wall Street Journal* poll indicated that Americans consider the microwave their favorite household product. In fact, the microwave in a McDonaldizing society is seen as an advance over the fast-food restaurant. Said one consumer researcher, "It has made even fast-food restaurants not seem fast because at home you don't have to wait in line." As a general rule, consumers are demanding meals that take no more than ten minutes to microwave, whereas in the past people were more often willing to spend about a half hour or even an hour cooking dinner. This emphasis on speed has, of course, brought with it poorer taste and lower quality, but people do not seem to mind this loss: "We're just not as critical of food as we used to be."...

FAST FOOD [AND HOMOGENIZATION]

Another dehumanizing effect of the fast-food restaurant is that it has contributed to homogenization around the country and, increasingly, throughout the world. Diversity, which many people crave, is being reduced or eliminated by the fast-food restaurant. This decline in diversity is manifest in the extension of the fast-food model to all sorts of ethnic foods. The settings are all modeled after McDonald's in one way or another and the food has been rationalized and compromised so that it is acceptable to the tastes of virtually all diners. One cannot find an authentically different meal in any of these ethnic fast-food chains.

The expansion of these franchises across the landscape of America means that one finds little difference among regions and among cities throughout the country. Tourists find more familiarity and predictability and less diversity as they travel around the nation, and this is increasingly true on a global scale. Apparently exotic settings are likely to be overrun with both American fast-food chains as well as indigenous varieties. The new and world's largest McDonald's and Kentucky Fried Chicken in Beijing are but two examples of this. . . . The spread of American and indigenous fast food throughout much of the world means that there is less and less diversity from one setting to another. The human craving for new and diverse experiences is being limited, if not progressively destroyed, by the national and international spread of fast-food restaurants. The craving for diversity is being supplanted by the desire for uniformity and predictability....

CONCLUSION

Although I have emphasized the irresistibility of McDonaldization, my fondest hope is that I am wrong. Indeed, a major motivation is to alert readers to the dangers of McDonaldization and to motivate them to act to stem its tide. I hope that we are able to resist McDonaldization and can create instead a more reasonable, more human world.

McDonald's was recently sued by the famous French chef, Paul Bocuse, for using his picture on a poster without his permission. Enraged, Bocuse said: "How can I be seen promoting this tasteless, boneless food in which everything is soft." Nevertheless, Bocuse seemed to acknowledge the inevitability of McDonaldization: "There's a need for this kind of thing . . . and trying to get rid of it seems to me to be as futile as trying to get rid of the prostitutes in the Bois de Boulogne." Lo and behold, two weeks later, it was announced that the Paris police had cracked down on prostitution in the Bois de Boulogne. Said a police spokesman, "There are none left." Thus, just as chef Bocuse was wrong about the prostitutes, perhaps I was wrong about the irresistibility of McDonaldization. Yet, before we grow overly optimistic, it should be noted that "everyone knows that the prostitutes will be back as soon as the operation is over. In the spring, police predict, there will be even more than before." Similarly, it remains likely that no matter how intense the opposition, the future will bring with it more rather than less McDonaldization.... [F]aced with Max Weber's iron cage imagery of a future dominated by the polar night of icy darkness and hardness, the least the reader can do is to follow the words of the poet Dylan Thomas: "Do not go gentle into that good night.... Rage, rage against the dying of the light."

READING 16

How Many Sexual Partners Do Americans Have?

Robert T. Michael, John H. Gagnon, Edward O. Laumann, and Gina Kolata

introduction

Human sexual behavior is one of the many fascinating aspects of social life that sociologists study. This aspect of social life is significant because it involves not only social relationships but also a central part of our personal identity—our feelings of self, of who we are. Yet when sociologists investigate this vital area of human behavior, they meet resistance and suspicion. Resistance comes from people who feel that human sexuality is solely a private matter and no prying sociologist should examine it. Suspicion is generalized, coming from a great number of people who feel that the sociologist's motives are somehow impure and improper. If sociologists do research on teenage sexuality, they are thought to harbor secret fantasies. If they do research on prostitutes, they are thought to visit prostitutes under cover of night. If they gather data on homosexual behavior, they are thought to be closet homosexuals. No matter what area of sexual behavior they investigate, they are suspected of fantasies, secret longings, or some sort of sexual deviation from the norm.

This risk to reputation and relationships (which often comes with snide remarks and smirking) is not faced by sociologists who investigate voting behavior or changes in food preference. These researchers do not come under suspicion or derision as people who may covertly want to undermine democracy or who harbor secret food longings. With this risk to reputation, few sociologists investigate human sexual behavior, despite its high significance for understanding social life. Some do, however, and this selection by Robert Michael, John Gagnon, Edward Laumann, and Gina Kolata provides an update on changing human sexual behavior.

Thinking Critically

As you read this selection, ask yourself:

1. In the introduction to this selection, the editor says that unlike those who do research on political behavior, sociologists who study human sexual behavior risk reputation and relationships. Why do you think this is so?
2. This selection underscores the significance and influence of marriage. What evidence do you find for this statement?
3. Based on this reading, how has the sexual behavior of Americans changed? Why?

Sometimes, the myths about sex contain a grain of truth. The common perception is that Americans today have more sexual partners than they did just a decade or two ago. That, it turns out, is correct. A third of Americans who are over age fifty have had five or more sexual partners in their lifetime. But half of all Americans aged thirty to fifty have had five or more partners even though being younger, they had fewer years to accumulate them.

Still, when we ask older or younger people how many partners they had in the past year, the usual reply is zero or one. Something must have changed to make younger people accumulate more partners over a lifetime, yet sustain a pattern of having no partners or only one in any one year. The explanation is linked to one of our most potent social institutions and how it has changed.

That institution is marriage, a social arrangement so powerful that nearly everyone participates. About 90 percent of Americans have married by the time they are thirty, and a large majority spends much of their adulthood as part of a wedded couple. And marriage, we find, regulates sexual behavior with remarkable precision. No matter what they did before they wed, no matter how many partners they had, the sexual lives of married people are similar. Despite the popular myth that there is a great deal of adultery in marriage, our data and other reliable studies do not find it. Instead, a vast majority are faithful while the marriage is intact....

So, yes, many young people probably are having sexual intercourse with a fair number of partners. But that stops with marriage. The reason that people now have more sexual partners over their lifetimes is that they are spending a longer period sexually active, but unmarried. The period has lengthened from both ends and in the middle. The average age at which people have their first sexual intercourse has crept down and the average age at which people marry for the first time has edged up. And people are more likely to divorce now, which means they have time between marriages when they search for new partners once again.

To draw these conclusions, we looked at our respondents' replies to a variety of questions. First, we asked people when they first had heterosexual intercourse. Then, we asked what happens between the time when people first have intercourse and when they finally marry. How many partners do they have? Do they have more than one partner at any one time or do they have their partners in succession, practicing serial monogamy? We asked how many people divorced and how long they remained unmarried. Finally, we asked how many partners people had in their lifetimes.

In our analyses of the numbers of sex partners, we could not separately analyze patterns for gay men and lesbians. That is because homosexuals are such a small percentage of our sample that we do not have enough people in our survey to draw valid conclusions about this aspect of sexual behavior.

If we are going to look at heterosexual partners from the beginning, from the time that people first lose their virginity, we plunge headfirst into the maelstrom of teenage sex, always a turbulent subject, but especially so now, in the age of AIDS.

While society disputes whether to counsel abstinence from sexual intercourse or to pass out condoms in high schools, it also must grapple with a basic question: Has sexual behavior among teenagers changed? Are more having sexual intercourse and at younger ages, or is the overheated rhetoric a reaction to fears, without facts? The answer is both troubling and reassuring to the majority of adults who prefer teenagers to delay their sexual activity—troubling because most teenagers are having intercourse, but reassuring because sexual intercourse tends to be sporadic during the teen years.

We saw a steadily declining age at which teenagers first had sexual intercourse. Men and women born in the decade 1933–1942 had sex [for the first time] at an average age of about eighteen. Those born twenty to thirty years later have an average age at first intercourse that is about six months younger, as seen in Figure 1. The figure also indicates that the men report having sex at younger ages than the women. It also shows that blacks report a younger age at first intercourse than whites.

Another way to look at the age at first intercourse is illustrated in Figure 2. The figure shows the proportions of teenagers and young adults who experienced sexual intercourse at each age from twelve to twenty-five. To see at what age half the people

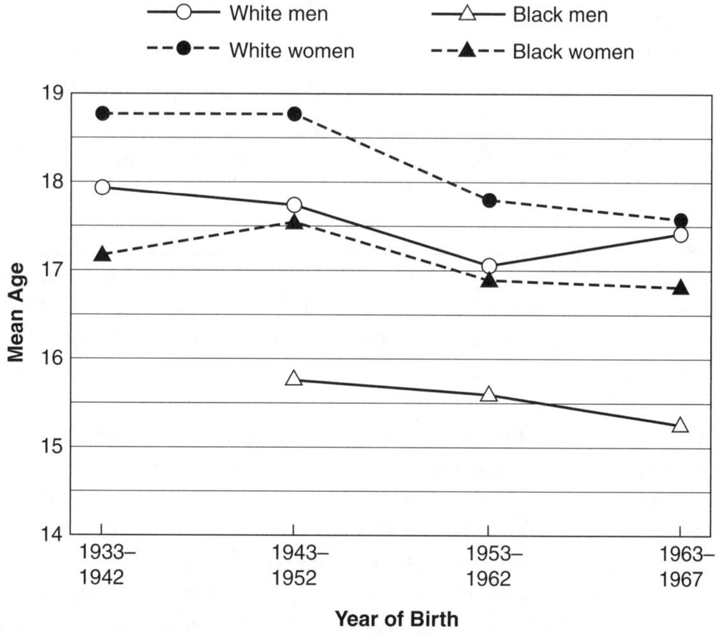

FIGURE 1 Mean Age at First Intercourse

Note: This includes respondents who had vaginal intercourse no later than age twenty-five and who have reached their twenty-fifth birthday by the date of the interview. [There were an] insufficient number of cases [to show Hispanics]. Whites computed from cross-section sample; blacks computed from cross-section and the over-sample.

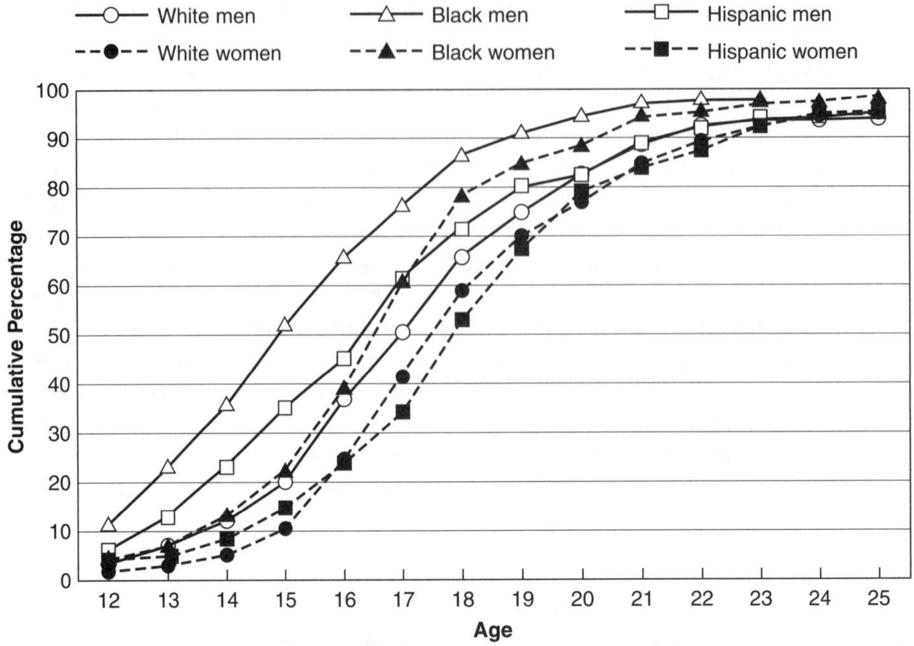

FIGURE 2 Cumulative Percentage Who Have Had Intercourse [by Age 25]

Note: Cumulative percentage indicates the proportion of respondents of a given group at a given age. This figure only includes respondents who have reached their twenty-fifth birthday by the date of the interview.

had intercourse, for example, follow the...horizontal line that corresponds to a cumulative frequency of 50 percent. It shows that half of all black men had intercourse by the time they were fifteen, half of all Hispanic men had intercourse by the time they were about sixteen and a half, half of all black women had intercourse by the time they were nearly seventeen, and half the white women and half the Hispanic women had intercourse by the time they were nearly eighteen. By age twenty-two, about 90 percent of each group had intercourse.

The patterns are crystal clear. About half the teenagers of various racial and ethnic groups in the nation have begun having intercourse with a partner in the age range of fifteen to eighteen, and at least four out of five have had intercourse by the time their teenage years are over. Since the average age of marriage is now in the mid-twenties, few Americans wait until they marry to have sex....

It's a change that built up for years, making it sometimes hard to appreciate just how profound it is. Stories of what sex among the unmarried was like decades ago can be startling. Even people who were no longer teenagers, and who were engaged, felt overwhelming social pressure to refrain from intercourse before marriage....

In addition to having intercourse at younger ages, many people also are marrying later—a change that is the real legacy of the late 1960s and early 1970s. This period was not, we find, a sexual revolution, a time of frequent sex with many partners for all. Instead, it was the beginning of a profound change in the sexual life course, providing the second reason why Americans have accumulated more partners now than in decades past.

Since the 1960s, the route to the altar is no longer so predictable as it used to be. In the first half of the twentieth century, almost everyone who married followed the same course: dating, love, a little sexual experimentation with one partner, sometimes including intercourse, then marriage and children. It also was a time when there was a clear and accepted double standard—men were much more likely to have had intercourse with several women before marrying than women were to have had intercourse with several men.

At the dawn of the millennium, we are left with a nation that still has this idealized heterosexual life course but whose actual course has fragmented in the crucial years before marriage. Some people still marry at eighteen, others at thirty, leading to very different numbers of sexual partners before marriage. Social class plays a role, with less-educated people marrying earlier than better-educated people. Blacks tend to marry much later than whites, and a large number of blacks do not marry at all.

But a new and increasingly common pattern has emerged: affection or love and sex with a number of partners, followed by affection, love, and cohabitation. This cycles back to the sexual marketplace, if the cohabitation breaks up, or to marriage. Pregnancy can occur at any of these points, but often occurs before either cohabitation or marriage. The result is that the path toward marriage, once so straight and narrow, has begun to meander and to have many side paths, one of which is being trodden into a well-traveled lane.

That path is the pattern of living together before marriage. Like other recent studies, ours shows a marked shift toward living together rather than marriage as the first union of couples. With an increase in cohabitation, the distinctions among having a steady sexual partner, a live-in sexual partner, and a marriage have gotten more fuzzy. This shift began at the same time as talk of a sexual revolution. Our study shows that people who came of age before 1970 almost invariably got married without first living together, while the younger people seldom did. But, we find, the average age at which people first move in with a partner—either by marrying, or living together—has remained nearly constant, around age twenty-two for men and twenty for women. The difference is that now that first union is increasingly likely to be a cohabitation....

With the increase in cohabitation, people are marrying later, on average. The longer they wait, however, the more likely they are to live with a sexual partner in the meantime. Since many couples who live together break up within a short time and seek a new partner, the result has been an increase in the average number of partners that people have before they marry....

Finally, we can look at divorce rates, another key social change that began in the 1960s and that has led to increasing numbers of partners over a lifetime.... For example, we can look at how likely it is that a couple will be divorced by the tenth anniversary of their marriage. For people born between 1933 and 1942, the chance was about one in five. For those born between 1943 and 1952, the chance was one in three. For those born between 1953 and 1962, the chance was closer to 38 percent. Divorced people as a group have more sexual partners than people who remain married and they are more likely, as a group, to have intercourse with a partner and live with a partner before they marry again.

These three social trends—earlier first intercourse, later marriage, and more frequent divorce—help explain why people now have more sexual partners over their lifetimes.

To discern the patterns of sexual partnering, we asked respondents how many sexual partners they had. We could imagine several scenarios. People could find one partner and marry. Or they could have sex with several before marrying. Or they could live with their partners first and then marry. Or they could simply have lots of casual sex, never marrying at all or marrying but also having extramarital sex.

Since our respondents varied in age from eighteen to fifty-nine, the older people in the study, who married by their early twenties, would have been married by the time the turbulent 1960s and 1970s came around. Their premarital behavior would be a relic from the past, telling us how much intercourse people had in the days before sex became so public an issue. The younger people in our study can show us whether there is a contrast between the earlier days and the decades after a sexual revolution was proclaimed. We can ask if they have more partners, if they have more than one sexual partner at a time, and if their sexual behavior is markedly different from that of the older generations that preceded them.

Most young people today show no signs of having very large numbers of partners. More than half the men and women in America who were eighteen to twenty-four in 1992 had just one sex partner in the past year and another 11 percent had none in the last year. In addition, studies in Europe show that people in the United Kingdom, France, and Finland have sexual life courses that are virtually the same as the American life course. The picture that emerges is strikingly different from the popular image of sexuality running out of control in our time.

In fact, we find, nearly all Americans have a very modest number of partners, whether we ask them to enumerate their partners over their adult lifetime or in the past year. The number of partners varies little with education, race, or religion. Instead, it is determined by marital status or by whether a couple is living together. Once married, people tend to have one and only one partner, and those who are unmarried and living together are almost as likely to be faithful.

Our data for the United States are displayed in Table 1.

The right-hand portion of Table 1 tells how many sexual partners people had since they turned eighteen. Very few, just 3 percent, had no partners, and few, just 9 percent, had a total of more than twenty partners.

The oldest people in our study, those aged fifty-five to fifty-nine, were most likely to have had just one sexual partner in their lifetimes—40 percent said they had had only one. This reflects the earlier age of marriage in previous generations and the low rate of divorce among these older couples. Many of the men were married by age twenty-two and the women by age twenty.

The left-hand portion of Table 1 shows the number of sexual partners that people had in the past twelve months. These are the data that show how likely

TABLE 1 Number of Sex Partners in Past Twelve Months and since Age Eighteen

	SEX PARTNERS PAST TWELVE MONTHS				SEX PARTNERS SINCE AGE EIGHTEEN					
	0	*1*	*2 to 4*	*5+*	*0*	*1*	*2 to 4*	*5 to 10*	*10 to 20*	*21+*
Total	12%	71%	14%	3%	3%	26%	30%	22%	11%	9%
Gender										
Men	10	67	18	5	3	20	21	23	16	17
Women	14	75	10	2	3	31	36	20	6	3
Age										
18–24	11	57	24	9	8	32	34	15	8	3
25–29	6	72	17	6	2	25	31	22	10	9
30–34	9	73	16	2	3	21	29	25	11	10
35–39	10	77	11	2	2	19	30	25	14	11
40–44	11	75	13	1	1	22	28	24	14	12
45–49	15	75	9	1	2	26	24	25	10	14
50–54	15	79	5	0	2	34	28	18	9	9
55–59	32	65	4	0	1	40	28	15	8	7
Marital status										
Never married, noncohabiting	25	38	28	9	12	15	29	21	12	12
Never married, cohabiting	1	75	20	5	0	25	37	16	10	13
Married	2	94	4	1	0	37	28	19	9	7
Divorced, separated, widowed, noncohabiting	31	41	26	3	0	11	33	29	15	12
Divorced, separated, widowed, cohabiting	1	80	15	3	0	0	32	44	12	12
Education										
Less than high school	16	67	15	3	4	27	36	19	9	6
High school graduate or equivalent	11	74	13	3	3	30	29	20	10	7
Some college, vocational	11	71	14	4	2	24	29	23	12	9
Finished college	12	69	15	4	2	24	26	24	11	13
Master's/advanced degree	13	74	10	3	4	25	26	23	10	13
Current Religion										
None	11	68	13	7	3	16	29	20	16	16
Mainline Protestant	11	73	13	2	2	23	31	23	12	8
Conservative Protestant	13	70	14	3	3	30	30	20	10	7
Catholic	12	71	13	3	4	27	29	23	8	9
Jewish	3	75	18	3	0	24	13	30	17	17
Other religion	15	70	12	3	3	42	20	16	8	13
Race/Ethnicity										
White	12	73	12	3	3	26	29	22	11	9
Black	13	60	21	6	2	18	34	24	11	11
Hispanic	11	69	17	2	4	35	27	17	8	9
Asian	15	77	8	0	6	46	25	14	6	3
Native American	12	76	10	2	5	28	35	23	5	5

Note: Row percentages total 100 percent.

people are to remain faithful to their sexual partner, whether or not they are married. Among married people, 94 percent had one partner in the past year. Couples who were living together were almost as faithful. Seventy-five percent of people who had never married but were living together had one partner in the past year. Eighty percent of people who were previously married and were cohabiting when we questioned them had one partner in the past year. Two-thirds of the single people who were not living with a partner had no partners or only one in the past year. Only a few percent of the population had as many as five partners for sexual intercourse in the past year, and many of these were people who were never married and were not living with anyone. They were mostly young and mostly male.

One way to imagine the patterns of sexual partners is to think of a graph, with the vertical axis showing numbers of partners and the horizontal axis showing a person's age. The graph will be a series of blips, as the person finds partners, interspersed with flat regions where the person has no partners or when the person has just one steady partner. When the person marries, the line flattens out at a height of one, indicating that the individual has only one partner. If the marriage breaks up, the graph shows a few more blips until the person remarries, and then it flattens out again.

For an individual, the graph is mostly flat, punctuated by a few areas of blips. But if we superimposed everyone's graph on top of each other, we would have a sort of supergraph that looked like it was all blips. That, in essence, is what has led to the widespread impression that everyone is having lots of partners. We see the total picture—lots of sex in the population—without realizing that each individual spends most of his or her life with only one partner.

These findings give no support to the idea of a promiscuous society or of a dramatic sexual revolution reflected in huge numbers of people with multiple casual sex partners. The finding on which our data give strong and quite amazing evidence is not that most people do, in fact, form a partnership, or that most people do, in fact, ultimately get married. That fact also was well documented in many previous studies. Nor is it news that more recent marriages are much less stable than marriages that began thirty years ago. That fact, too, was reported by others before us. But we add a new fact, one that is not only important but that is striking.

Our study clearly shows that no matter how sexually active people are before and between marriages, no matter whether they lived with their sexual partners before marriage or whether they were virgins on their wedding day, marriage is such a powerful social institution that, essentially, married people are nearly all alike—they are faithful to their partners as long as the marriage is intact. It does not matter if the couple were high-school sweethearts who married after graduation day or whether they are in their thirties, marrying after each had lived with several others. Once married, the vast majority have no other sexual partner; their past is essentially erased. Marriage remains the great leveler.

We see this, for example, when we ask about fidelity in marriage. More than 80 percent of women and 65 to 85 percent of men of every age report that they had no partners other than their spouse while they were married....

The marriage effect is so dramatic that it swamps all other aspects of our data. When we report that more than 80 percent of adult Americans age eighteen to fifty-nine had zero or one sexual partner in the past year, the figure might sound ludicrous to some young people who know that they and their friends have more than one partner in a year. But the figure really reflects the fact that most Americans in that broad age range are married and are faithful. And many of the others are cohabiting, and they too are faithful. Or they are without partners altogether, a situation that is especially likely for older women.... We find only 3 percent of adults had five or more partners in the past year. Half of all adult Americans had three or fewer partners over their lifetimes.

Name Index

Subject Index